# Queering the Prophet

# Queering the Prophet

*On Jonah and Other Activists*

Edited by
L. Juliana Claassens
Steed Vernyl Davidson
Charlene van der Walt
Ashwin Thyssen

scm press

Published in 2023 by SCM Press
Editorial office
3rd Floor, Invicta House,
108–114 Golden Lane,
London
London EC1Y 0TG, UK

www.scmpress.co.uk

SCM Press is an imprint of Hymns Ancient & Modern Ltd
(a registered charity)

Hymns Ancient & Modern® is a registered trademark of
Hymns Ancient & Modern Ltd
13A Hellesdon Park Road, Norwich,
Norfolk NR6 5DR, UK

British Library Cataloguing in Publication data.

A catalogue record for this book is available
from the British Library

ISBN 978-0-334-06513-5

Typeset by Regent Typesetting
Printed and bound by
CPI Group (UK) Ltd

# Contents

## Part 2: Becoming Queer Prophets

# Contributors

**Madré Arendse**, MTh Student in Old Testament, Faculty of Theology, Stellenbosch University.

**Hendrik L. Bosman**, Emeritus Professor of Old Testament, Faculty of Theology, Stellenbosch University.

**L. Juliana Claassens**, Professor of Old Testament/Head of Gender Unit, Faculty of Theology, Stellenbosch University.

**Hanzline R. Davids**, Lecturer at the Department of Gender and Sexuality Studies, College of Human Sciences University of South Africa.

**Steed V. Davidson**, Professor of Hebrew Bible/Old Testament/ Vice President for Academic Affairs and Dean of the Faculty, McCormick Theological Seminary, Chicago, IL/Extraordinary Visiting Professor, Old Testament, Department of Old and New Testament, Stellenbosch University.

**Sheurl Davis**, PhD Student in Old Testament, Stellenbosch University/Junior Lecturer in Old Testament, North-West University.

**Rhiannon Graybill**, Marcus M. and Carole M. Weinstein, and Gilbert M. and Fannie S. Rosenthal Chair of Jewish Studies, University of Richmond, Richmond, VA.

**Crystal Hall**, Independent Scholar and a Certified Coach for Women in Ministry, Philadelphia, PA.

**Jione Havea**, Trinity Methodist Theological College (Aotearoa New Zealand), Centre for Religion, Ethics and Society of Charles Sturt University (Sydney, Australia).

**Stephen Kapinde**, Lecturer of Religion and Public life, Pwani University, Kenya, and LUCAS/LAHRI Research Fellow 2021, University of Leeds.

**Adriaan van Klinken**, Professor of Religion and African Studies, School of Philosophy, Religion and History of Science, University of Leeds, Extraordinary Professor in the Desmond Tutu Centre for Religion and Social Justice, University of the Western Cape.

**Jacob Meiring**, Research Fellow in Systematic Theology and Ecclesiology, Faculty of Theology, Stellenbosch University.

**Nokuthula Mjwara**, Process Coordinator: Civil Society Partnerships, Inclusive and Affirming Ministries.

**R. Louis van der Riet**, Process Coordinator: Collaborative Faith Partnerships, Inclusive and Affirming Ministries/Research Associate, Systematic Theology and Ecclesiology, Faculty of Theology, Stellenbosch University.

**Rosa Ross**, Graduate Student, Princeton Theological Seminary/Adjunct Professor, Humanities Department, Marshall University.

**Tracey Sibisi**, Ujamaa Centre/School of Religion, Philosophy and Classics, University of KwaZulu-Natal.

**Sizwesamajobe (Sizwe) Sithole**, School of Religion, Philosophy and Classics, University of KwaZulu-Natal.

**Ashwin Thyssen**, Junior Lecturer in Church Polity, Church History, Religion and Law, Faculty of Theology, Stellenbosch University.

**Lena-Sofia Tiemeyer**, Professor of Old Testament Exegesis at ALT School of Theology, Örebro, Sweden, and Research Associate at the Department of Old Testament and Hebrew Scriptures, Faculty of Theology and Religion, University of Pretoria.

**Charlene van der Walt**, School of Religion, Philosophy and Classics, University of KwaZulu-Natal.

**Gerald West**, Emeritus Professor of Old Testament, Ujamaa Centre/School of Religion, Philosophy and Classics, University of KwaZulu-Natal.

**Sithembiso Zwane**, Ujamaa Centre/School of Religion, Philosophy and Classics, University of KwaZulu-Natal.

# Acknowledgements

In an expansive project such as *Queering the Prophet*, there are many people who played an indelible role in bringing the book to life. We express heartfelt appreciation to the following.

The former (Professor Eugene Cloete) and the current (Professor Sibusiso Moyo) Deputy Vice-Chancellor of Research at Stellenbosch University, for your ongoing support of the Gender Unit of the Faculty of Theology, which helps bring projects such as this one to fruition.

The Faculty of Theology, Stellenbosch University, and especially the Dean, Professor Reggie Nel, and the Director of the Beyers Naudé Centre for Public Theology (which houses the Gender Unit), Professor Dion Forster, for your encouragement and appreciation for the work we do.

Estelle Muller, Marita Snyman, Simba Pondani, Tannie Minnie Philander, Joseph Fillies and Zandré Marais, who provided invaluable administrative assistance before and during the conference.

SCM Press, and especially David Shervington, who saw the potential of this project and encouraged us to bring even more voices into the conversation. Rachel Geddes for shepherding this project to publication.

Alexandra Banks, the newly appointed postdoctoral fellow in the Gender Unit, for compiling the indexes before you even started working with us.

Nickole Brown for permission to use the poem 'A Jonah' (2020), Norwegian Writer's Climate Campaign (available online: https://forfatternesklimaaksjon.files.wordpress.com/2020/08/nickolebrown-poemforfreddy1.pdf), which first appeared in the *Birmingham Poetry Review* 46 (2019).

Cosimo Miorelli for permission to use the image *Jonah Flyer* from his 'live-painting-concert', which 'combines live digital painting projected on a screen and live music' that 'invites the audience to interpret the narrative as the events unfold on the screen'. Readers are invited to look at Cosimo Miorelli's website for his reinterpretation of the Jonah story, with its themes of 'conflict, compassion, atonement and hope'. As he writes in the description of his project: 'The storyline follows a modern-day Jonah, through her perilous journey, reviving and reinterpreting the passages of the biblical story' (see http://www.cosimomiorelli.com/jonah/).

Finally, to everyone who over the years participated in the annual Gender Unit conferences (some every year), who have found joy and inspiration and renewed courage in our individual and collective efforts for justice and the establishment of a kinder, more equitable world: we are deeply grateful for the community we have built.

Aluta Continua.

Juliana Claassens
Steed Vernyl Davidson
Charlene van der Walt
Ashwin Thyssen

*Stellenbosch/Chicago/Cape Town*
*11 September 2023*

# Introduction
# Queering Jonah and Other Activists

Oh, help me, Jonah,
patron saint of cowards
who didn't ask to carry
the message

or worse
who tore through
town screaming
and was thought
insane,

because now I can't help
but feel that for these storms to
cease, that I

and – God forgive
me – maybe
all of us

might have to beg
to be thrown
overboard

('A Jonah', Nickole Brown, 2019)[1]

In her evocative poem, 'A Jonah', Nickole Brown imagines her-self in the final stanza, driving away fast with a full tank of gas as the radio reports one huge storm after another. She says this prayer as she keeps thinking:

And I'm a Jonah, I'm
a Jonah

> my head frenzied
> with this prophecy
> but afraid
> no one will hear and not
> knowing what to do

Brown writes her poem in the context of the devastating consequences of climate change. She, for instance, imagines herself fleeing away upon hearing the news about 'the numbers of carbons and acids, of temperatures and fish, of bears the colour of snow staggering, the wet slop left of their coats slung loose across their starved hips'. She realizes that she is a Jonah, and while fleeing, she thinks:

> and still, I down
> sweet, carbonated water from
> plastic, enough bottles to choke
> the sea with a whole island
> of my sprawl.

And I'm a Jonah,
I'm a Jonah
my hunger big
as any and my trashcan full.

Brown's Jonah is a reluctant prophet, an angry activist who many might think is insane. Brown's Jonah is inevitably hurled in a climate crisis that will mean disaster for all, as cities are overthrown, and the most vulnerable suffer precisely because they cannot protect themselves from the consequences of the disaster. But those who are embroiled in battles for justice, equality, and the recognition of human dignity irrespective of factors such as race, class, sexual orientation, and physical and mental ability, all too often may say to themselves:

And I'm a Jonah,
I'm a Jonah

Through Brown's interpretation of Jonah, the poet and others who enter the narrative world, given new significance by her fresh interpretation, may find a kindred spirit in Jonah, 'the patron saint of cowards who didn't ask to carry the message', but nevertheless did against their will and initial inclinations.

## Queering the prophet Jonah

If the figure Jonah seems all too common, Jonah in fact stands out more for how different he is from the norm. Jonah is more queer than normal. In her monograph on *Masculinity in the Hebrew Bible Prophets*, Rhiannon Graybill notes that all too often in the biblical prophets, the prophetic body is also the wounded body, violated, and carrying the wounds of the people in his person (2016, p. 11). A sample of prophets in the Bible reveals individuals willing at times, and at other times forced, to put their bodies on the line. These prophets do not always represent the normative position of prophets who served established ancient institutions of the palace and temple. In their roles, prophets supported the status quo. The representative figures in the Bible stand out because their words and actions survived generations to become relevant for times that needed something different, something not normal. Graybill argues that 'it is the very difficulties that prophets experience with their bodies – nakedness, suffering, pain – that render these bodies queer'. Although prophets are often understood in contemporary interpretative settings as heroes or larger-than-life figures of faith, Graybill's work highlights the vulnerability of these figures as they embody a lived reality that runs counter to the dominant construction of masculinity. Prophets, as subordinate to God, surrendered (willingly or otherwise) their bodies to a male deity in a hierarchical relationship that more often than not feminized their male personas and bodies. Nevertheless, the honest embrace of woundedness, this unique social position, offers the potential for something new to emerge.

*Queering the Prophet: On Jonah and Other Activists* considers the role of queer interpretation as it also intersects with feminist and postcolonial biblical interpretation in reframing what it means to be a prophet in these exceedingly queer times in which we are living. In the first part of this collection of essays that emerged from a conference hosted in March 2022 by the Gender Unit of the Faculty of Theology, Stellenbosch University, contributors draw attention to various aspects associated with reading the story of Jonah through a queer lens. The traumatized prophet Jonah, on the one hand, represents the anger and frustration of many ordinary Judean inhabitants who had to deal with the ongoing presence of the Persian Empire in their daily lives. However, the rather strange sight of a perpetually angry prophet, perched on the hill outside of the capital city of the Assyrian Empire that remains present (despite having been destroyed in real life), attests to the importance of queering prophetic identity in contexts in which new forms of empire inflict a great deal of individual and collective suffering. In these queer times, where normalcy means the support for death-dealing systems for vulnerable humans, threatened species and a fragile planet, reading a dominant book like the Bible from a queer perspective counts as protest action. The embrace of queer positionalities provided by LGBTIQA+ and formerly colonized people of various sorts confronts the prevailing world systems that ensure the interests of a narrow group of people.[2] These small groups, located in different systems of modern life, continue to argue that their version of reality represents the only normal worthy of existence. A queer reading of Jonah challenges the religious systems that resulted in the social constructions that maintain mechanisms of exclusions for those who opt out of these norms. Jonah's strange posture at the end of the book helps us as contemporary interpreters to see in sharper focus the systemic realities that function as backdrop to this narrative. These systems of oppression are pervasive and insidious. A Queer approach helps us to engage them in a more forceful way.

Queer biblical hermeneutics has come a long way. The second edition of the *Queer Bible Commentary* was published in 2022 by SCM Press with authors uncovering rich perspectives on the various biblical books read in terms of the lived experiences of

LGBTIQA+ communities.[3] The numerous books and collections of essays that have appeared in recent years[4] speak to the depth and the breadth of queer biblical interpretation that extends beyond the biblical texts to other theological disciplines and hermeneutical approaches.[5] Although Queer biblical interpretation is primarily concerned with the work of troubling, destabilizing and challenging normative ideas and constructions of gender and sexuality and embodiment within the text, it has been helpful for the work of other biblical scholars, including postcolonial, feminist and gender-critical scholars who find a queer lens productive for their interpretative endeavours.

Publishing in the field of Jonah studies has been prolific in recent years. In a two-year period, at least eight commentaries either appeared in print or were awaiting publication[6] – contributors to this volume engage with four of these commentaries. Of particular interest for this current collection are contextual approaches, which have in common reading *against* the grain of the text, *from* below, and *for* the most vulnerable – individuals and groups who all too often have been considered bodies out of place (Ahmed 2006). Coming from a place of pain and attentive to those individuals and communities being negated and disrespected by those in power, these approaches help us to question hegemonic interpretations of biblical texts such as Jonah, and specifically what is considered to be 'normal' and normative, central, and marginalized.

In terms of queer biblical interpretation, several elements in the book of Jonah can be considered unstable, incoherent, ambiguous, or one could say queer, and offer fertile ground for interpretations that challenge, trouble or interrogate seemingly fixed, set-in-stone (heteronormative) power structures and norms (Williams 2006, p. 528). In particular, the bodies of the exclusively male prophets in the Hebrew Bible have traditionally been overlooked and, when considered, seen in a heteronormative light. That a male deity co-opts the bodies of these men in an intimate relationship already sets the stage for reconsidering presumptions of normativity, particularly gender normativity.

A queer orientation opens up new vantage points in the text and the world of the text. Together with the labours of postcolonial and feminist interpreters, queer readings give us new eyes for reading the book of Jonah, the prophet and God presented in it, and also the rest of the characters. From the exceedingly great city of Nineveh to the big fish, as well as minor characters such as the militarized worm and the defenceless plant (Jonah 4), and also the mariners in Jonah 1 and the people of Nineveh in Jonah 3, all receive a second look. Contextual interpreters are hence united by the common task of reading a book like Jonah against the grain, interrogating white, male, cisgender, heteronormative privilege as these interpretations strive to imagine and represent other ways of being in the world.

A good example of the new layers of meaning that queer interpretation of Jonah can open up is to be found in Samuel Ross's recent study, 'Queer Themes in the Book of Jonah and its Contemporary Analogues'.[7] He writes that 'reading Jonah through queer eyes' provides us with 'a myriad of opportunities to reflect upon many facets of queer experience' (2019, p. 2). Ross views Jonah's escape from God and abusive home environments in terms of the LGBTIQA+ experience of leaving home, yet not always finding a welcoming community in queer places (2019, p. 8). He imagines the belly of the big fish as 'a psychiatric ward, and Jonah has become an inpatient' to reflect on the abuse many LGBTIQA+ patients experience that pathologize the queer experience (2019, p. 46). And in his reading on Nineveh, he reflects on the complex relationship between queer communities and the city, proposing that the latter functions as a refuge for those communities but challenging the idea that 'this queer metronormativity could be considered an unqualified good as a safe haven' (2019, p. 85). In his final chapter, he considers Jonah's portrayal in chapter 4 in terms of queer anger, also reflecting on what Jonah's disappearance, or one could say death, at the end of the book might mean for queer people's ongoing experience of life in a hostile world (2019, p. 87).

We need more of these types of innovative readings of the text and the world in which readers live. A queer reading strategy is more important than ever – to some extent queering is about all of us. The increased anti-LGBTIQA+ legislation in the United States, which also has a profound impact on individuals and communities around the world though funding regimes and the export of cultural hegemony, once more confirms what we know all too well; that is, that the world is not a safe space for women and those minoritized by the forces of normalcy. Sadly, the church has not been at the forefront of effecting change, and either has been silent or, worse, complicit.

This collection aims therefore, particularly in the first part of the book, to continue the conversation on the importance of queer biblical hermeneutics by employing the book of Jonah as a reflective surface to demonstrate and practise skills afforded to us by queer biblical hermeneutics.

For instance, *Charlene van der Walt* finds 'a queer kindred in the book of Jonah' as she reflects 'on themes such as calling, conversation, coming-out, belonging, embodiment, repentance, forgiveness, and despondence' in the context of 'a number of auto-ethnographical snapshots' in terms of her own struggle to be included in the Dutch Reformed Church of South Africa. *Rhiannon Graybill* offers 'a feminist and queer reading of consent in the book of Jonah', which 'reveal[s] the (sexual and sexualized) violence of the prophetic call story, the centrality of ambiguity and ambivalence, and the complex representations of harm' in the prophetic traditions. *Steed Vernyl Davidson* explores the notion of 'queer heterotopias in Jonah', which centres on 'Jonah's consistent search to find alternative spaces to imagine the potentiality of another world' in contrast to 'the imperialist discourse that underlies prophetic literature'. *Juliana Claassens*, in conversation with Sara Ahmed's *Queer Phenomenology*, explores how categories of time, space and the prophetic body are undone in the book of Jonah, or one could say, through a lens of queer hermeneutics, rendered 'queer'. *Hendrik Bosman* draws upon queer interpretation to reflect on the ambiguous portrayal of Nineveh as a 'great city' in the book of Jonah as a subtle critique of power relations in Yehud and thereafter. *Lena-Sofia Tiemeyer* examines how interpreters read the book of Jonah against its grain, either to make it conform to standard theological views or to destabilize those same views.

These reading strategies ultimately result in the queering of the straight prophet: the conformist Jonah is given roles and viewpoints that he would never have dreamt of having. Finally, *Jione Havea* in a transtextual reading is bothered by the question of why in certain traditions, the big fish died after delivering Jonah ashore. Read in terms of other religious traditions, Havea reads for the healing of Jonah, as well as for the 'poor fishie'.

## ... and other activists

*Queering the Prophet* is not just about queering Jonah. As evident in the second part of this book, the goal of this engagement with a biblical book like Jonah in all of its complexity as it pertains to our respective contemporary context(s) is to inspire more students, faith and community leaders, parishioners, concerned citizens to become thought leaders and change agents. Or one could say to become (queer) prophets, who are innately strange because of who they are and what they have seen; who carry the wounds of being on the front of the battle for justice in their bodies and psyches. As Bessel van der Kolk famously has written, 'the body keeps the score' (2014, p. 46).

In the conclusion of his study on queer themes in Jonah that brings the diverse life experiences of the LGBTIQA+ community into the conversation drawing on literature and music, Ross offers the following important observation that aligns well with what we aim for with *Queering the Prophet*:

> I feel that one of the most important lessons to be taken from this project is that the formation of a queer Biblical studies must be collaborative, inclusive, and international. We must continue to elevate the voices of marginalised LGBT+ people worldwide, to ensure that queer Biblical studies does not become another field dominated by a hegemony of white, Western academics, and so does not come to resemble the very structures we intend for it to struggle against. (2019, p. 88)

*Queering the Prophet* is unique in the sense that it is able to bring together a wide variety of scholars from different parts of the world, experienced scholars as well as up-and-coming theologians, queer, feminist and postcolonial interpreters, reflecting a diversity of ethnicity, culture, gender, sexual and nationality identities. In the second part of this book, *Queering the Prophet* crosses disciplinary divides as it brings together biblical scholars with scholars from Systematic Theology, History of Christianity, Ethics, Religion and Society, as well as academics with practitioners and activists. Given the original context of the Gender Unit conference that inspired this volume, one finds a strong emphasis on the (South) African context, particularly in Part 2. However, the ongoing battle for justice, inclusion, representation and equality transcends borders and is a constant concern in many contexts around the world.

In this regard, contributors explore the ways in which the role of the prophet is being queered, in our time. Offering a definition for the term 'post-truth', Vittorio Bufacchi (2020) writes:

> Post-truth is a deliberate strategy aimed at creating an environment where objective facts are less influential in shaping public opinion, where theoretical frameworks are undermined in order to make it impossible for someone to make sense of a certain event, phenomenon, or experience, and where scientific truth is delegitimized.

In a time when the lives of queer people – sexual and gender minorities, also referred to as LGBTIQA+ people – are marked by violence and death, contributions consider the ways truth (or the lack thereof) shapes public discourse.

Contributions to the second part of the volume centralize the body and the inescapable reality of context as a starting point for these examples of contemporary truth-telling. The body is understood as a dynamic site of meaning-making, and rather than talking about the bodies of queer people, the volume centres the embodiment and agency of those speaking from a place of queer being and resistance.

For instance, in an example of collaborative authorship,

*Gerald West, Charlene van der Walt, Sithembiso Zwane, Crystal Hall, Sizwe Sithole* and *Tracey Sibisi* reflect on the Contextual Bible Study praxis of the Ujamaa Centre; that is, rereading biblical texts with organized formations of African queer communities. Collectively, these authors resist the 'I' of Paul, trusting in the trickiness of Jesus – and the praxis of the Ujamaa Centre – to summon us as a prophetic plural as we move, slowly, from within an embodied queer 'people's theology' to forms of hetero-patriarchal transformative 'prophetic theology'. *Ashwin Afrikanus Thyssen* reflects 'On the Public Intellectual as Queer Prophet' by considering the pioneering work of two intellectuals – Zethu Matebeni and Charlene van der Walt – who, in terms of their important contribution to the communities of LGBTI+ people, are queering our 'conception of the public intellectual' and thus the prophet. *Jacob Meiring* reflects on the life and legacy of Desmond Tutu as a queer prophet as he increasingly came to embody and speak out for LGBTIQA+ equality. And the chapter from *Stephen Kapinde* and *Adriaan van Klinken*, in the context of anti-queer campaigns dominant in African Pentecostal traditions, draws a spotlight on the ministry of a queer prophet in Kenya, Apostle Darlan Rukih of the Bride of the Lamb Ministries International Church, 'who openly identifies as intersex and performs gender ambiguity'. And *Rosa Ross* brings into conversation biblical circumcision and gender-affirming surgery in the context of transgender identity.

Finally, a central feature of the book's second part is the two roundtables that allow readers to hear the voices of young scholars, activists and people of faith who are front and centre in the struggle for justice. We hear, for instance, of what it means to be a womanist scholar in an (academic) world still dominated by white and/or male scholars. And we hear from practitioners who are, or have been, involved with the work of IAM (Inclusive and Affirming Ministries), a non-profit partner doing excellent work in raising awareness and changing hearts and minds regarding diversities of all kinds.

These roundtables are informed by the collaborative, critically reflective scholarship that is characteristic of the multi-authored contribution coming from the Ujamaa Centre, whose work in Contextual Bible Reading bridges academic and ecclesial/community contexts. These examples of collective writing in and of themselves offers a methodological challenge to the often-pervasive solitary understanding of prophecy. Rather than thinking of the prophet as the lone figure of truth-telling, the collective essays speak to the embodied and collective process of contemporary truth-telling. Beyond content, *Queering the Prophet* offers queer scholarship in terms of style, genre and methodological orientation.

## Notes

1 This poem, 'A Jonah', is used with the permission of the author. It appeared in the *Norwegian Writer's Climate Campaign* in 2020, available at https://forfatternesklimaaksjon.files.wordpress.com/2020/08/nickolebrown-poemforfreddy1.pdf, and was previously published in *The Birmingham Poetry Review* 46 (2019).

2 LGBTIQA+ is used as shorthand referring to sexual and gender minorities, who may identify as lesbian, gay, bisexual, transgender, intersex, queer and asexual; the plus (+) signifies those who may not identify with the previous markers yet who consider themselves minorities.

3 Goss and West (eds) 2022; see also the earlier edition, Guest (ed.) 2006.

4 See, for instance, Hoke 2021; Marchal 2020; Marchal (ed.) 2019; Townsley 2017; Macwilliam 2016; Hornsby and Guest (eds) 2016; Cornwall (ed.) 2015; Hornsby and Stone (eds) 2011; Stone 2005; Goss and West (eds) 2000.

5 See, for instance, Van Klinken 2021; Paul 2020; Nolasco 2019; Tonstad, Matyila, Sithole and Van der Walt 2019; Tonstad 2018; Thatcher 2011; Cheng 2011; Loughlin (ed.) 2009); Althaus-Reid 2002.

6 See Niditch 2022; Hunter 2022; Erickson 2021); Tiemeyer 2021; Havea 2020; Graybill et al. 2023; Fischer forthcoming; Claassens forthcoming.

7 Ross 2019.

# References

Ahmed, Sara, 2006, *Queer Phenomenology: Orientations, Objects, Others*, Durham, NC: Duke University Press.

Althaus-Reid, Marcella, 2002, *Indecent Theology*, London & New York: Routledge.

Brown, Nickole, 2019, 'A Jonah', *The Birmingham Poetry Review* 46.

Bufacchi, Vittorio, 2020, 'Truth, Lies and Tweets: A Consensus Theory of Post-Truth', *Philosophy & Social Criticism* 47/3, https://doi.org/10.1177/0191453719896382, accessed 15.12.2022.

Cheng, Patrick S., 2011, *Radical Love: An Introduction to Queer Theology*, New York: Seabury.

Claassens, L. Juliana, forthcoming, *Jonah*, OTL, Louisville, KY: Westminster John Knox Press.

Cornwall, Susannah (ed.), 2015, *Intersex, Theology, and the Bible: Troubling Bodies in Church, Text, and Society*, New York: Palgrave Macmillan.

Erickson, Amy, 2021, *Jonah: Introduction and Commentary*. Illuminations, Grand Rapids, MI: William B. Eerdmans.

Fischer, Irmtraud, forthcoming, *Jonah*, Internationaler Exegetischer Kommentar zum Alten Testament; Stuttgart: Kohlhammer Verlag.

Goss, Robert and Mona West (eds), 2022, *The Queer Bible Commentary*, 2nd edn, London: SCM Press.

Goss, Robert E. and Mona West (eds), 2000, *Take Back the Word: A Queer Reading of the Bible*, Cleveland, OH: The Pilgrim Press.

Graybill, Rhiannon, 2016, *Are We Not Men? Unstable Masculinity in the Hebrew Prophet*, Oxford: Oxford University Press.

Graybill, Rhiannon, John Kaltner and Steven L. McKenzie, 2023, *Jonah*. Anchor Yale Bible Commentaries, New Haven, CT: Yale University Press.

Guest, Deryn (ed.), 2006, *The Queer Bible Commentary*, London: SCM Press.

Havea, Jione, 2020, *Jonah: An Earth Bible Commentary*, London: T&T Clark.

Hoke, Jimmy, 2021, *Feminism, Queerness, Affect, and Romans: Under God?* Atlanta, GA: SBL Press.

Hornsby, Teresa J. and Deryn Guest (eds), 2016, *Transgender, Intersex and Biblical Interpretation*. Semeia Studies 83, Atlanta, GA: SBL Press.

Hornsby, Theresa J. and Ken Stone (eds), 2011, *Bible Trouble: Queer Reading at the Boundaries of Biblical Scholarship*. Semeia Studies 67, Atlanta, GA: SBL Press.

Hunter, Alastair G., 2022, *The Judgement of Jonah: Yahweh, Jerusalem and Nineveh*, London: T&T Clark.

Loughlin, Gerard (ed.), 2009, *Queer Theology: Rethinking the Western Body*, Malden, MA: Blackwell Publishing.

Macwilliam, Stuart, 2016, *Queer Theory and the Prophetic Marriage Metaphor in the Hebrew Bible*, London and New York: Routledge.

Marchal, Joseph A. (ed.), 2019, *Bodies on the Verge: Queering Pauline Epistles*. Semeia St 93, Atlanta, GA: SBL Press.

Marchal, Joseph A., 2020, *Appalling Bodies: Queer Figures Before and After Paul's Letters*, Oxford: Oxford University Press.

Niditch, Susan, 2022, *Jonah*, Hermeneia, Minneapolis, MN: Fortress Press.

Nolasco, Rolf, 2019, *God's Beloved Queer: Identity, Spirituality, and Practice*, Eugene, OR: Wipf & Stock.

Paul, Greg, 2020, *Queer Theology: The Bible's Surprise Ending to the Story of Sexuality and Gender*, Eugene, OR: Wipf & Stock.

Ross, Samuel, 2019, 'Queer Themes in the Book of Jonah and its Contemporary Analogues', MTh thesis, School of Critical Studies College of Arts, University of Glasgow.

Stone, Kenneth, 2005, *Practicing Safer Texts: Food, Sex and Bible in Queer Perspective*, London: Bloomsbury T&T Clark.

Thatcher, Adrian, 2011, *God, Sex, and Gender: An Introduction*, Hoboken, NJ: Wiley-Blackwell.

Tiemeyer, Lena-Sofia, 2021, *Jonah Through the Centuries*, Wiley Blackwell Bible Commentaries, Hoboken, NJ: John Wiley & Sons.

Tonstad, Hanzline R., Abongile Matyila, Sindi Sithole and Charlene van der Walt, 2019, 'Stabanisation: A Discussion Paper about Disrupting Backlash by Reclaiming LGBTI Voices in the African Church Landscape', Johannesburg: The Other Foundation.

Tonstad, Linn Marie, 2018, *Queer Theology: Beyond Apologetics*, Eugene, OR: Wipf & Stock.

Townsley, Gillian, 2017, *The Straight Mind in Corinth: Queer Readings Across 1 Corinthians 11:2–16*. Semeia Studies 88, Atlanta, GA: SBL Press.

Van der Kolk, Bessel A., 2014, *The Body Keeps the Score: Brain, Mind, and Body in the Healing of Trauma*, New York: Viking.

Van Klinken, Adriaan, 2021, *Kenyan, Christian, Queer*, University Park, PA: Penn State University Press.

Williams, Jennifer, 2006, 'Queer Readings of the Prophets' in Carolyn Sharp (ed.), *Oxford Handbook to the Prophets*, Oxford: Oxford University Press, pp. 527–45.

# PART I

# Queering the Prophet Jonah

# These Are the Days of Raw Despondence: Finding a Queer Kindred in the Book of Jonah

CHARLENE VAN DER WALT

## Introduction

*It was clearly communicated that I and those like me were not welcome to the special General Synod meeting of the Dutch Reformed Church that took place in Pretoria in 2016. The special synod was called precisely to deal with the disruption of LGBTIQA+ people and their unruly bodies that were welcomed and affirmed during the 2015 synod, but that subsequently created a great deal of conflict and strife and therefore necessitated a special Synod meeting. The Sunday newspaper announced that no disruption would be tolerated and that those with #Liefdeisliefde T-shirts would not be allowed to enter the meeting. Upon arrival at the meeting venue the reception was chilling and the aggression tangible. I slipped past those who were stationed with strict orders not to allow us into the meeting venue and found a seat at the edge of the pew on the balcony. A man, not much older than me, probably an elder in the church structures, approached me and demanded that I leave the meeting venue. He insisted that it was clearly communicated that I was not welcome and that I should leave. In response to my refusal, he took me by the arm and indicated that if I refused, I would be forcefully removed. In the midst of this threatening encounter, the moderator of the church meeting started proceedings on the meeting floor and welcomed all present. He indicated that the meeting would start by all those present sharing the signs of the Eucharist and that also the guests to the Synod meeting on the balcony would be invited to partake in the communal sacramental meal. In what felt like a heartbeat, the hand that was instructed to forcefully remove me became the hand that had to share the broken body of Christ with me in the signs of bread and wine. To this day words escape me to express the violence, the disjunctedness and the strange grace of these moments.*

As I, surrounded by and embedded within a community of LGBTIQA+ change-makers within the landscape of the Dutch Reformed Church in South Africa, paged through the book of Jonah in preparation for developing this contribution, I noted points of resonance. We collectively noted points of resonance. I found spaces in the text where I could relate. Spaces where the membrane of my own experience wore thin as it brushed up against the story of the solitary, stubborn, unruly and vulnerable prophet that we encounter in the book of Jonah.

Hartmut Rosa in an interview with Schiermer reflects on the importance of the concept of resonance when elucidating on the implied meaning of 'resonance':

First, af ← fection: we feel truly touched or moved by someone or something we encounter ... Second, e → motion: we feel that we answer this 'call', we react to it with body and mind, we reach out and touch the other side as well – in a word, we experience self-efficacy in this encounter ... Third, in this process of being touched and affected by something and of reacting and answering to it, we are transformed – or we transform ourselves in the sense of a co-production. However, and this is the fourth element, resonance is always characterised by an element of elusiveness. ... [T]his elusiveness also means that it is impossible to predict or control what the result of an experience of resonance will be, what the process of transformation will result in. (Schiermer and Pettenkofer 2017, p. 3)

Possibly one of the strongest points of resonance for me personally at the time was the raw despondence that we note in the posture of the prophet at the end of the book. I could relate to Jonah, sitting dejected to the east of the city in the glaring sun after being a witness to his own journey's unfolding. The raw despondence, the disappointment and the disillusionment as he sat suspended in a moment, not overjoyed by grace and not yet ready to move on. Just sitting to the east of the city in the sun. Something of that posture resonated with me and I found within the contours of this ancient narrative a kindred spirit.

As argued elsewhere, I believe that text holds the possibility for encounter, sense-making and meaning-making (Van der Walt 2015, pp. 66–7; Van der Walt and Terblanche 2016, pp. 177–9 and Van der Walt 2018, pp. 170–74). The resonances that we feel and the recognitions that we register imply finding a space for the unexpected and the tacit, the aesthetic and the relational. The hermeneutical process to my mind is an invitation to enter into conversation and to make meaning of the 'narrative gaps and textual silences' that prevail in the book of Jonah, and other biblical narratives, as highlighted by Elizabeth Boase and Sarah Agnew (2016, p. 4). As such, I have always been drawn to approaches that take seriously the role of the reader in the interpretative process and that acknowledge that readers show up to the process of interpretation with tools, contextually cultivated resources, and most importantly life experiences. Such approaches understand and take cognizance of the fact that readers and their contexts shape readings. Not everyone who is concerned with the hermeneutical process acknowledges this reality of course. Some still argue for objectivity in the interpretative process, for truths in the text that exist beyond the process of interpretation. Some deny the fact that what you see depends on where you stand.

In line with the counter-normative impulses of Queer Theory, this essay queerly takes back the biblical text that has often been appropriated as a weapon to justify the exclusion and violence directed towards the bodies of African LGBTIQA+ people, or *Izitabane*, as they are often referred to in a derogatory manner. As already noted, I understand texts as reflective surfaces that invite encounter and interpretation. As such, the biblical narrative is used as a reflective surface to enable an auto-ethnographical *stabanizing* encounter with the queer kindred in the book of Jonah. I deliberately choose to employ indigenous terminology such as *Izitabane* and the act of *stabanizing* or queering, to situate this contribution in the South African context and to push back in a decolonial manner against ideas that LGBTIQA+ is a Western construct not present in the African context. The essay leans into the disruptive and transgressive nature of queer by offering a mashup of style and genre to reflect on themes such as calling, conversation, coming-out, belonging, embodiment, repentance, forgiveness and despondence. Several auto-ethnographical snapshots emerge as intertextual narratives when engaging the book of Jonah in the context of the struggle for full *Izitabane* inclusions in the Dutch Reformed Church of South Africa. The essay blurs the lines between what is considered personal and political and offers the first attempt at an unruly reading of the book of Jonah in this volume.

The audacity to do this, to take up the text, to read, to discover myself and my life within the pages of the biblical text, has not always been straightforward or a given reality. In what feels like a lifetime ago, I discovered the wonder of a diversity of interpretative tools that could be appropriated in the process of reading the biblical text in the Department of Old and New Testament at the Faculty of Theology at Stellenbosch University in South Africa. I was guided by generous and gifted scholars such as Hendrik Bosman, Bernard Combrink, Louis Jonker and later Elna Mouton and Julie Claassens. I was introduced to a rich diversity of interpretative approaches and methods that allow for more in-depth engagement with the text and more 'responsible and accountable' contextual interpretations (Schüssler Fiorenza 1988, pp. 16–17).

I have always been drawn to the narrative world of the Old Testament, but ironically enough it was through engaging in the little book *Opsoek na Jona: Verskilllende Benaderings tot die Interpretasie van die Bybel* (ed. Ernst Conradie, Louis Jonker and Douglas Lauwrie 1995 – later translated into English with the title *Fishing for Jonah*, and even later *Fishing for Jonah*

*Anew*) that things fell into place for me. The book illustrated the contours of different interpretative approaches by using the book of Jonah as the foundational text.

It was a great locally developed introduction to the hermeneutical process that illustrated how different methods and approaches contribute something unique and significant to the project of the interpretative process. *Opsoek na Jona* started by reflecting on classical approaches and then gradually moved to more contemporary and experimental approaches. It allowed me to grapple with the importance of the historical-critical approach and to take seriously the world of the text in literary critical approaches. However, approaches focusing on the reception of the text and approaches that seriously considered power in the interpretative process animated me and brought something alive in me.

Through reading and engaging the book and following the trails it offered into other theoretical landscapes I discovered feminist, postcolonial, contextual and African interpretative strategies. I discovered that I could take up the invitation, from my particular contextual place to read the biblical text. That the interpretation of the text did not belong to cisgender, white, heterosexual men who were either sanctioned by the church or the academy to read the biblical text on my behalf or for me. Until this discovery, I believed (as so many continue to do) that the text can only be read by those whom God has chosen or those who navigate the corridors of academia. I realized through the exploration that the book made possible that the text held an invitation to me.

Fundamentally, I think the point that the book was trying to make in the end was that there is no single, exclusive or super-approach to reading the text. That there is no one-size-fits-all approach and that not even the extreme attempts by some to master a diversity of different interpretative approaches and techniques would lead to the complete, correct or final interpretations of the text. The book pointed out the flaws, shortcomings, challenges and dangers of all the various individual approaches. In time, I started to realize that the point was not to be an expert on every single approach or dimension of the interpretative process, but rather to hold a gentle balance between different approaches to reading the text and to value the variety of gifts that a diverse interpretative community hold.

Many contemporary discussions on the nature and validity of the interpretative endeavour especially as it relates to ethical matters have become highly contested and polarized. Interpreters from various sides of the interpretative process make enemies of each other and cast suspicion on one another. To my mind, *Opsoek na Jona* and other subsequent resources, however, argued for a collective and communal interpretative process. In this process, we realize that the text does not only hold an invitation to me or those like me but rather it holds an invitation to all of us and it holds an invitation for community. This early lesson sparked in me a commitment to power-critical contextual and communal approaches to the interpretation of scripture.

Although some dimensions of my person and contextual situatedness and interpretative concerns were addressed by a few of the latter approaches discussed in *Fishing for Jonah*, there were dimensions of my life and my person that I did not find reflected in the book.

It is safe to say that when I first read *Fishing for Jonah* queer biblical hermeneutics was not an interpretative approach that many took cognizance of, certainly not in the South African context. However, even in subsequent editions of the book queer biblical hermeneutics still has not been considered as something noteworthy for inclusion (Jonker and Lawrie 2005). As argued elsewhere, I propose that:

(Q)ueer biblical hermeneutics is a helpful theoretical tool because it questions dominant ideas rooted in heteronormativity by critiquing hegemonies that exist in the use of biblical texts or even within biblical texts themselves, and it also enables the opening of space for more experiences to matter in the interpretation process. (Van der Walt 2022, p. 102)

The deconstructivist approach draws foundationally on the work of the French philosopher Michel Foucault and troubles, destabilizes and disrupts everything that is considered normative, natural or matter of fact. When drawing on the imperatives of this approach in the engagement of the biblical text queer hermeneutics invites us as diverse interpreters to sit with the discomfort of those things that seem strange, out of place, or counter-normative within the text but also with the diversity of interpretations that develop as others take up the text and read it for themselves. For our modern sensibilities, the text is full of strange things. Strange things like someone who runs away from a divine calling. Someone who would rather dive into the deep, than going to deliver a message to those who have been oppressed and dehumanized. The book of Jonah notes, with concern, the divine correction, forcing Jonah to make his way to the oppressor despite his protest.

The approach deliberately and subversively brings stories into conversation that on the surface have little to do with each other. Queer hermeneutics searches for points of resonance between the seemingly unconnected, like between the prophet Jonah in this strange little book in the Hebrew Bible and a white Afrikaans-speaking Dutch Reformed Church lesbian socially engaged biblical scholar who has tried to labour in community with others for full inclusion of LGBTIQA+ people in the Dutch Reformed Church.

A queer approach picks up on these dimensions and rather than trying to gloss over it or pretend like it is not an outrageous hyperbolic tale, it starts the process of interpretation at the point of discomfort and asks what possibilities for meaning exist if we disrupt the status quo, if we read against the normative, the decent and the expected. What happens if we risk creativity, if we imagine, if we dream, if we think beyond prose to poetry?

We see traces of this through the work offered by queer biblical scholars and those who draw on the theoretical insights offered by queer scholarship. In this essay, I contribute to this ongoing and developing project by offering some reflections on the points of resonance for me as I bring memories, stories, images, forgotten and half-remembered song lyrics to the point of intersection with the Jonah narrative.

The book of Jonah is a narrative that developed within a specific context and was intended to be read and reread and is to this day still read by people who are disenfranchised and marginalized. Numerous postcolonial and decolonial scholars pick up on the reality of empire that functions as the backdrop to this story (Havea 2013; 2016; Ryu 2016; Claassens 2021). They note in the background of the narrative people who suffer or who have suffered and who tell these stories to make sense and to deal with the wordlessness that is left when you experience earth-shattering trauma. The background of the book consists of people trying to make sense, and make meaning in the light of despair, dehumanization and death.

## Being considered a disobedient problem

The first point of resonance for me with Jonah is being considered a disobedient problem. Disobedience connects me to Jonah and serves as a link to the short personal narrative that introduces this essay. In his reception by traditional and mainstream interpreters, Jonah is often considered an example of a disobedient problem (Keller 2018; Laurie 2014). He is highlighted as an example of one who does not listen to God's voice in calling and who has to 'be brought into line' to fulfil his purpose. Boase and Agnew reflect on this when stating: 'Too often, however, readers read against Jonah and Jonah's community, filling the textual silences in ways that portray this prophetic figure and his community as anti-heroes – object lessons on how not to behave' (2006, p. 6).

Feminist, postcolonial and trauma theorists ask if this line of interpretation is a fair reflection on the complexity that the prophet navigates in this narrative. If we take seriously the work of trauma and postcolonial theorists, can we blame Jonah for not being so excited about the prospect of going to the heart of the empire and to go and preach to those who continue to exploit, misrecognize and benefit from this exploitation?

Being considered a disobedient problem is not something new for African LGBTIQA+ people. LGBTIQA+ people are often seen; our difference is written on the body and our otherness leaves us vulnerable and open to being wounded (Van der Walt and Davids 2022). As referred to above, we see this well illustrated in the derogatory naming of African LGBTIQA+ people as *Izitabane* but also in the alarming increase of violence committed against LGBTIQA+ people in the African context (Igual 2022). Of course, this visible difference also inspires agency, creativity, and the possibility for connection and meaning-making, but overwhelmingly it often inspires vulnerability. Although it is not the case for everyone and some indeed can 'pass', fitting the prescribed mould for the expression of gender identity and sexual orientation prescribed by heteropatriarchy, for most this is not the case.

For most of us, our otherness and our visible difference are something that people know, even before they know that they know it. Is it in the way you walk, talk, dress, carry yourself, speak, situate yourself or camouflage yourself? Perhaps it is the sum of all of these things, or maybe not even one single thing. This otherness that is written on the body is often a source of shame, not only for the self but also for the family, community and faith community that you are born into.

Underlying this problematic status or classification as unruly is a normative system. To understand the mechanisms of control and the susceptibility of violence for *Izitabane* people one has to take cognizance of the systemic reality informing it. The increasingly explored term econo-heteropatriarchy or CisHetPatCap aims to express the systemic affinities and life-denying realities that develop when patriarchy, heteronormativity and socio-economic models informed by these ideologies combine (West 2021; Van der Walt 2021). When it comes to the navigation of sexual orientation and gender identity this systemic reality relies on the foundational understanding that sex is biologically essentialist and finds expression in the binary categorization of sex as male and female. Such categorizations inform an insistence on the alignment of biological sex with gender identity and sexual orientation. This in turn informs hegemonic constructions of masculinity that frame men primarily as powerful providers, protectors, and penetrators (Ngcobo 2022). Within this frame, reproduction is understood as a moral imperative and this in turn leads to stable notions of what constitutes a 'natural family'.

Those who embody and story life at the margins or counter the heteronormative ideal are often stigmatized, marginalized or at worst violently annihilated. One of the key mechanisms identified by theorists like Foucault and others to protect and maintain the normative operates through the gaze of surveillance. Quite often, through surveillance individuals are systemically kept in check especially when it comes to embodiment, sex and pleasure. The normative gaze of surveillance aims to keep the norm intact by undermining, discrediting, undoing or violently annihilating or correcting all that is considered counter-normative or perverted. Strategies designed at keeping the norm intact are not neutral or innocent but are prone to violence and find expression in homophobic hate speech, violence and hate crimes that are ultimately intended for erasure. Corrective or curative homophobic hate crimes and practices of conversation therapy represent the same systemic impulse that underlies it, namely, to force those who are different to conform or return to the norm or golden standard as prescribed by heteronormativity and patriarchy. These strategies often play out in our intimate spaces and intimate relationships, within the confines of spaces that we would naturally deem safe.

Jonah's counter-normative behaviour and how he is corrected within the narrative and also by subsequent communities of traditional interpreters offer a reflective surface to contemporary queer interpreters like me to think about difference and how those who are considered a disobedient problem are often responded to with deliberate violence.

## Conversion moment?

The second point of resonance pertains to the notion of calling. Jonah receives a divine calling into a less-than-desirable landscape when he is called to deliver the divine message of judgment to the heart of the exploiting force in Nineveh. For LGBTIQA+ people who feel a sense of calling or who receive a calling into formal ministry, the precarity of context might seem similar to what is expected of Jonah. Econo-heteropatriarchy as a foundational ideology is bolstered by religion and culture in the African context. Being called, as a queer person, to serve within faith institutions that are foundationally underpinned by notions of patriarchy and heteronormativity is often at best a complex reality to navigate and at worst a violent one.

While being stationed as a minister of religion in Grahamstown (Makanda) in the Eastern Cape of South Africa, I recall a subtle change that took place in me over time as I navigated the complexity of Dutch Reformed ministry as a queer person. This season was made particularly complicated for me because I knew that the formal position of the Dutch Reformed Church at the time was not welcoming and to live out my sense of calling, I felt that I could not fully and freely express my sexual orientation as a lesbian woman (Van der Walt 2015).

*Sunday after Sunday as I would walk up the pulpit to offer the weekly sermon I would pray: 'Dear God, you know my life and you know the journey of this week, but, please, let something happen here today despite of who I am.' In time, this prayer shifted to not asking for something to happen here despite of who I am, but rather because of who I am and because I knew what it meant to be below and outside. 'Dear God,' I would pray, 'Let something happen here today, because of the gift that my different-kind-of-life-and-love can be to this community.'*

In Jonah 2, we find Jonah queerly suspended in time and space, in a sort of in-between state, in the belly of the fish. Jonah, where natural imagery abound, is exploring the contours of his calling in a conversational prayer to God. He is neither fleeing any longer nor yet going to where he is called to. In the belly of the fish, Jonah is busy with the work of sense-making and reframing.

This state of being queerly in-between and navigating calling is something that I could relate to, and to a certain extent still do. Although having a strong sense of personal calling, I could not find a safe foothold within the faith community that I was serving. I found myself disorientated by the heteronormative mould and the desired profile that this ideology created for an ideal minister of religion. This ideal image of a minister of religion as cisgender, male, heterosexual and married with children often finds clear expression in the job search advertisements that one finds in the church job application sites and bulletins within faith communities.[1] The ideology that functions behind these hiring profiles is explored by both Ashwin Thyssen (2020) and Hanzline Davids (2020) in the context of the Uniting Reformed Church in Southern Africa.

When reading Jonah's prayer from the position of my navigation and reflections on calling in a hostile context, I found myself asking if what we are witnessing here is a true and heartfelt moment of conversation. Is Jonah aligning himself with the divine calling? Is he going to conform to the expected prophetic standard of obedience? From my perspective and also considering his posture in delivering and digesting the response to his task at the end of the book, it seems like he is trying hard to convince himself of something that might imply more of a process of discovery than a one-off event. So rather than reading this prayer as a radical moment of transformation, it sounds more like an expression of hope to gain some faith or conviction. The prayer seems fleeting and unfolding in its expression and something that might gain form or contours in its unfolding.

As part of a current collective project, I interviewed 20 Dutch Reformed LGBTIQA+ clergy, theological students, proponents of ministry, and theologians for a project to develop a Queer Digital Archive of the stories of queer clergy in the Dutch Reformed Church (Van der Walt and Van der Riet 2022). Some of the themes explored in the individual interviews include the navigation and integration of sexuality and spirituality, the process of 'coming out' or maybe rather 'letting-in', and the meaning and experience of calling and imagination for an inclusive and affirming Dutch Reformed Church. While conducting the interviews I discovered strong points of connection and similarity in how queer clergy within the contours of the Dutch Reformed Church navigate calling. Although each story is unique and offers insight into different eras of the faith communities' ongoing process of navigating LGBTIQA+ inclusion, in general, three trends could be observed. For most of those who participated in the interviews, the understanding of calling remains an ongoing process and has shifted in shape and meaning over time. For most respondents, the first understanding of calling strongly related to the formal and structural congregational ministry context, but in time this notion shifted to less institutionalized understandings of calling. Second, almost all of the interviewees expressed a sense of fit between their gifts, skills, or abilities and the needs that are prevalent in faith communities or the ministerial context. Despite resistance, hostility, or violence experienced within the ministerial context, most had a sense of natural suitability within the context of ministry. Third, for most respondents, their situatedness within a formal institutional ministerial context remains a queer disconnected reality. Most find themselves unable to sustain life for prolonged periods within the confines of a heteronormative and patriarchal institution and therefore are often situated in in-between spaces or find themselves dabbling in a variety of structures and contexts at the same time. For those who belong without belonging, Jonah seems an appropriate queer kindred as we witness his navigation of calling in a life-denying context.

## An embodied sermon

Interpreters of the Jonah narrative make much of the brevity and powerful impact of the sermon delivered by the solitary Jonah to the city of Nineveh. Without an outpouring of words and emotions, the lone Jonah evokes in the people and animals that call Nineveh home such remorse and insight that his words lead to a mass conversion and acts of deep repentance and penitence.

In contrast to the lone prophetic figure in the book of Jonah, in the work for LGBTIQA+ inclusion in the Dutch Reformed Church, there exists a counter community of care. A queer collective of change-makers with a diversity of positionalities, strategies for change, gifts and abilities to point out blind spots. Rather than a lone hero for change, this work has implied collective engagement and collaborative decrement and action. The work progresses through a community that I am part of, that I sometimes disqualify myself from, that I hide from, but one that I always seem to return to for encounter, for restoration, for care, for community, for re-humanization and for action.

Jonah's unconventional sermon made me think of an organic change-making strategy that spontaneously developed among members of the queer collective who were present at the watershed 2015 Dutch Reformed Synod in Pretoria. The so-called issue of 'same-sex relationships' was again on the agenda and despite numerous attempts to move the conversation about us to a conversation with us, the container of the discussion was again limited to church leaders of the Dutch Reformed Church speaking about LGBTIQA+ people. Rather than talking with us or allowing us to find words for our own experience in conversation, there was again an attempt to pretend we did not exist, as if we were not present amid the Dutch Reformed Church as clergy, theological students, theologians and change-makers. Within the contours of our change-making process, we collectively came to the end of words and, without a specific mandate, we knew that our presence at that meeting was non-negotiable. After some discussion, we came up with a t-shirt design and the slogan #LiefdeisLiefde (#LoveisLove) to articulate something of our common humanity and our collective desire for love and belonging. Initially, we sat at the back of the meeting venue as observers, wordlessly, present. After some time, to enhance our visibility, we moved to the gallery space of the meeting venue and remained present throughout the discussion as embodied examples of the 'issue' that was being discussed.

Figure 1: Original image by Dr Elize Morkel, used with written consent, capturing the embodied protest at the 2015 Dutch Reformed Church General Synod meeting in Pretoria, South Africa.
Pictured, left to right, are Charlene van der Walt, Michelle Boonzaaier, Hennie Pienaar and Lulani Vermeulen.

The image, captured by Elize Morkel from the meeting floor, has become an iconic image of LGBTIQA+ embodied change-making in the Dutch Reformed Church. The image represents something beyond talking and the embodied resistance that remains when one comes to the end of words in the face of injustice. Settler and Engh reflect on the possibility of embodied agency when staking: 'The body is not simply a site of inscription but also significantly, a site of performance, resisting and self-asserting' (2015, p. 132).

In Jonah's case, the response to his call for repentance is a hyperbole of repentance and acts of remorse. We see an outpouring of regret and also embodied acts of penitence. Not everyone, however, is convinced by these over-the-top motions of repentance. Chesung Ryu, a Korean postcolonial scholar, writes:

All the Ninevites, including their kin, don sackcloth and pro-claim a fast. In their fear and effort to display their repentance clearly, they ludicrously even put sackcloth on their beasts! Their repentance, however, fails to target their brutal plunder of their weaker neighbors including Israel. There is no indication of restitution towards their victims. To Jonah and the implied readers, the repentance of Nineveh is hypocritical repentance, repentance only for a domestic matter, totally lacking the compensatory action to the people they violated. It is a temporary repentance, perhaps even only for the sake of deception ... (2016, p. 230)

Within the Dutch Reformed Church, there have been numerous formulations of apology and repentance.[2] In 2002 the Dutch Reformed Church moved away from its initial stance of con-demnation as articulated in the 1986 concept document about homosexuality and offered an apology with sadness and regret because of a stance that did not speak of a posture of love and care. In 2004 there was a statement of apology because of the hurt caused to LGBTIQA+ members and their families. In 2015 when the Dutch Reformed Church took a progressive decision to include and affirm LGBTIQA+ ministers and members, there was again an apology because of homophobic language and behaviour that has been prevalent in the faith community. All of these expressions of apology speak of the awareness of a breakdown in relationships.

I think it reasonable to reflect on the validity and authenticity of these acts and words of repentance in the light of ongo-ing LGBTIQA+ exclusion and how formal faith structures, role players, and leaders continue to pander to a vocal, well-organized, oppositional minority.

Ryu continues his argument and writes in the context of the expressions of remorse witnessed in the city of Nineveh:

... to the oppressed whose lands had been plundered or exploited, who had experienced slavery or colonization, and who were still suffering from the long-lasting scars left by the actions of their oppressors, this type of repentance without any reference to restitution would have been considered insincere and totally unacceptable. (2016, p. 230)

The call for repentance and acts of remorse that we witness in the book of Jonah, read against the backdrop of systemic exploitation and injustice as highlighted above, offers us a dynamic reflective surface to think about the role of others' emotions and tears in the process of change-making. In conclusion of this section, I offer three short reflections that warrant our collective attention and critical engagement.

First, within the process of working for LGBTIQA+ liberation in faith spaces, there is often an expectation that LGBTIQA+ people must tell their stories or offer their narratives to educate the majority on their experience of injustice. This burden of education is not only placed on LGBTIQA+ people in the context of homophobia and heteronormativity, but we can trace these same realities in conversations about gender, race, class, ability and ethnicity. There remains an expectation that the vulnerable, marginalized and disenfranchised must 'perform their pain'. This raises important questions about where the burden of responsibility rests when we are working for change. Is it the work of the wounded minority or the marginalized to educate those in power? Or do we need to cultivate a culture of greater interrogation of our privilege and positionality so that we don't have to rely on the wounded to stay captured in a state of woundedness for our education?

Second, and particular to the context of the LGBTIQA+ discussion in the Dutch Reformed Church, there has been an appropriation of emotion that has been used to frustrate and derail processes aimed at restoring human dignity and LGBTIQA+ inclusion. Most recently there has been a spate of conservative faith communities, most noteworthy the Moreleta Kairos Network, which has started a process of 'mourning and weeping' because of the more inclusive direction that the Dutch Reformed Church has been taking towards LGBTIQA+ people since 2015.[3] The use of tears and lamentation to derail efforts for inclusion and justice to my mind warrants serious interrogation and critical reflection and I think the systemic realities informing the injustice that Jonah's community experiences could be a helpful starting point for reflections of this nature.

Finally, there is a need for reflection on the embodied nature, implications and cost of our processes of self-actualization, identity construction and community formation. The embodied nature and cost of change-making in dehumanizing systems is something that asks for acknowledgement and the development of communities of care and support. The liberation struggle implies the long haul and this requires more urgent and authentic reflections on how we care for change-makers and how we offer support to those in the trenches.

I don't think our grappling with hurt inflicted and injustice committed as change-makers within the Dutch Reformed Church is unique, but I think the book of Jonah offers an important reflective surface to ask serious questions about the process of forgiveness, healing and restoration and what this endgame of inclusion and celebration of LGBTIQA+ lives in the Dutch Reformed Church looks like. There is a need to ask serious questions about the balance between words and deeds of regret and repentance and the process of restoration and restitution. There is a need to move beyond touching formulations to change in behaviour. And foundationally there is a need to reflect on who determines the agenda for this process of recognition and inclusion and maybe also a pertinent question about how long you hang on to be seen. How long do we stay at the table if respect is not being served?

## Raw despondence

As stated at the beginning of this contribution, the first thing that drew me to Jonah was his anger, despondence and silence in the final part of the book. I found resonance with his posture, sitting to the east of the city, in the sun. Raw, angry desponded. Not leaving, but rather angrily being there. This scene brought to memory a song by the Canadian artist and poet, Alanis Morissette, who brings to words something of what is often left unsaid at the end of a relationship. Something of the formulation seemed appropriate and reminiscent of the posture that we witness in Jonah at the end of the book. Captured in the title of this contribution, Morissette sings that 'These are the days of raw despondence.' She continues that she never could have imagined having to lay down her torch for her beloved.[4]

Jione Havea helped me to grapple with the bad break-up that we witness at the end of the book when he writes:

> The thorn in my side is not that i do not want a merciful G*d, but that it rubs salt into my native eyes when mercy trumps justice for desperate and colonized peoples. The poor and downtrodden obviously need mercy. But mercy benefits those who have done wrong more than those who are desperate. If i have to choose between mercy and justice, i pick justice because it benefits those who have been wronged and with whom i am in solidarity. (2013, p. 50)

Havea helped me to recognize the contours of my silent anger. Anger, not so much directed at people or role-players or those situated 'at the other side' of the fight for liberation, but rather at the systems of oppression that functions as the heart of empire and how God is/is made complicit to these systems.

The story offers me a reflective surface to move beyond the individual to the systemic. Normative systems of power are exceptionally pervasive and insidious. The stories they tell are hard to refute. They gaslight and discredit those who do not conform or who do not fit in. These systems are complex and intersect with each other in pervasive and surprising ways. One can be marginalized by some of these systems and benefit profoundly from others, and to this complexity, I am not blind.

But I am currently finding myself sitting to the east of the Dutch Reformed Church, in the blistering sun, being devastated because and with those who still suffer violence and dehumanization because of the dominant systems that constitute realties of race, class, gender and sexual orientation. I find myself angry at those not willing to interrogate the privileges and benefits that come from an alignment with these systems and I find myself wordless for how God and the World continue to be shaped by that which is white, male, heterosexual, capitalist, Western, cisgender.

## Notes

1 For a Dutch Reformed Church example of an exclusive job-search placement, see https://kerkbode.christians.co.za/2018/02/26/lynnwoodrif-gemeente/, accessed 7.06.2023. The pervasive nature of job-search advertisements of this nature in the Dutch Reformed Church has led to the development of a new style guide in order to enhance equality and inclusion: https://kerkbode.christians.co.za/2021/06/18/vakatures-nuwe-gids-vir-gelykheid-van-geleenthede/.

2 For more on the process and the formal decision-making timeline in the Dutch Reformed Church about so-called 'same-sex relationships', see the document produced by its General Synod (Algemene Sinode Moderamen 2020).

3 For more on the Kairos Network, see: https://kairosnetwerk.net/.

4 Alanis Morissette, 'Torch', track 8 on Alanis Morissette's album *Flavours of entanglement* (The Village Recorder, 2011).

## References

Algemene Sinode Moderamen, 2020, 'Agtergrond en Inligting: Die Algemene Sinode se 2019-besluit oor selfdegeslagverhoudings', https://www.scribd.com/document/478109801/Selfdegeslagverhoudings-GIDS-Vir-Gesprek-Sept-2020, accessed 7.06.2023.

Boase, Elizabeth and Sarah Agnew, 2016, '"Whispered in the Sound of Silence": Traumatising the Book of Jonah', *The Bible and Critical Theory* 12/1, pp. 4–22.

Claassens, L. Juliana, 2021, 'Surfing with Jonah: Reading Jonah as a Postcolonial Trauma Narrative', *Journal for the Study of the Old Testament* 45/4, pp. 576–87.

Conradie, Ernst, Louis C. Jonker, Lawrie Douglas and R. Arendse (eds), 1995, *Op Soek Na Jona: Verskilllende Benaderings tot die Interpretasie van die Bybel*, Cape Town: UWK Publications.

Davids, Hanzline R., 2020, 'Recognition of LGBTIQ Bodies in the Uniting Reformed Church in Southern Africa: An Indecent Proposal?', *Stellenbosch Theological Journal* 6/4, pp. 301–17.

Havea, Jione, 2013, 'AdJusting Jonah', *International Review of Mission* 102/1, pp. 44–55.

Havea, Jione, 2016, 'Sitting Jonah with Job: Resailing Intertextuality', *The Bible and Critical Theory* 12/1, pp. 94–108.

Igual, Roberto, 2022, 'Human Rights Watch asks SA govt what it's doing to stop LGBTIQ murders', *MambaOnline.com*, https://www.mambaonline.com/2022/01/27/hrw-asks-sa-govt-what-its-doing-to-stop-lgbtiq-murders/, accessed 7.06.2023.

Jonker, Louis C. and Douglas G. Lawrie (eds), 2005, *Fishing for Jonah (anew): Various Approaches to Biblical Interpretation*, Stellenbosch: African Sun Media.

Keller, Timothy, 2018, *The Prodigal Prophet: Jonah and the Mystery of God's Mercy*, New York: Penguin.

Laurie, Greg, 2014, *A Fresh Look at the Book of Jonah: The Hard to Swallow Truth About Disobedience*, Dana Point, CA: Allen David Books, Kerygma Publishing.

Ngcobo, Siwakhile, 2022, 'Powerful, Penetrator, Provider: A Religio-cultural Analysis of Masculinity Production in Men's Conference Promotional Media in the African Pentecostal Context', Master's thesis, University of KwaZulu-Natal.

Ryu, Chesung J., 2016, 'Divine Rhetoric and Prophetic Silence in the book of Jonah', *The Oxford Handbook of Biblical Narrative*, Oxford: Oxford University Press, pp. 226–35.

Schiermer, Bjørn and A. Pettenkofer, 2017, 'Acceleration and Resonance: An Interview with Hartmut Rosa (by B. Schiermer). In Four Generations of Critical Theory', *Acta Sociologica*, pp. 1–7.

Schüssler Fiorenza, Elizabeth, 1988, 'The Ethics of Biblical Interpretation: Decentering Biblical Scholarship', *JBL* 107/1, pp. 3–17.

Settler, Federico and Mari Haugaa Engh, 'The Black Body in Colonial and Postcolonial Public Discourse in South Africa', *Alternation Special Edition* 14 (2015), pp. 126–48.

Thyssen, Ashwin, 2020, 'Children of God: Exploring URCSA's Catechetical Sexual Ethic', *Studia Historiae Ecclesiasticae* 46/3, pp. 1–12.

Van der Walt, Charlene, 2015, '"It's the Price I Guess for the Lies I've Told that the Truth It No Longer Thrills Me…" Reading Queer Lies to Reveal Straight Truth in Genesis 38' in L. Juliana Claassens and Bruch C. Birch (eds), *Restorative Readings: The Old Testament, Ethics, and Human Dignity*, Eugene, OR: Wipf & Stock, pp. 57–74.

Van der Walt, Charlene, 2018, '"To the Wonder." Finding God in the Most Unexpected Places' in L. Juliana Claassens and Frits de Lange (eds), *Considering Compassion: Global Ethics, Human Dignity, and the Compassionate God*, Eugene, OR: Pickwick, pp. 170–86.

Van der Walt, Charlene, 2021, 'Come On, Come Out, Come Here, Come Here … Queer Expressions of Desire in Genesis 28–31' in L. Juliana Claassens, Christl M. Maier and Funlola O. Olojede (eds), *Transgression and Transformation: Feminist, Postcolonial and Queer*

*Biblical Interpretation as Creative Interventions*, London: Blooms-bury T&T Clark, pp. 145–60.

Van der Walt, Charlene, 2022, '"The Bra Is Wearing a Skirt!" Queering Joseph in the Quest to Enhance Contextual Ethical Gender and Sexu-ality Engagements' in Manitza Kotze, Naida Marais and Nina M. van Velden (eds), *Sexual Reformation? Theological and Ethical Reflec-tions on Human Sexuality*, Eugene, OR: Wipf & Stock, pp. 94–109.

Van der Walt, Charlene and R. Hanzline Davids, 'Heteropatriarchy's Blame Game: Reading Genesis 37 with Izitabane during COVID 19', *Old Testament Essays* 35/1, pp. 32–50.

Van der Walt, Charlene and R. Louis van der Riet, 2022, 'A New Narra-tive for Queer Clergy in the Dutch Reformed Church', *IAM Blog post*, https://iam.org.za/a-new-narrative-for-queer-clergy-in-the-dutch-re formed-church/, accessed 7.06.2023.

Van der Walt, Charlene and Judith Terblanche, 2016, 'Reimagining a Solitary Landscape: Tracing Communities of Care in Exodus 1–2 and the Film Shirley Adams,' *OTE* 29/1, pp. 176–94.

West, Gerald O., 2021, 'A Trans-textual and Trans-sectoral Gender-economic Reading of the Rape of Tamar (2 Sam 13) and the Expropriation of Naboth's Land (1 Kings 21)' in Jin Young Choi and Joerg Rieger (eds), *Faith, Class, and Labor: Intersectional Approaches in a Global Context*, Eugene, OR: Wipf & Stock, pp. 105–21.

# 2

# Prophecy and Consent:
# The Case of Jonah

## RHIANNON GRAYBILL

## Introduction

The book of Jonah is the story of a man compelled to do
something he does not want to do, at significant personal cost.
Jonah eventually becomes a prophet, but not before fleeing and
attempting to avoid both prophecy and the God who has called
him. While he does eventually accept his calling – or at least
accept that he cannot flee it any longer – larger questions of
choice, coercion and consent remain unresolved in the text.

'Bloodchild', Octavia Butler's acclaimed short story, is the
story of a boy compelled to do something he does not want to
do, at significant personal cost. Gan, the teenage protagonist of
Butler's Hugo and Nebula award-winning story, first published
in 1984, is no prophet: instead, his 'calling' is to become the
human host for an alien creature's fertile egg. Like Jonah, Gan
tries to flee before eventually accepting his fate; like Jonah, it is
not clear whether he acts willingly, or submits to insurmount-
able circumstances. As with the book of Jonah, 'Bloodchild'
is a story shot through with extreme power imbalances, with
choices that are not fully autonomous choices, with obligations
to community and a deep uneasiness over what is the 'right'
thing to do, and at what cost. It is not only the prophet or pregnant human who must pay the price, but also his community
– Jonah's prophecy leads to Nineveh's repentance and deliverance, a deliverance directly contrary to the interests of the

Israelite community, as interpreters since the Rabbinic period have observed (see Zlotowitz 1988, p. xxxiii). And Gan's act of gestation means collaboration with the alien race that control humans, their actions and their movements.

We can read both 'Bloodchild' and the book of Jonah as stories about consent and its limits. The central question of Butler's plot, *Will Gan consent to be implanted with the egg?* overlays a more fundamental ethical question: *Can Gan consent at all?* Or, put differently, *Is consent a meaningful framework for a relationship with such an imbalance of power (not to mention alien species)?* This is – not coincidentally – also one central question of the book of Jonah. On the level of plot, *Will Jonah consent to be a prophet?* is the question that drives the first half of the book. But as with Gan in 'Bloodchild', this question overlays a more fundamental question: *Can we meaningfully speak of consent in cases of prophecy?* And if not, then *What, if anything, distinguishes prophecy from coercion, exploitation and abuse?* And finally, the fundamental question I explore here, *How can critiquing consent help us think more richly and robustly about biblical prophecy?*

In asking these questions, I am inspired not only by the ambiguities of the two texts under consideration, but also by broader feminist and queer critiques of consent. In my previous work, I draw on critiques of consent and queer responses to sexual violence to propose a new paradigm for understanding biblical rape stories. As part of this project, I argue that consent is both *insufficient* and *insufficiently feminist* as a means of diagnosing or responding to sexual violence (Graybill 2021, pp. 5, 31). Here, I extend this argument and suggest that consent is *insufficient to the problem of the prophetic calling*. Confronted with this failure, feminist and especially queer critiques of consent can help us understand more fully the scene of prophetic calling and its relations to prophecy.

The book of Jonah tells a story about saying yes when the cost of saying no is too high, in which consenting to prophecy is better understood as consenting *to avoid* violence. To suggest the contrary – that prophets freely accept the divine calling – is to maintain a cruelly optimistic attachment to consent.

Such attachment has real consequences: it devalues survivors, including Jonah himself, and it leaves the ickiness of the story unresolved.[1] More broadly, analysing Jonah's prophetic calling through the framework of consent reveals the sexualized violence of the prophetic call story genre, the centrality of ambiguity and ambivalence, and the complexity of harm.

The essay unfolds as follows. I begin with a brief overview of some of the difficulties with consent. My discussion focuses on Octavia Butler's short story 'Bloodchild', which offers a compelling example of consent's complexities and failures. It also offers a point of entry into questions of consent in the prophetic literature, the focus of the majority of the essay. After discussing consent in prophecy in general, I turn to Jonah in particular, reading the prophet's story as a subtle critique of the overvaluing of consent. The essay concludes with some general reflections on prophecy and consent, as well as considering what might come after consent.

## The trouble with consent, as explained through 'Bloodchild'

Consent is a peculiar, powerful thing. Heidi M. Hurd (1996, p. 121) has famously described consent as 'moral magic' that possesses transformative power. As Hurd observes, 'Consent turns a trespass into a dinner party; a battery into a handshake; a theft into a gift; an invasion of privacy into an intimate moment; a commercial appropriation of name and likeness into a biography' (1996, p. 123). And, of course, it is consent that distinguishes sex from rape – or so it is commonly believed (Fischel 2019; Kessel 2020). When we look more closely at consent, however, it turns out that things are not so simple.[2] In fact, consent is a strikingly limited framework for understanding sexual violence. The notion of consent assumes a liberal Enlightenment understanding of the subject as an autonomous moral agent, which makes little sense when reading the Bible (or in many other contexts, including analysing alien pregnancy in science fiction). Consent is not uniformly or equally available to all people or all categories of people (gender and race are especially important here). And the fact that something is consensual does not mean it is not problematic or troubling in other ways – the so-called 'moral magic' of consent only extends so far. As I conclude in my book about sexual violence and the Hebrew Bible, 'Consent discourses fail to accommodate complexity' and offer an insufficient framework for understanding sexual violence (Graybill 2021, p. 39). Unlike the biblical stories I analyse there, neither 'Bloodchild' nor the book of Jonah is a story of sexual violence. But these are both stories of consent, nonetheless. To draw out this point further, I expand the critique of consent to accommodate four additional points. I trace these difficulties with consent as they play out in Butler's story before turning to Jonah.

Understanding the difficulties of consent in 'Bloodchild' requires a few additional details about the plot. The story describes the relationship between a community of humans living on an alien planet and the Tlic, giant, insect-like aliens. The relationship is not equal: the Tlic hold the power. However, they also rely on humans to help them reproduce. Because it is difficult for the Tlic to gestate their own eggs, they implant them in human hosts; male hosts are especially valuable. In the past, humans were treated similarly to livestock; however, the Tlic now establish ongoing relationships with human families and provide them with patronage and protection. The narrator of the story is a teenage boy named Gan, who has been chosen by T'Gatoi, a powerful Tlic female, to carry her egg. Gan's mother, Lien, grew up with T'Gatoi and the two were once close friends; Lien promised that one of her children would be T'Gatoi's surrogate. Now, however, she is reluctant and fearful – the process of being implanted with and carrying Tlic eggs is not fatal to humans, though it does carry risks. Gan's siblings also have a range of reactions: his sister Hoa is jealous, while his brother is outwardly scornful and filled with hatred towards the Tlic. Gan himself is uncertain if he wants to go through with carrying the egg; his fear grows as he encounters another human host, a man named Bran Lomas, who is being eaten alive from the inside by improperly hatched Tlic offspring.

Despite his hesitations, Gan eventually consents to having the egg implanted, in part to protect his sister, in part out of love for T'Gatoi. He describes the moments immediately before implantation:

> 'Now!' I let her [T'Gatoi] push me out of the kitchen, then walked ahead of her toward my bedroom. The sudden urgency in her voice sounded real. 'You would have done it to Hoa tonight!' I accused.
> 'I must do it to someone tonight.' I stopped in spite of her urgency and stood in her way. 'Don't you care who?'
> She flowed around me and into my bedroom. I found her waiting on the couch we shared. There was nothing in Hoa's room that she could have used. She would have done it to Hoa on the floor. The thought of her doing it to Hoa at all disturbed me in a different way now, and I was suddenly angry. Yet I undressed and lay down beside her. (Butler 2005, p. 27)

And given the context of *consenting to avoid (sex)*, it is perhaps notable that the act of implantation that follows is described in quite sexual terms:

> I felt the familiar sting, narcotic, mildly pleasant. Then the blind probing of her ovipositor. The puncture was painless, easy. So easy going in. She undulated slowly against me, her muscles forcing the egg from her body into mine ... Then I let go, moved inadvertently, and hurt her. She gave a low cry of pain and I expected to be caged at once within her limbs. When I wasn't, I held on to her again, feeling oddly ashamed. 'I'm sorry,' I whispered.
> She rubbed my shoulders with four of her limbs.
> 'Do you care?' I asked. 'Do you care that it's me?'
> She did not answer for some time. Finally, 'You were the one making the choices tonight, Gan. I made mine long ago.' (Butler 2005, pp. 27–8).

Shortly after the implantation, the story ends.

Butler described 'Bloodchild' as 'basically a love story' (Potts and Butler 1996, p. 336). Readers and critics, however, have often suggested that it is a story about exploitation or sexual abuse under slavery.[3] Butler, in turn, has criticized this reading; as she remarks in an interview, 'So many critics have read this as a story about slavery, probably just because I am black ... The only places I am writing about slavery is where I actually say so' (Potts and Butler 1996, p. 332). But love does not mean consent is necessarily present, secure or sufficient. Love may well be inextricable from exploitation or even abuse. All this points to the matter of consent. As I have already suggested, the question, *Does Gan consent?* is in many ways the central issue of the tale.[4] And, relevant to the exploration here, the story also thematizes several of the points critiquing consent.

## Consent can mean saying yes when the cost of saying no is too high

Sexual health educators often stress that consent should be enthusiastic and freely given. But this ideal of consent is not always met in practice. Instead of an enthusiastic yes, consent can also be a reluctant last resort, a *yes* that is fundamentally about the cost of a *no*. As Sara Ahmed writes:

> A feminist account of gender as a social relation might need to include analysis of how women willingly agree to situations in which their safety and well-being are compromised. For understandable reasons, feminist work on violence against women in dealing with questions of law and legal redress has focused on consent and on the violence of men hearing no as yes ... We certainly need to hear the violence that con-verts no into yes. My additional suggestion is modest: we also need to hear the cases in which yes involves force but is not experienced as force, when for instance a woman says yes to something as the consequences of saying no would be too much (loss of access to children, to resources or benefits, to residence, etc.). (Ahmed 2014, p. 55).

Ahmed's comments here are part of a broader feminist critique of wilfulness and the question of what it means to be a willing subject. Elsewhere, I have used her analysis to highlight the importance of *discomfort* as it relates to consent and non-consent (Graybill 2021, pp. 35–6). To this analysis, which privileges feeling, I add *cost*: consent may come about because the cost or consequence of non-consent is too high. This cost can take many forms: financial, legal, social, personal. I may be worried about losing my child, or my home, or my job – or my sense of myself, my sense of the situation, my understanding of how to be in the world. The cost of saying no can take many forms, or come at too high a price in many ways.

This is certainly the case in 'Bloodchild'. Gan's consent to carry T'Gatoi's egg is in many ways an example of *saying yes when the cost of saying no is too high*. Amanda Thibodeau observes that in the relationship between T'Gatoi and Gan, 'it is Gan who seeks validation and equality, for he has the most to lose – his social status, his family's livelihood, and his life' (2012, p. 272). Gan says yes to protect those things – and, I would add, to protect his understanding of his relationship with T'Gatoi as a relationship of love and care. Gan consents to the egg because to do otherwise would be to give up on the fantasy of love and care that animates their relationship.

## Consent can be 'consenting to avoid'[5]

A second problematic dynamic of consent is the practice of *consenting to avoid*. My analysis here builds on feminist psychologist Nicola Gavey's work on the phenomenon she calls 'consenting to avoid rape'. In interviewing women about their sexual histories, Gavey is struck by the frequency with which her interview subjects describe consenting to have sex so as to avoid sexual violence. As one woman tells Gavey, 'If I tried it, if I'd resisted, then he might rape me, you know' (2013, p. 161). Gavey describes this sort of 'consenting to avoid' as 'point[ing] to a complex gray area between … mutually consenting sex, on the one hand, and rape or sexual coercion on the other'

(2013, p. 136). Such 'consenting to avoid' is a deeply unsettling concept, as Gavey herself describes. For the feminist scholar of sexual violence, it is troubling to accept the idea that sex that is consented to in order to avoid rape is consensual at all. At the same time, it is also troubling to suggest that people do not understand their own experiences, or are unable to interpret them correctly.

Gavey's focus is on sex and sexual violence, but it is not only in sex where this dynamic is at work. Instead, as with many questions of consent, the example of sex illuminates the working of consent more broadly.[6] I suggest later in this essay that prophecy offers another potent example of *consent to avoid*. This is also present in 'Bloodchild.' Because the Tlic hold the power – physically, politically, pharmacologically – in Gan's world, human consent to implantation can take the form of *consenting to avoid*. And given the context of *consenting to avoid (sex)*, it is perhaps notable that the act of implantation is, as already observed, described in quite sexual terms: Thibodeau describes it as 'heavy with clichéd erotic language and imagery, more a scene of lovemaking than of alien or insect implantation', and notes 'The act itself resembles sex' (2012, p. 271). Our (over)emphasis on consent renders this scene as sex, rather than rape, but the dichotomy is often illusory. Thus, the act shows not so much Gan's consent – although he does consent – as much as consent's meaninglessness.

There are also suggestions in the story that Gan may not have the power to say no, contrary to his own belief. T'Gatoi pierces his mother, Lien, without her consent and injects her with a drug. And even before Gan's birth, his mother has promised one of her children to T'Gatoi; it is inevitable that someone will carry the egg. Consent thus avoids only the appearance of force, not the underlying force itself.

## Consent is a form of cruel optimism

Consent is not always about cost or avoidance; sometimes, it is a positive or even hopeful gesture. But this is not always straightforward: a third problem with consent is that it represents a form of cruel optimism. 'Cruel optimism' originates with queer theorist Lauren Berlant, who explains that 'a relation of cruel optimism exists when something you desire is actually an obstacle to your flourishing' (2001, p. 1). It is optimistic because it encodes a hope or desire for something other than the present; it is cruel because this hope does not come to pass. Many kinds of cruel optimism are possible: 'It might involve food, or a kind of love; it might be a fantasy of the good life, or a political project' (2001, p. 1). Or, of course, consent. Alisa Kessel has demonstrated that the attachment to consent as a straightforward and effective means of differentiating sex from rape is itself a form of cruel optimism. As she writes, 'This is the cruel optimism of sexual consent: [we] sustain an optimistic attachment to consent as the evidence of agency that distinguishes sex from rape, when in fact the perverse construction of victim/survivor-as-agent and of perpetrator-as-victim has, for centuries, facilitated the persistence of sexual violence' (Kessel 2020, p. 361). The problem is that despite our investment in it, consent is unable to do the work that we ask it to do (to distinguish between rape and sex).

Kessel's focus is on sexual consent. But cruel optimism explains different forms of consent as well. Gan's consent to T'Gatoi signals his investment in a more expansive fantasy of Terran [Earth]/Tlic coexistence and even mutual flourishing. But other characters in the story suggest other, darker possibilities, among them Gan's brother, who fears and hates the Tlic, and Bran Lomas, who is murdered by the alien young gestating within his body. While it is tempting to write off these voices as xenophobic (the brother) or insufficiently trusting (Lomas, who runs away from his Tlic host), it is equally possible to read them as (failed) protesters against a system of exploitation. And their perspectives suggest that Gan's attachment to T'Gatoi, and to what Berlant calls the 'fantasy' or 'that moral-intimate-economic thing called "the good life"' is in fact a cruelly optimistic attachment indeed (2011, p. 2). Cruel optimism? Is, moreover, in keeping with larger trends in Butler's works: Gerry Canavan notes the '*troubled* affirmation of survival' that characterizes much of Butler's published fiction, observing that 'hers is a futurism that is never 100% sure, where "optimism" always threatens to tip over into "cruel optimism" instead' (n.d., p. 52; emphasis original).

## Focusing on the moment of consent neglects what happens after[7]

Beyond cruel optimism, consent can be cruel in other ways as well. In order to work, consent has to be clear – I either consent to X, or I don't. There is little space for ambiguity, for uncertainty, or for changing one's mind.[8] Because of the premium placed on certainty and clear boundaries, any suggestion that the aftermath may be uncertain or different from what comes before is met with suspicion and anger. 'Bloodchild' ends with Gan still pregnant; Butler does not invite us into the *after*. But the character of Gan's mother, Lien, gives some hint at what this after may consist of. Lien and T'Gatoi were once close friends; T'Gatoi still regards Lien with significant affection and love. Lien, however, has changed. Having consented – before their births – to give one of her children to T'Gatoi to impregnate, she is now filled with anger and fear. Against Gan's optimism and love, she shows the cruelty of the Terrans' optimistic attachments to a certain fantasy of Terran/Tlic coexistence, as well as the fundamental limits of consent.

## Consent does not resolve ickiness

Finally, and related to all of the previous points: consent does not resolve ickiness. Icky sex can be consensual; consensual sex can be icky (Graybill 2021, pp. 16–17). Consent will not abolish disgust and discomfort, no matter how much we might hope it would do so. And our obsession with consent can become icky when it leads us to judgement or limits the capaciousness of our sexual politics and our feminist and queer sexual imagination. There is a lingering ickiness in 'Bloodchild', even or especially if we take seriously Butler's characterization of her work as a love story.

## Do prophets consent to prophecy? Does Jonah?

The question *Does Gan consent to pregnancy?* sets up a related biblical question: *Do prophets consent to prophecy?* A good starting point to answer this question is to look at the call stories of the Major Prophets. The clearest example of consent comes with Isaiah. Isaiah has a vision of God in the temple, seated on his throne and surrounded by adoring seraphim. When the prophet laments his 'unclean lips' (Isa. 6.5), a seraph flies over and touches them with a coal, cleansing them. And then, 'I heard the voice of the Lord saying, "Whom shall I send, and who will go for us?"' to which Isaiah replies 'Here I am! Send me!' (Isa. 6.8). This is consent that would please any college sexual health educator – unambiguous, verbal and enthusiastic. But there is one complicating detail: Isaiah consents without knowing *what he is consenting to*. The prophetic task is only described in 6.9–13; furthermore, it seems impossible. This raises the question as to whether he would have said yes if these details were provided – a question that hangs uneasily over the text.

Consent is also complicated for Jeremiah and Ezekiel. Jeremiah and Ezekiel offer somewhat more complex examples. Jeremiah, famously, is called before birth:

> Now the word of the LORD came to me saying,
> 'Before I formed you in the womb I knew you,
> and before you were born I consecrated you;
> I appointed you a prophet to the nations.' (Jer. 1.4–5)

Upon hearing these words, Jeremiah protests; a negotiation with God ensues (not unlike Moses' prophetic calling at the burning bush). God also places his words in Jeremiah's mouth: 'Then the LORD put out his hand and touched my mouth; and the LORD said to me, "Now I have put my words in your mouth"' –

opening his body without necessarily seeking consent to do so. Still, Jeremiah quickly takes to prophecy.[9] Ezekiel, meanwhile, hardly speaks in his call story (Ezek. 1—3); his only objection involves the specific details of food preparation during his symbolic actions (Ezek. 4.9–12). His specific objection to this one portion of the call can be interpreted as his general acceptance of the prophetic calling more broadly.[10]

Jonah's case, however, is more complicated. Two key scenes are the prophetic calls Jonah receives, in the beginning of chapter 1 and then again at the beginning of chapter 3. Consider the opening lines of the book:

> Jonah the son of Amittai received the message from YHWH that said, 'Get up and go to Nineveh, the great city, and cry out against it, because its evil has come to my attention.' So Jonah got up – to flee to Tarshish, away from YHWH. Going down to Joppa, he found a ship heading to Tarshish. He paid the fare and boarded it to travel with them to Tarshish, away from YHWH. (Jonah 1.1–3)[11]

Jonah's attempt at flight, as we all know, fails – God sends a storm and waylays the ship, Jonah reveals his identity, is thrown overboard at his demand, and is swallowed by a giant fish. After three days in the fish, he is vomited out, and when 'Jonah received the message from YHWH a second time' (3.1), he does not attempt to flee again.

Jonah's actions are often read as signs of his intransigence, or his unsuitability as a prophet. Sometimes, they are even interpreted comically – Jonah, the prophet who does everything wrong and yet succeeds; the inverse of a prophet such as Jeremiah or Ezekiel, who prophesies correctly and nevertheless 'fails' (see Miles 1975; Sasson 1990; Marcus 1995, p. 95; Garber and Zuckerman 2017, p. 198, among others). Another trajectory of interpretation treats Jonah's actions as righteous protest: Jonah will not prophesy because, out of solidarity with Israel, he does not want Israel's enemy, the wicked Assyrians, to receive mercy (Rosen 1992, p. 87; Gaines 2003; Ryu 2009, pp. 196–9).[12] I suggest, however, that we can read Jonah's actions differently:

as tactics of resistance that signal his non-consent to prophecy, while also revealing the inappositeness of consent in the
scene of prophecy at all. Jonah, no less than Gan, exists in a
world where the notion of consent is equal parts seductive and
impossible.

*Jonah's consent to prophecy is an example of saying yes when
the cost of saying no is too high.* There is no actual choice in the
scene of prophetic calling, as Jonah learns in chapters 1 and 2,
when he rejects God's calling and finds himself first in a terrifying storm, then inside a (no doubt also terrifying) fish. Even
the psalm that Jonah sings in chapter 2, which thanks God for
saving his life, cannot really cover over the fact that it is God
who has also threatened his life.[13] The cost of saying no is too
high: what is at stake is life itself, both the life of the prophet
and, potentially, the lives of the innocent sailors on the ship.
Having seen the consequences of non-consent in chapters 1 and
2, Jonah does not resist in chapter 3. Here, *saying yes when the
cost of saying no is too high* crosses over with *consenting to
avoid*. In this case, Jonah consents to avoid a repetition of the
outrageous divine punishment he receives in chapter 2. While
the fish is often presented as a respite, and perhaps even a cosy
abode, some sources stress the ways the experience resembles
torture.[14]

Reading Jonah with 'Bloodchild' suggests, as well, another
way of understanding both *the cost of saying no* and *consenting
to avoid*. In Butler's story, Gan consents at least in part so as
to preserve his understanding of his relationship with T'Gatoi
as based in love and mutuality. And yet he also recognizes, on
some level, that this is a fiction – a fiction that is concealed by
consent. So too, perhaps, with Jonah. By consenting (through
non-refusal) to prophesy to Nineveh in Jonah 3, Jonah preserves
an understanding of what it means to be a prophet, as well
as what it means to be in relation with the God who calls a
prophet. His fury in chapter 4 can be understood, at least in
part, as fury about the fact that he has played along, but has
nevertheless been forced to pay the cost as if he had not.

The events of Jonah 4 also point to *the cruel optimism of
consent*. I have already in this essay made clear that suggesting

Jonah had the option to consent to prophecy, or not, requires a cruelly optimistic attachment to consent. But now I add that prophecy itself is a cruelly optimistic endeavour. Jonah himself makes this clear in chapter 4, after he has prophesied to Nineveh (in chapter 3) and succeeded in bringing about their repentance, causing God to change his mind about the destruction. Jonah angrily announces, 'Oh YHWH, this is what I thought when I was in my country, isn't it? This is the reason I fled towards Tarshish before – because I knew you to be a gracious and merciful God, slow to get angry, very kind, and changing your mind about bringing harm' (4.2) and then expresses his desire to die. With his speech and actions in chapter 4, Jonah exposes the lie of prophecy, and the cruel optimism of believing it changes anything.

Furthermore, the fact that Jonah complies with the (second) prophetic calling and thus 'consents' does not address the problem of *what happens after*. We do not know how Gan reacts after the implantation; the story ends shortly after the act itself. But with Jonah, we are given a view of the after. But the view afforded by chapter 4 is complicated. What is clear is that Jonah's attitude seems wholly inappropriate to the situation. He vacillates wildly between anger and joy – and joy over an inappropriate object, a simple plant, no less. Mostly, he expresses the desire to die.[15] Previously, I have described Jonah as a prophetic failure, characterized by his refusal, and by his status as an affect alien and a melancholic migrant (these last two categories come from Ahmed 2010) (Graybill 2016, pp. 132–4; Graybill 2019). In a somewhat related vein, Karen Bray describes Jonah as 'moody' (2019, pp. 120, 124). And John Kaltner, Steven L. McKenzie and I explore Jonah as suffering from trauma (Graybill et al. 2023). Now I bring these readings together and link them explicitly to the problem of the *afters* of consent.

And finally, but importantly: *Jonah's consent does not resolve ickiness*. Even if we accept that Jonah freely and enthusiastically consents in chapter 3 – an assumption I put pressure on – all is not well. The story maintains its ickiness, whether we understand this ickiness as residing in the sparing of the wicked

Ninevites (icky in the pity shown to terrible people), in Jonah's response (icky in its refusal to accommodate mercy), or in the unfinished ending of the story (icky in its failure to find closure).

## Do prophets consent to prophecy? Reconsidered

The book of Jonah resists any attempt to read the prophet's story as a story of consent. To the contrary: even attempting to explore how consent works in Jonah leaves us, instead, interrogating the notion of consent itself. In fact, the failures of consent that this brief prophetic book stages are enough to call into question consent as a framework for approaching any biblical accounts of prophecy or prophetic calling. Prophecy is, from the coming of the call, a situation of coercion. It is, strictly speaking, impossible to consent to prophecy because prophecy is outside of consent. The appearance of consent, even more of enthusiastic consent (as when Isaiah cries out 'Send me!') is simply a strategy of concealment and avoidance. And when we cling to consent, or to the even more basic idea that prophets accept prophecy, we are left perpetuating cruel optimism.

And so: *consent fails as a framework for prophecy*. But this failure can teach us, even beyond teaching us about the limits of consent. Consider three brief insights:

First, *the prophetic call story as a genre structurally resembles a scene of sexual non-consent*. Using Jonah to interrogate prophecy and consent reveals the violence, including sexual-ized violence, of the prophetic call story genre. The calling of a prophet instigates a relationship of intimacy. But it is inarguably a relation shot through with vertical power hierarchies; it is a scene in which consent is impossible. Though there is no actual sexual violence in the prophetic call stories, the structural similarities are nevertheless striking.

Second, *consent and non-consent help focalize the centrality of ambiguity and ambivalence to prophecy more broadly*. One reason that consent is so appealing as a notion is that it suggests clear delineation between appropriate and inappropriate, between sex and rape, between lovers and perpetrators, between victims and willing participants (Kessel 2020, pp. 361, 364). But consent is not straightforward, and neither is prophecy. Jonah 4 is an extended staging of the prophet's ambivalence and anger. The gratitude the speaker expresses in the psalm in chapter 2 is at odds with the remainder of the book. We find similar ambiguities and ambivalences across the prophetic corpus. Earlier, I referred to Jeremiah's regret over accepting the prophetic word, and his sense of being overpowered and deceived.

Third, *taking non-consent seriously demands that we complexify and queer our understanding of harm.* Of all the ways that an easy, simplistic reliance on consent can be damaging, one of the most significant, to my mind, is the way that consent discourses flatten the idea of harm. It is tempting, in the case of Jonah, to seek a straightforward representation of harm, whether harm to the prophet (by God, by commentators, by his own actions), harm to the Israelites by the Assyrians, harm to the notion of mercy (by Jonah's small-mindedness), or harm to meaning (by the book's frustrating ending). Queer readings are not immune to this desire: we understand Jonah's hurt through his queerness, or his queerness as a form of harm. Queer readings become frustrated readings and melancholic readings.[16] Or, alternatively, they cling to utopian possibilities, but in ways that can downplay real evidence of harm.

Queer writing about consent, non-consent and the afters of sexual violence help us to thread this needle. Consider, for example, a suggestion from Leah Lakshmi Piepzna-Samarsinha, writing about trauma and being a survivor:

> I want to venture: What if some things aren't fixable? What if some things really never will be the same – and that might not be great, but it might be okay? ... What if some trauma wounds really never will go away – and we still might have great lives? (2018, p. 235)

What if Jonah does not consent, is traumatized and harmed, and never recovers? And what if that *after* is also not a sentence to pain and nothing more? What if, instead, we take harm seriously without allowing it to be the only thing we are able to think about, in prophecy and (non)consent and in prophecy more broadly? Consent does not give us answers. But it does, at least, help us to ask questions.

## After consent

From the perspective of consent, Gan's ultimate willingness to be implanted with T'Gatoi's egg is frustrating. He consents, but under conditions that make us question the sincerity or reliability of his consent – conditions that perhaps call consent into question altogether. There are many threads here, perhaps impossible to untangle: the general conditions of human life under Tlic control, the specific situation of Gan and his family, who benefit from the patronage of the powerful T'Gatoi; the long history of his mother's relationship with T'Gatoi, Gan's sense of protection (and rivalry) towards his sister, Gan's love for T'Gatoi, the demands of masculinity, of family, of reproduction, and more. It is difficult to say why Gan agrees to the egg, or which of these many factors is the determining one.

Like Gan, Jonah flirts with refusal before eventually agreeing to what is asked – in his case, to become YHWH's prophet and prophesy to Nineveh. There are many threads here as well: the general conditions of prophecy, Jonah's own personal history, Jonah's view of foreigners (first the sailors, then the Ninevites), the status of Nineveh as a historical enemy of Israel, the significance of the fish and the time Jonah spends within it. Why does Jonah refuse the first time he is called and then consent the second? It is difficult to say.

While they share important parallels, the two stories are not identical. 'Bloodchild' is narrated by Gan, giving us as readers access to his thoughts and his understanding of his own situation. Of course, false consciousness is possible; nevertheless, we have significant access to how Gan understands things. Jonah, in contrast, is a frustratingly opaque character. The only real glimpses into his interiority come in chapter 4 and focus on his anger at YHWH's forgiveness, as well as the incident with the plant. We do not know how he feels when fleeing in chapter 1, or when agreeing in chapter 3. What the book of Jonah provides that 'Bloodchild' does not is some accounting for what comes after the moment of consent. Butler's story ends shortly after Gan has been implanted with the egg, long before the young are born. The final lines are T'Gatoi's promise to look after Gan: 'I'm healthy and young,' she said. 'I won't leave you as Lomas was left – alone, N'Tlic [implanted/pregnant]. I'll take care of you' (Butler 2005, p. 29). This is an optimistic ending to an often dark story. With Jonah, in contrast, we have a fuller sense of what happens after: a full quarter of the book (chapter 4) takes place after Jonah has acted. Furthermore, and importantly, Jonah is deeply unhappy for much of what comes after; more than once he expresses his desire to die. The 'moral magic of consent', it seems, has limits: Jonah may consent to prophecy, but it does not secure his happiness.

Reading Jonah and 'Bloodchild' together exposes the limits of consent, as well as the queer possibilities that inhere in the moments when consent is insufficient. These are two stories about consent as a form of avoidance, about saying yes when the cost of saying no is too high, about the cruel optimism of consent. But they are also stories that show us moments of queer possibility, pleasure, and love – not separate from exploitation, but curled up within it. In 'Bloodchild' as in Jonah, loyalty and love may well be inextricable from exploitation or even abuse. In questioning consent, scrutinizing its limits, and looking beyond them we begin to sketch this space of queer possibility.

## Notes

1 On ickiness and *icky* as a critical category, see Graybill 2021, pp. 16–17.

2 This paragraph summarizes my extended critique of consent in Graybill, *Texts after Terror*, pp. 34–9. See, in addition, Graybill 2017.

3 For a review of readings (as well as an analysis of the story from Hortense Spillers), see Lillvis 2014; Jenkins and Sciurba 2022. On consent, see Minister 2019; Joe Heidenescher 2020.

4 Minister 2019, pp. 162–70; Heidenescher 2020, p. 56.

5 For a related analysis of this dynamic, see also Graybill 2021, p. 13.

6 Though sex is also 'special', as Fischel points out (2019, pp. 27–8).

7 On the question of the after, see also Graybill 2021, pp. 3–4, 171.

8 For a thoughtful reflection on these issues, see Musser 2017.

9 The issue with Jeremiah is not in his refusal to consent at the beginning of his prophetic calling but rather in his changed understanding later on, as in Jeremiah 20.7, 'You seduced me, you overpowered me, and you prevailed.'

10 I argue for reading Ezekiel's body as voluptuous, unmanned and shot through with ecstatic pleasure. Though I do not address consent specifically there, I add that this reading of Ezekiel also shows the limits of consent and its inability to allow space for shattering pleasures and *jouissance*. See Graybill 2016, pp. 112–16.

11 Translations original. For discussion of specific translational issues and choices, see Rhiannon Graybill, John Kaltner and Steven L. McKenzie, 2023, *Jonah: A New Translation with Commentary*, Yale Anchor Bible, New Haven, CT: Yale University Press.

12 This is also common in the classical Jewish sources such as Ibn Ezra and the Mekhilta of Rabbi Ishmael; see Bob 2013, pp. 19–21.

13 There are other problems with the psalm as well, including that it seems originally to describe a different sort of deliverance entirely, from drowning. See further Graybill, Kaltner and McKenzie 2023.

14 This is especially common in the premodern sources, both Jewish and Christian. According to Ibn Ezra, 'because he stood in the belly of the fish for a long time the skin of his flesh was tender and could not stand heat' (Ibn Ezra, trans. Bob 2013, p. 39). The fish's gastric juices are understood to have burned away Jonah's skin. Jonah's time in the fish may also contribute to his trauma. For a reading that brings together humour and suffering, see Claassens 2015, p. 657.

15 For further analysis of this motif, see Levinson 2021.

16 I myself am guilty of this in some of my own work, e.g. Graybill 2019. In navigating this question, I have found especially helpful Jennifer Knust's reflections on the anxieties of reparative reading, as well as Maia Kotrosits' sensitive weaving together of personal reflection and theory. See Knust 2014; Kotrosits 2018.

# References

Ahmed, Sara, 2010, *The Promise of Happiness*, Durham, NC: Duke University Press.

Ahmed, Sara, 2014, *Willful Subjects*, Durham, NC: Duke University Press.

Berlant, Lauren, 2011, *Cruel Optimism*, Durham, NC: Duke University Press.

Bob, Steven, 2013, *Go to Nineveh: Medieval Jewish Commentaries on the Book of Jonah*, Eugene, OR: Pickwick Publications.

Bray, Karen, 2019, *Grave Attending: A Political Theology for the Unredeemed*, New York: Fordham.

Butler, Octavia E., 2005, *Bloodchild and Other Stories*, 2nd edn, New York: Seven Stories Press.

Canavan, Gerry, n.d., 'The Octavia E. Butler Papers', *Eaton Journal of Archival Research in Science Fiction* 3/1, pp. 42–53.

Claassens, L. Juliana M., 2015, 'Rethinking Humour in the Book of Jonah: Tragic Laughter as Resistance in the Context of Trauma', *Old Testament Essays* 28/3, pp. 655–73.

Fischel, Joseph J., 2019, *Screw Consent: A Better Politics of Sexual Justice*, Oakland, CA: University of California Press.

Gaines, Janet Howe, 2003, *Forgiveness in a Wounded World: Jonah's Dilemma*, Atlanta, GA: SBL.

Garber, Zev and Bruce Zuckerman, 2017, 'The Odd Prophet Out and In' in Frederick E. Greenspahn and Gary A. Rendsburg (eds), *Lema'an Ziony: Essays in Honor of Ziony Zevit*, Eugene, OR: Cascade Books, pp. 175–202.

Gavey, Nicola, 2013, *Just Sex? The Cultural Scaffolding of Rape*, New York: Routledge.

Graybill, Rhiannon, 2016, *Are We Not Men? Unstable Masculinity in the Hebrew Prophets*, New York: Oxford University Press.

Graybill, Rhiannon, 2017, 'Critiquing the Discourse of Consent', *Journal of Feminist Studies in Religion* 33/1, pp. 175–6.

Graybill, Rhiannon, 2019, 'Prophecy and the Problem of Happiness: The Case of Jonah' in Fiona C. Black and Jennifer L. Koosed (eds), *Reading with Feeling: Affect Theory and the Bible*, Semeia Studies, Atlanta, GA: SBL Press, pp. 95–112.

Graybill, Rhiannon, 2021, *Texts after Terror: Rape, Sexual Violence, and the Hebrew Bible*, New York: Oxford University Press.

Graybill, Rhiannon, John Kaltner and Steven L. McKenzie, 2023, *Jonah: A New Translation with Commentary*, Yale Anchor Bible, New Haven, CT: Yale University Press.

Heidenescher, Joe, 2020, 'Problematizing Consent in the Posthuman Era: Octavia E. Butler's "Bloodchild" and "Amnesty"' in Gregory J. Hampton and Kendra R. Parker (eds), *The Bloomsbury Handbook to Octavia E. Butler*, New York: Bloomsbury, pp. 55–70.

Hurd, Heidi M., 1996, 'The Moral Magic of Consent,' *Legal Theory* 2/2, pp. 121–46.

Jenkins, Jerry Rafiki and Katie Sciurba, 2022, 'Body Knowledge, Reproductive Anxiety, and "Paying the Rent" in Octavia E. Butler's "Bloodchild"', *Science Fiction Studies* 49/1, pp. 120–37.

Kessel, Alisa, 2020, 'The Cruel Optimism of Sexual Consent', *Contemporary Political Theory* 19/3, pp. 359–80.

Knust, Jennifer, 2014, 'Who's Afraid of Canaan's Curse? Genesis 9:18–29 and the Challenge of Reparative Reading', *Biblical Interpretation* 22/4–5, pp. 388–413.

Kotrosits, Maia, 2018, 'Penetration and its Discontents: Greco-Roman Sexuality, the Acts of Paul and Thecla, and Theorizing Eros without the Wound', *Journal of the History of Sexuality* 27/3, pp. 343–66.

Levinson, Hanne Løland, 2021, *The Death Wish in the Hebrew Bible: Rhetorical Strategies for Survival*, Cambridge: Cambridge University Press.

Lillvis, Kristen, 2014, 'Mama's Baby, Papa's Slavery? The Problem and Promise of Mothering in Octavia E. Butler's "Bloodchild"', *MELUS* 39/4, pp. 7–22.

Marcus, David, 1995, *From Balaam to Jonah: Anti-Prophetic Satire in the Hebrew Bible*, Atlanta, GA: Scholars Press.

Miles, John A., 1975, 'Laughing at the Bible: Jonah as Parody', *The Jewish Quarterly Review* 65/3, pp. 168–81.

Minister, M. Cooper, 2019, 'Sex and Alien Encounter: Rethinking Consent as a Rape Prevention Strategy' in Rhiannon Graybill, M. Cooper Minister and Beatrice Lawrence (eds), *Rape Culture and Religious Studies: Critical and Pedagogical Engagements*, Feminist Studies and Sacred Texts, Lanham, MD: Lexington Books, pp. 157–74.

Musser, Amber, 2017, 'Consent, Capacity, and the Non-Narrative' in Cyd Cipolla, Kristina Gupta, David A. Rubin and Angela Willey (eds), *Queer Feminist Science Studies: A Reader*, Seattle, WA: University of Washington Press, pp. 222–33.

Piepzna-Samarasinha, Leah Lakshmi, 2018, *Care Work: Dreaming Disability Justice*, Vancouver: Arsenal Pulp Press.

Potts, Stephen W. and Octavia E. Butler, 1996, '"We Keep Playing the Same Record": A Conversation with Octavia E. Butler', *Science Fiction Studies* 23/3, pp. 331–8.

Rosen, Norma, 1992, *Accidents of Influence: Writing as a Woman and a Jew in America*, Albany, NY: SUNY Press.

Ryu, Chesung Justin, 2009, 'Silence as Resistance: A Postcolonial Reading of the Silence of Jonah in Jonah 4:1–11', *Journal for the Study of the Old Testament* 34/2, pp. 195–218.

Sasson, Jack M., 1990, *Jonah*, Anchor Bible vol. 24B, New York: Doubleday, pp. 348–50.

Thibodeau, Amanda, 2012, 'Alien Bodies and a Queer Future: Sexual Revision in Octavia Butler's "Bloodchild" and James Tiptree, Jr's "With Delicate Mad Hands"', *Science Fiction Studies* 39/2, pp. 262–82.

Zlotowitz, Meir, 1988, *Jonah: A New Translation with a Commentary Anthologized from Talmudic, Midrashic and Rabbinic Sources*, 2nd edn, New York: Mesorah.

# 3

# Under a Desert Plant: Queer Heterotopias in Jonah

## STEED VERNYL DAVIDSON

## Introduction

The intimacies of touch invested human bodies with lethal potential. The orthodoxies of proximity upended, left few bodies safe. Queer times! In these queer times in search of the perfect place, we discovered the no place of the virtual world. In place of Foucault's mirrors, we had webcams that projected our bodies unto screens and into places, over there where we are not (Foucault and Miskowiec 1986, p. 24). Heterotopias abound! Life in a twenty-first-century pandemic should grant almost certain security against viral infection. Instead, the modern world relied upon medieval solutions for several months to forestall scenes of ancient carnage. Bustling cities turned into bleak landscapes where silence crowded out noise and the earth inhaled its first breath of fresh air in centuries.

Our present global challenges threaten to overwhelm a small biblical book like Jonah. Odd as the book may seem, our present outstrips the book's peculiarities. To engage the spatialities and temporalities of the book – depth, height, breadth, past, futures – makes us even more aware of the enormity of our own reality. The strange story no longer seems strange. A queer Jonah, a fish's stomach as worship space, an imperial city in drag, a desert plant for shade are exactly the *'spaces of alternate ordering'* that Kevin Hetherington understands as heterotopias (1997, p. 8; emphasis original). Our many experiments in sociality over the course of the Covid-19 pandemic and its lockdowns pushed us into new norms, into deviant spaces that make heterotopias all too real and a queer Jonah ordinary. The extensive studies of the reception of Jonah show us how easily the exceptional aspects of the book can be appropriated by the normative; to dull its edges even while sharpening its bite to keep certain groups in line. As Jasbir Puar notes, 'queer times require even queerer modalities of thought' (2005, p. 121), justifying the work we do in this volume.

In this essay, I make the claim that queerness serves as a useful tool in the politics of freedom precisely because social ordering benefits from difference. Despite these contributions, queerness achieves little gains. In building this claim I look at heterotopic spaces in the book and Jonah's relationship to these spaces and objects. My central focus is the space outside of the city of Nineveh in chapter 4. I begin with how I understand heterotopia and which spaces in the book I consider fall into this category. In the next section, I describe Jonah as queer and his relationship to these heterotopic sites that I also see as queer spaces. In the following section, I analyse the space in the desert where Jonah's relationship with the plant interrogates the material dimensions of divine power as a source of freedom. I explore queer space in relation to the city of Nineveh as drag space to fill out how divine power deploys queerness to enforce orthodoxy.

## Jonah's heterotopias

Like other prophetic literature, Jonah contains utopian ideals. This book asks its readers to imagine a world where the power of empire exists in a different way. If not a destroyed Assyrian Empire, then a reformed empire that does good in the world. That the book ends, seemingly, in a debate about these two options suggests the aspiration for a world where empires are subject to divine power. The disputed histories regarding the existence or non-existence of Nineveh at the time of the writing of the book confirm the broad utopian impulses of original texts and histories of interpretation (Tiemeyer 2022; Erickson,

2021; Sherwood 2000). Engagement with the empire should make Jonah postcolonial utopian literature, following Bill Ashcroft for whom postcolonial utopianism 'offers a particularly intense rhetoric of the future characterized by its engagement with imperial power' (Ashcroft 2017, p. 4). As such, postcolonial literature and prophetic literature imagine futures rid of the imperial impositions. Ironically, the book of Jonah seems more like an imperial utopia with the concerns of 'the tension of freedom and coercion; the struggle between the education and manipulation of desire; the necessity of the Law and the rule of the enlightened' being more formative (Ashcroft 2017, p. 10). These concerns come into focus in the final chapter under the desert plant. In that space Jonah disputes divine grace, his autonomy as a man, albeit a man forced to the prophetic task, and whether deities can approach omniscience. Nonetheless, there is much in the book regarding preferred futures even as it struggles with the imperfect present.

Utopias and heterotopias may not be opposite sides of the same coin. Instead, they sit in relation to each other along a spectrum of change. If, as Kenneth Surin offers, utopias point to a better future as the escape from an awful present, then heterotopias offer real glimpses of those possibilities (2009, p. 268). As sites where real and fairy-tale-like freedom exists (so Foucault and Miskowiec 1986, p. 24), heterotopic spaces are where the virtual and real mix together because the real, meaning true freedom, has not yet happened or may never happen (Surin 2009, pp. 269, 272). Rather than spaces that accommodate the next best thing, heterotopias are 'a queering or a desubjugating practice' as Jennifer Ingrey suggests (Ingrey 2016, p. 152). Queer spaces that privilege the embodied knowledge of queer folk and at the same time refuses to accede to the power of gender orthodoxies (Ingrey 2016, p. 152). The attractiveness of these spaces as counter-sites may not always capture the interlocking web of oppressions that need to be dismantled in order to achieve a modicum of freedom (Surin 2009, p. 282). In other words, heterotopias are not utopic even as they gesture to spaces that 'do not make deviants out of its entrants' (Ingrey 2016, p. 153). At best, they are spaces of deferral, as Hetherington indicates that experiment with ideas and practices in search of freedom that may or may not achieve any success (1997, p. ix).

Several spaces in the book of Jonah resemble heterotopias. The ship with the sailors is an obvious choice (Jonah 1.4–16), if only for the fact that Foucault names ships as 'the heterotopia *par excellence*' (Foucault and Miskowiecv 1986, p. 27). Ships in general and the ship in Jonah are closed sites that are at the same time open to possibilities to achieve perfection. The ship provides Jonah a pathway to another city, a place where his confession is neither mocked nor taken too seriously, a company of seekers ready to engage with the divine as a means to manipulate nature. The 'gut of the fish' (Havea 2020, p. 30) holds some of the same possibilities as the ship. Fish entrails, if ever one should find it a place to inhabit, are adaptable spaces that accommodate near orthodox confession and commitment of the sort Jonah performs. A site that allows only the type of forced entry that Jonah experiences (Foucault and Miskowiec 1986, p. 26). The city of Nineveh combines both temporal and spatial features of heterotopia. In its appearance in the book, Nineveh (Jonah 3.1) is also what Foucault calls a heterochronie, a place where time accumulates (Foucault and Miskowiec 1986, p. 26). Nineveh in the book is both dead and living, destroyed in 612 BCE but a menacing imperial city at its height. Nineveh in its many histories and as an imagined space in this book matches the extensive afterlives of Jonah as a book. This dead city exerts this pull in the book to reveal to us, through the actions of its residents, the many ways imperial civilizations try to remake themselves in order to stay alive and even when they are dead and gone still live on in museums and libraries. Jane Lydon and Uzma Z. Rizvi observe how modern museums curate Western knowledge, 'perpetuating the desire to commemorate ancestors, museums have become Eurocentric regimes of memory' (2010, p. 26).

The desert plant is the final heterotopia that I name. I am aware that my thought of the landscape outside of Nineveh leads me to make several interpretative conclusions. At the same time, I reserve judgement about other disputed aspects of this plant.[1] The space outside of the city may or may not be a desert. From the descriptions of Jonah's physical needs in the book, I conclude that he is in a space with little vegetation that can provide shade. Additionally, my use of 'desert plant' draws attention to how major cities – ancient and modern – contribute to the degradation of the environment on their outskirts that can lead to processes resembling desertification. I restrain myself on the matter of the Hebrew term *qiqayon*. I translate it 'a slender desert plant' without making too much commitment as to naming the vegetation. Whatever else our limited knowledge of this word unique to the book of Jonah tells us, we know that it is not luxuriant growth; more cactus than baobab.

Several incompatibilities come together in the space that forms the scene of the final chapter – a hurriedly made booth decorated by a plant with an odd lifespan at the edges of an imperial city. This disparate landscape scene serves as the setting for a compressed expression of life and death with the potential to go in either direction: The city can be destroyed, the wind should topple the booth, the plant should live longer than a single day, and the misanthropic Jonah would receive reproof from the divine. These anticipated verities do not occur. That they do not happen suggests that the space is not simply heterotopic but queer. For in this space Jonah's 'orientation device' as Sara Ahmed calls it, the object that extends his body into space renders him queer, that object being the desert plant. Jonah's affective attachment to the object gives us one of the few insights into his emotional state (Ahmed 2006, p. 11).

## Jonah's queerness

Is Jonah also one of the prophets? This question gets not only to Jonah's performance in the episodes of the book, but also to Jonah in general. At verse three of chapter 1, Jonah demonstrates a penchant to depart from normative prophetic behaviour. Set within the cultural norms of the prophetic vocation where the divine commission anticipates some resistance, Jonah crosses the line into blatant refusal. As Ahmed tells us, 'The queer subject within straight culture hence deviates and is made socially present as a deviant' (2006, p. 21). If Jonah enters the book queerly through his refusal of the Nineveh commission, the book's end should leave no doubt about his queerness. Perhaps as he exits the city, Jonah vents that the events come to pass as he anticipated while he was still on 'his home ground' (Havea 2020, p. 49). This comment reveals not so much Jonah's prescience as much as the practised ways of trying unsuccessfully to fit queerly into straight spaces. Where else might Jonah have questioned the use of divine power or the imposition of the divine will to straighten the lives of people? Jonah's practice of queerness might place him in proximity with those that do not fit into normative spaces. Yet he hardly expresses any affinity with those who might be his people. Jonah buries himself in the hold of the ship away from the sailors who take an 'all hands' approach to combatting the storm (Jonah 1.5). Unafraid to defy norms, expectations, and not cowed by the divine presence, Jonah takes a while before he confronts coercive power and its demands over non-conforming bodies.

In the commission to Jonah, Nineveh is set up in the form of Foucault's crisis heterotopia, those places for people and their practices that are outside the norms of society. Foucault lists these spaces in the ancient world as those set aside for 'menstruating women, pregnant women, the elderly, etc.' (Foucault and Miskowiec 1986, p. 24). To the extent that crisis heterotopias exist in the modern world, he names those as boarding schools or reform schools of the reform types; places deemed as 'nowhere' since the normal rules seem not to apply there. As a crisis heterotopia, Nineveh is a nowhere place until it becomes almost everywhere. This spatial anomie of the book that Amy Erickson describes as 'tied to no place and no time and yet to many places and many times' (2021, p. 37) means that recognition signals dire implications for Nineveh. In the Hebrew text the foundation for Jonah's commission to Nineveh's lies in the disturbing reality that its 'evil' (רעה) stood in the face of the deity (Jonah 1.2). Sasson translates כי—עלתה רעתם לפני as 'the wickedness of its citizens is obvious to me' (1990, p. 3). We never know fully what constitutes Nineveh's 'evil' (רעה) (Jonah

1.1). By the end of the book, though, we get the sense that the divine comment about their confusion of the right and the left (Jonah 4.11) reflects their pre-Jonah character. The inability to make these distinctions suggest for Ahmed a fluidity of orientation. Seemingly, the Ninevites lack the type of neutrality that Ahmed understands Immanuel Kant presumes comes with the distinction of right and left: 'This lack of neutrality is what grounds the distinction between right and left: the right becomes the straight line, and the left becomes the origin of deviation' (Ahmed 2009, p. 14). Even if this feature of Nineveh remains true after the national acts of repentance, this description represents what José Esteban Muñoz regards as ephemera, 'things that are left hanging in the air like a rumor' (Muñoz 2009, p. 65). Nineveh consists of real persons; lives that Jonah could touch and influence. A queer city. To the extent that Jonah's mission involved straightening Nineveh, then this crisis heterotopia and the types of interventions it requires would not be compatible for the way Jonah inhabits queerness.

Prophets are intensely lonely and isolated figures. Jonah, though, seems to find human relationships difficult.[2] He avoids the sailors on the ship until he no longer can. He speaks sparingly in his proclamation to Nineveh. The range of emotions that Jonah displays under the slender plant highlights a man devoid of human ties. Apart from the details of his patrilineage, nothing is known of Jonah's family. Camaraderie and any interests in the cycles of human life appear not to interest him as much as the life cycle of the plant does. The queerness of the interspecies intimacy Jonah displays in the final chapter calls attention to a particular display of what Muñoz regards as queer futurity filled with 'political resonance' (2009, p. 87). Awaiting the obliteration of an entire city, Jonah's intimacy with the slender plant in its decided preference for vegetal intimacy rejects reproductive futurity. The elimination of reproductive futures for Nineveh stands alongside of Jonah's awkward signal of a queer futurity where hope persists through other relational forms. More than a cynical embrace of death, Jonah's queer futurity marks a rejection of forms of reproduction that can prevent interspecies affiliations. Neel Ahuja points out how 'bodies and atmospheres reproduce through complex forms of socio-ecological entanglements' (2015, p. 368). Jonah may stumble awkwardly into human relationships and advocacy, yet may well gesture to a queer political stance that Esteban argues is 'a relational and collective modality of endurance and support' (Muñoz 2009, p. 91).

A queer prophet seems like a contradiction in terms. The prophetic task of calling out failures and pressing communities back into the line of normalcy seems an ill fit for Jonah. Not the first prophet to disavow the title (see Amos 7.14), even the text itself cannot name him prophet. Jonah's prophetic performances are either deviant or simply forced. We are not privy to all the locations where the divine word encounters prophets in order to name a normal site for these get-togethers. For Jonah, the guts of the fish offer his best experiences of a divine meeting. Otherwise, Jonah's divine encounters seem tiresome and unproductive. Absent the performances of rituals and only the hint of future sacrifice (Jonah 2.9), Jonah strikes no pose as the most observant of prophets or even someone who is devout. 'Reluctant prophet' insufficiently captures the sight of Jonah cringing through Nineveh with his brief word of denunciation. Forcibly brought in line from his deviations, Jonah takes a day's journey through the city before he could start issuing the threat of destruction (Jonah 3.4). Was his day's walk of silence a queer yet effective form of proclamation? Or maybe, as Havea suggests, he did not even need to speak since the transformations occur before Jonah reaches the other side of the city in two days' time (2020, p. 43).

Jonah perverts divine orthodoxies in ways that reveal his latent queerness. The central confrontation in the book revolves around the divine nature codified into dogma.[3] The inadequacies of this dogmatic declaration seem to have been a longstanding problem for Jonah even before the events unfold (don't unfold) in Nineveh. Ahmed offers that perversion in its spatial sense means 'the willful determination to counter or go against orthodoxy' (2006, p. 78). This perspective provides a useful way to understand Jonah's queerness. If divine grace then functions as a tool of manipulation to bring those who have crossed the line into deviance back in line (that is, straight), then that explains the extraordinary efforts to ensure that Jonah carries out this mission. What's more appropriate for the deviant city of Nineveh than for the spared deviant prophet to announce through a body disciplined into normative conformity that they too can be recipients of divine grace? In effect, Jonah's refusal of the commission represents a rejection of what Puar regards as 'homonationalism', which she describes as the normalization of queerness in the service of imposing national ideals upon other nations that subjugate racial and sexual otherness (2007, p. 2). The deviant prophet performs the useful function to threaten the imperial city with lethal divine power.

Jonah becomes the homonational, at least from the perspective of anti-Semitic interpreters. The heroic Jonah, more particularly what Sherwood views as the 'Jonah the Jew' stream of interpretation (2000, p. 27), successfully achieves what other prophets failed to accomplish – lead an entire nation to repentance. His success confirms for several Christian polemicists, Jewish deficiencies. Tiemeyer cites the example of Jerome: 'Nineveh believed but not Israel; the foreskin believed, but circumcision remained without faith' (Tiemeyer 2022, p. 179). Jonah functions as a template for the believers of exported morality; 'a proto-missionary text' (Sherwood 2000, p. 79). This export product, marketed by a carefully selected spokesperson who aligns well with the target group, facilitates the type of 'soft diplomacy' that works alongside of lethal military power.[4] Jonah's disciplined body performs prophecy with all the sexual hierarchical implications contained in that role to display to Nineveh the results of the application of different forms of coercive power. Any sense of Jonah as disappointment or success fails to come to terms with the essential role he is called to play; make an entire nation 'line up' rather than be 'slantwise' (Ahmed 2006, p. 107). Ehud Ben Zvi talks of this mission as the perception that the Ninevites as foreigners are 'Israelitizable, that is, as having the potential to behave as an Israelite, to talk and act as a good Israelite' (Ben Zvi 2003, p. 89).

In response to the threat of overwhelming force, Nineveh accepts the superiority of divine power and saves itself from destruction through rituals that at best seem like a drag performance. The commonness of sackcloth and ashes, notwithstanding, the piety of the Ninevites seems both forced and unnatural. The inclusion of animals in the fast from food and water (Jonah 3.7) means that everyday Ninevites performed imposed ways of being upon their animals. Their performances of piety include forms of dress that transform their bodies as well as the animals into the conformity required by their king's capitulation to the divine threat. In effect, they play at being Israelite in the way that drag performers manipulate gender performances. While drag for some persons may be a form of play and entertainment, in other cases drag allows someone to enter into what Muñoz regards as 'the antinormative disjuncture between their biological gender and their performed or lived gender' (2009, p. 76). The term 'evil' (Jonah 1.2), to describe the Ninevites, easily forecloses on the broad stroke tendencies of orthodoxies. The book and its histories of interpretations are not always as adept at separating out the citizens of the city from the excess of the Assyrian Empire. Guilt by association, stereotyping, collective punishment generates passing, hiding, drag as forms of survival. In this case, drag that gestures to queer performances of compulsory straight orthodoxies to forestall sanctified violence. The divine threat forced Nineveh's perversions, 'the willful determination to counter or go against orthodoxy' – whatever these would be – back into the closet (Ahmed 2009, p. 78). The peevish response 'I told you so', at Jonah 4.1–3, reveals the futility of violence to achieve meaningful transformation. The response also questions the role of queerness in the divine economy and how grace is dispensed in pursuit of queer liberation. To the extent that queerness can be a useful transformative trait to entrench dominant orthodoxies, what is the investment the divine economy makes towards queer liberation. Where does the dominant culture break, bend, crack or slant?

## Plant heterotopia

The desert location serves as the most generative of heterotopic spaces in the book of Jonah since it is also the space of real disputation in the book. A face-to-face encounter occurs here (Jonah 4.1–4), unlike the dispatches through messenger formulas and prayers that formed earlier communications. This meeting place emerges at the hands of both protagonists. Jonah selects the location outside the city, constructs it, and later the deity decorates it with a plant. The invocations of a wilderness setting – outside of built-up spaces – point to this location as a normative place for prophetic discernment. However, Jonah contests these expectations by placing himself on the outskirts of Nineveh and even more, outside the divine relationship emerging with Nineveh. His crisis does not resemble Elijah's existential angst of being an ineffective prophet (1 Kings 19.10) and therefore he does not need a non-specific wilderness in the form of a cave (1 Kings 19.9). The environs of Nineveh form the context for his venting to double down on marginalization through the erection of a booth (סכה) for he truly resents the role of prophet and his deployment to Nineveh. The location serves in many ways as an ideal heterotopia of deviation to embrace several forms of exclusions, particularly after the discomforts that result from the inclusion of Nineveh in the divine economy. Foucault thinks of heterotopias of deviation as spaces where people with deviant behavior belong, such as 'rest homes, psychiatric hospitals, and of course prisons' (Foucault and Miskowiec 1986, p. 25). Foucault's quirky definitions belie the dominance of cultural norms that might appear innocuous or innocent but in fact instead enforce harsh standards. He includes retirement homes among deviant spaces since idleness stands as an aberration in a culture where pleasure is the norm.

The arrival of the plant enhances the space for Jonah because he now has an object that orients him to the world. His body can occupy space and shape its way in the world in response to what Ahmed regards as a queer object (2006, p. 91). In the rarity of the plant lies its queerness, since queer objects are not easily accessible. For the first time, we see Jonah experience authentic joy in relation to another living being in his rejoicing over the plant. His reaction stands in contrast to his deferred 'thanksgiving voice' (Jonah 2.9), the only other place where he seems to breathe from the consistent demand to prove difference. Muñoz plays with the word *jouissance* to express queer joy. He goes further than Lee Edelman in *No Future: Queer Theory and the Death Drive*. Muñoz critiques Edelman's call to surrender politics and hope in order to embrace the abjection of queerness to experience true pleasure as insufficient (2009, p. 91). To experience queer *jouissance* means living within the now and the not yet (Muñoz 2009, p. 94); a refusal and at times an inability to ignore current realities and contexts. Jonah simply standing in anticipation of the destruction of Nineveh poses an atemporal guise. The figure locked into the endless debates of the dates of the book in relation to the destruction of Nineveh. In those debates lie a specificity of history that brackets any sense of historical accountability. Instead, the book of Jonah moves the easily forgettable Jonah into a scene that fixes him among those who understand that empires leave their victims uncompensated, their legacies intact in the pages of history, only to be reincarnated in other cultures and in other locations.[5] The pouting Jonah, dissatisfied with the developments in Nineveh and clutching his queer object, disturbs theological normalcy. The prophet at odds with his deity disrupts a happy ending for this book and bends prophetic expectations to a slant. This scene evokes a momentary glee that not even divine power can stage-manage straightness. Queer objects like a slender desert plant spring forth for a brief moment to generate joy. At best, we can say that Jonah as queer finds his home under a plant.

As much joy that Jonah finds in the plant, the space highlights several realities of queer life. Real community with like-minded humans remains absent for Jonah. While he encounters several humans in the course of his travels, he never finds his people. The vegetal intimacy that he experiences here only serves to remind us of his queerness and how isolating queerness can be in a world overdetermined by straightness. The fleeting moments of joy, brought to him compliments of divine intervention in the form of the slender plant, only highlight the complicating role of theological orthodoxy. Should the plant be a source of Jonah's object lesson? If the entire prophetic odyssey[6] serves only as the learning outcome for a deviant prophet, then it only enforces what Jonah already knows, that queerness has a particular utility in the divine economy. The source of his queer joy, the object that truly shapes his orientation to the world, lasts only so long because divine action prevents its permanent place in his life. Even more, that queer object surfaces in the conversation in a way that reinforces the divine project in Nineveh. The divine contention over the slender plant suggests eliminating, if not diminishing, Nineveh's capabilities to stray away from the straight line was the goal of the prophetic commission. In the end, the point is made that only so much deviance is allowed before whole cities and prophets are brought back into the straight line. Queerness is at best only fleeting, a utility, a teaching tool, with little permanence in normative spaces.

The loss of the plant pleads Jonah's case for divine attention to queerness. If the material dimensions of power mean that divine attention will focus largely upon concerns on a grander scale, what does this mean for queer life that always exist in minoritized spaces. Jonah's repeated death wish[7] in the book indicates the sad reality of the insufficient value placed upon queer life. That Jonah speaks the death wish directly to the divine and his life is valued in the balance with others begs the question of not only how far the theological dogma of divine grace goes, but how far grace goes to sustain or even create a particular social order. As a marker of difference, rather than extending and diversifying the social order, queerness can be easily co-opted as the sign of all that stands in opposition to the social order as the means to reinforce the existing social order. Hetherington notes how heterotopias are implicated in the processes that renew the social order to ensure the maintenance of the status quo (1997, p. 7). The plant allows for an interrogation of what divine provisions support queerness to exist as an alternative ordering. The clearer answer may come from translating the final sentence of the book as a declaration rather than a question (Jonah 4.11). As a question, queerness never qualifies for divine attention except as a useful tool. As a declaration of divine callousness and caprice,[8] then queerness has a shot because it means that Jonah is seen.

## Conclusion

Limitations abound in Jonah. A small book with brief glimpses of possibilities. A book marked intensely by queer times in the way Muñoz understands queer times: 'Queerness is not yet here. Queerness is an ideality' (2009, p. 1). In the oddity of mixing medieval medical practices with modern scientific approaches lies the incongruity of sexual orthodoxies that insist on the rightness of pre-scientific biological determinism. These odd times persist and, in their endurance, underwrite lethal and other forms of violences that surveil bodies and their relationships with all things living. Jonah as a prophetic book presses the boundaries of the practices of prophets. As a doubtful and perhaps doubting prophet, we only guess at the reasons for his recalcitrance. His brooding personality hardly endears him to religion built upon prosperity and neoliberal ways of being. In such cultures, a figure like Jonah suffers endless taunts and ridicule for not being normal. Cathleen Kaveny offers that Jonah is 'not a petulant malingerer; he is a tragic hero' (2016, p. 402). As a tragic hero, Kaveny understands Jonah as a cheerleader for all those who question the verities of culture. His refusal to immediately comply and to conform reluctantly sets him apart from other prophets. In his work Jonah makes suspicion of divine motives and knowledge a worthwhile feature of the prophet as one who engages 'prophetic indictments ironically' (Kaveny 2016, p. 406). Yet Kaveny pauses on the utility of Jonah's orientation, seeing it as doing only so much. Drawing upon Kierkegaard, she limits Jonah: 'Irony is a tool to demolish rigidity, not a way of life' (2016, p. 415). Queerness is useful until it no longer works.

However, readers approach Jonah as queer determines how we understand the utility of queerness in a straight world. With a tightly constrained mission, Jonah serves a particular purpose to deliver a message to Nineveh. Once done he should exit the scene and cede the stage to divine action. Neither happens as expected. Jonah remains stage side. An empty centre stage. The action takes place in the wings to cajole Jonah that the vacant stage makes sense. To witness this uncomfortable drama play out forces viewers to write a negative review of the stage play. Neither as avant-garde theatre or prophetic literature does Jonah discomfort viewers/readers with the impermeability of orthodoxies, normativity or straightness. The more liberal view of incremental change and temporal elasticity too easily stand in for meaningful transformation and liberation. Despite the potential limitlessness of the book, Jonah as queer serves a pre-scribed utility as much as queerness slowly ekes out spaces in a heteronormative world.

As a contrast to straight time that denies queers any claim to the future, Muñoz invests queer times with potential for some-thing better: 'The future is queerness's domain' (2009, p. 1). His utopic vision captures the qualities of heterotopia and invites our reading to continue beyond the pages of the book. We can focus what is fleeting in the book to build a sense of possibility about the future.

## Notes

1 Jack Sasson notes with scepticism the ease with which interpreters, unfamiliar with ancient botany, make assertions about the identity of vegetation 'displayed with minimal realism'. As such he follows the lead of Aquila and Theodotion to transliterate the Hebrew word *qiqayon* (Sasson 1990, p. 292). Tiemeyer presents the fascination of interpreters who debate the identity of the plant that can range from ivy to gourd (Tiemeyer 2022, pp. 219–24).

2 The striking feature of Jonah's emotional vacuity when compared with other prophets lies in the absence of specific divine prohibitions. The deity orders Ezekiel not to mourn the death of his wife (Ezek. 3.10–16), then denies Jeremiah the experience of marriage for himself (Jer. 16.1) and any participation in communal celebrations (Jer. 16.8–9).

3 The 'intertextual web' spans several biblical texts from Exodus to several prophetic and psalm texts (Tiemeyer 2022, p. 209).

4 Thomas Bolin indicates that among Christian interpreters, Jonah's mission to Nineveh plays a more prominent role than his stay in the fish (1997, p. 20).

5 Erickson shows how the promise of death after resurrection features in several Christian homiletical and art depictions of the final scenes of Jonah. The dissatisfied prophet reconciles with his God based upon reading 4.11 as a declarative statement that resolves any lingering notions that Nineveh escapes divine judgement. She notes: 'The image of Jonah at peace, having been assured that God will reveal God's sovereignty over the empire-of-the-moment by destroying it in time, may have projected to early Roman Christians that they could peacefully anticipate God's coming reign and the future destruction of their Roman oppressors' (2021, p. 153).

6 Janet Howe Gaines thinks that 'the book of Jonah is an excellent illustration of journey literature.' She links it to books such as *Adventures of Huckleberry Finn* (Mark Twain) and *Heart of Darkness* (Joseph Conrad), where central characters mature and as a result 'earn a second chance to do the right thing, to increase knowledge and tolerance, and to realize freedom from ignorance and bigotry' (2003, p. 11). This type of literature also falls into the Robinsonade genre, where distant places through their exoticism function as sites as rehabilitation for a central character to re-enter into normative society. See DeLoughrey 2007, p. 12.

7 James Nogalski notes the various biblical characters who request their lives be taken by God (2011, p. 446).

8 Alan Cooper reads Jonah 4.11 as a declarative rather than interrogation. From this perspective he sees the divine acting in wild and unpredictable ways: 'God's wrath is just as inexplicable and uncontrollable as his love, but that, too, is part of what it means for him to be freely and truly God' (Cooper 1993, p. 163).

# References

Ahmed, S., 2006, *Queer Phenomenology: Orientations, Objects, Others*, Durham, NC: Duke University Press.

Ahuja, Neel, 2015, 'Intimate Atmospheres: Query Theory in a Time of Extinctions', *GLQ: A Journal of Lesbian and Gay Studies* 21/2–3, pp. 365–85.

Ashcroft, B., 2017, *Utopianism in Postcolonial Literatures*, London: Routledge.

Ben Zvi, Ehud, 2003, *The Sign of Jonah: Reading and Rereading in Ancient Yehud*, Sheffield: Sheffield Academic Press.

Bolin, Thomas M., 1997, *Freedom Beyond Forgiveness: The Book of Jonah Re-Examined*, Sheffield: Sheffield Academic Press.

Cooper, Alan, 1993, 'In Praise of Divine Caprice: The Significance of the Book of Jonah' in Philip R. Davies and David J. A. Clines (eds), *Among the Prophets: Language, Image and Structure in the Prophetic Writings*, Sheffield: Sheffield Academic Press, pp. 144–63.

DeLoughrey, Elizabeth M., 2007, *Routes and Roots: Navigating Caribbean and Pacific Island Literatures*, Honolulu: University of Hawai'i Press.

Erickson, Amy, 2021, *Jonah: Introduction and Commentary*, Grand Rapids, MI: Eerdmans.

Foucault, M. and J. Miskowiec, 'Of Other Spaces', *Diacritics* 16/1 (1986), pp. 22–7.

Gaines, Janet Howe, 2003, *Forgiveness in a Wounded World: Jonah's Dilemma*, Leiden: Brill.

Havea, Jione, 2020, *Jonah: An Earth Bible Commentary*, London: T&T Clark.

Hetherington, K., 1997, *The Badlands of Modernity: Heterotopia and Social Ordering*, London: Routledge.

Ingrey, J. C., 2016, 'Heterotopia' in N. M. Rodriguez, W. J. Martino, J. C. Ingrey and E. Brockenbrough (eds), *Critical Concepts in Queer Studies and Education: An International Guide for the Twenty-First Century*, London: Palgrave Macmillan, pp. 149–59.

Kaveny, Cathleen, 2016, *Prophecy Without Contempt: Religious Discourse in the Public Square*, Cambridge, MA: Harvard University Press.

Lydon, Jane and Uzma Z. Rizvi (eds), 2010, 'Introduction: Postcolonialism and Archaeology' in *Handbook of Postcolonial Archaeology*, Walnut Creek, CA: Left Coast Press, pp. 17–33.

Muñoz, J. E., 2009, *Cruising Utopia: The Then and There of Queer Futurity*, New York: New York University Press.

Nogalski, James D., 2011, *The Book of the Twelve: Hosea – Jonah*, Macon, GA: Smyth & Helwys.

Puar, J. K., 2005, 'Queer Times, Queer Assemblages', *Social Text* 23/3–4 (2005), pp. 121–30.

Puar, J. K., 2007, *Terrorist Assemblages: Homonationalism in Queer Times*, Durham, NC: Duke University Press.

Sasson, Jack M., 1990, *Jonah: A New Translation with Introduction, Commentary, and Interpretation*, New York: Doubleday.

Sherwood, Yvonne, 2000, *A Biblical Text and its Afterlives: The Survival of Jonah in Western Culture*, Cambridge: Cambridge University Press.

Surin, K., 2009, *Freedom Not Yet: Liberation and the Next World Order*, Durham, NC: Duke University Press.

Tiemeyer, Lena-Sofia, 2022, *Jonah Through the Centuries*, Hoboken, NJ: Wiley.

# 4

# 'When the World No Longer Appears the Right Way Up': Queering Time, Space and the Prophetic Body in Jonah 2

## L. JULIANA CLAASSENS

## Introduction

There is much in the book of Jonah that can be considered funny, strange or, one could say, queer. These peculiarities lead interpreters to continue to return to this intriguing book, as evident in the thousands of pages of scholarly reflection that include at least seven new major commentaries in a two-year period, adding to the already expansive interpretation history of this book as documented by Amy Erickson (2021) and Lena-Sofia Tiemeyer (2021).

These out-of-the-ordinary elements in Jonah also offer fertile ground for queer biblical interpreters, who are precisely drawn to those instances in the text that may be considered unstable, incoherent, ambiguous or complex to, as Sean Burke says, 'deconstruct and to denaturalize identities to demonstrate that what are claimed to be natural and normal essences are actually arbitrary and fluid social constructions' (2011, p. 176). Much is at stake in terms of this way of reading that seeks to challenge or interrogate seemingly fixed, set-in-stone, structures. As Burke notes, queer biblical interpretation's ultimate concern is 'to make it possible for more bodies to matter – for more bodies to be recognized as fully human' (2011, p. 176). These bodies are sexualized bodies, though queer interpretation also holds distinct implications for other bodies who are rendered 'other', including gendered bodies, racialized bodies, colonized bodies, migrant bodies and disabled bodies.[1]

For this essay, and with an eye to my own ginormous task of writing yet another commentary on Jonah (Ecclesiastes was right that 'Of making many books there is no end' (Eccles. 12.12)), in conversation with Sara Ahmed's seminal book *Queer Phenomenology*, I consider the queer moments, the queer turns and the queer effects in the book of Jonah as categories of time, space, and the prophetic body of the prophet itself, are rendered queer. Drawing on her own experience of coming out as a lesbian, as well as her mixed-race heritage (English mother/Pakistani father), Ahmed poetically, and quite poignantly, explores how we think about orientations, lines, directions and norms that hold distinct implications for what it means for bodies to fit, or more often than not, not fit, in terms of what society deems to be the normative.[2] I propose that some of Ahmed's insights in *Queer Phenomenology* may help us to 'redirect our attention toward different objects, those that are "less proximate" or even those that deviate or are deviant' as it pertains to sexual orientation, as well as gender, race and class (2006, p. 3).

In the first part of this essay, I highlight how some of these queer elements specifically pertaining to the confusion of categories of time and space in the book of Jonah are responsible for some queer turns, or queer (re)orientations, not only by the characters in the text but potentially also by its readers who are encouraged to redirect their gaze. A queer orientation opens up new vantage points in the text and the world, helping one to see things one ordinarily would not see. Accordingly, in the final section of this essay, I consider the queer effects of attending to such queer moments and queer turns in the interpretation of Jonah, which includes drawing our attention to feminist bodies, postcolonial bodies and queer bodies who all too often have been considered bodies out of place.

## Queer moments

There are several instances in the book of Jonah that align with what Sara Ahmed describes as queer moments, that is, those 'moments in the text where the world no longer appears "the right way up"' (2006, p. 65). Ahmed here is in conversation with Maurice Merleau-Ponty as she contemplates the relationship between bodies, time and space (2006, p. 66). She argues that '[t]hings as well as bodies appear "the right way up" when they are "in line".' However, bodies and, I add for the purpose of this paper, also categories such as time and space, that do not 'line up', appear 'slantwise' and hence could be considered 'queer'. As Ahmed writes: 'it is not just that thing that appears oblique but the world itself might appear on a slant, which disorientates the picture and even unseats the body' (2006, p. 67).

A good example of where categories of time and space do not align in the book of Jonah concerns the symbolic representation of the Assyrian capital Nineveh in which lines between past, present, and future are blurred, as Nineveh not only represents an empire long gone but also empires present and empires to come. Jonah's post-exilic readers would have known all too well that the Nineveh to which Jonah is called to proclaim its destruction long since had been destroyed. But future readers find themselves wrestling to discern which empire, and perhaps empires plural, loomed so large not only in the minds of first readers but also in readers since who have been dealing with empires of their own.[3]

Categories of time and space are equally confounding when it comes to Jonah's descent into the belly of the whale in Jonah 2 that continues Jonah's journey from Tarshish and his flight away from the presence of God (Erickson 2021, p. 299). The exceedingly strange moment of being swallowed by a big fish is coupled with a description of Jonah sinking ever deeper, descending into the hull of the ship, further down as he is hurled overboard, and deeper yet into the depths of the ocean, the Deep, or Sheol. But this queer moment of being swallowed by a whale becomes even stranger when one realizes that as scholars like Amy Erickson argue, this is no ordinary fish, but a gender-bending fish. Commentators throughout the ages have been intrigued, or one could say confounded, by the fact that it is a male fish that swallows Jonah (Jonah 2.1), but that Jonah then proceeds to pray from the belly, or rather the womb, of a female fish (Jonah 2.2), so opening up a range of metaphorical associations that fruitfully may be explored in a queer interpretation of the prophet and the book (Erickson 2021, p. 292; Graybill 2016, p. 132).[4]

Another queer moment in this text, regarding time and space, occurs in the incongruity between Jonah's act of calling out for deliverance and speaking of drowning when the sea already has calmed down (Jonah 2.3, cf. Jonah 1.15). Or even more strange, how he can perform liturgical acts of thanksgiving associated with a worship service, praising God for being saved all the while still being trapped inside a big fish. Scholars draw attention to how this place of captivity in the innards of a mythical sea monster serves as a space of divine encounter – in some traditions even going so far as imaging this space being transformed into a place of worship (Hendel 2019, p. 1; Pyper 2007, p. 337; Bolin 1997, p. 101). For instance, Yvonne Sherwood cites an imaginative interpretation by Pirke de Rabbi Eliezer in which 'Jonah finds himself in a synagogue, a place of study, illuminated by eye-windows and by a pearl that hangs from the stomach roof' (1998, p. 65). And Erickson views 'Jonah's performance of worship' as reminiscent of 'a thanksgiving service' that transforms the space he occupies, turning the belly of a whale into 'a recognizable temple space' (2021, pp. 286, 308).

Elsewhere, I suggest how this confusion of categories of time and space can be interpreted as a narrative strategy typical of a trauma novel to mimic the world-turned-upside down effects of trauma on the body and psyche.[5] However, read through a queer lens, such moments of disorientation in which time and space seem out of alignment, may compel us to reconsider what it means to be orientated in the first place. In this regard, I consider in the next section how these queer moments in the text contain potentially transformative effects as the prophetic body is submerged in the queer space of a big fish, that serves as a site of orientation, or rather reorientation or transformation.

## Queer turns

A central premise in Sara Ahmed's work is how bodies are shaped by the space they inhabit. She argues that 'bodies are submerged, such that they become the space they inhabit; in taking up space, bodies move through space and are affected by the "where" of that movement. Through this movement the surface of spaces as well as bodies takes shape' (2006, p. 53).

Bodies, in particular, are affected by spatial orientation. Ahmed reflects, for instance, on the role of turning in subject formation that might take a subject into a different direction – '[d]epending on which way one turns, different worlds might even come into view' (2006, p. 15). Particularly, those queer moments when the world appears slantwise, or when the subject is 'knocked off course' take responsibility for the subject facing in new directions. Ahmed, speaking from personal experience, writes that such queer moments may likely be quite traumatic and anxiety-inducing. However, 'queer orientations that don't line up', that compel one to look at 'the world "slantwise"', may make it possible for 'other objects to come into view' (2006, p. 107). Moreover, if these queer turns are repeated over time, it may well happen that 'bodies acquire the very shape of such direction'. Ahmed notes that by 'moving in this way, rather than that, and moving in this way again and again', bodies may be reorientated, redirected, as evident in the idea of 'changing course' (2006, p. 15).

When it comes to the book of Jonah, the queer moments in the text in which categories of time and space do not align have distinct implications of how one thinks about the prophetic body that hardly fits the typical profile of the Israelite prophet. This undoing of Jonah's identity as a prophet in the past has been characterized by scholars as a hallmark of satire, parody, or humour. However, in terms of Ahmed's point of bodies submerged into space, and how bodies take the shape of this space, one could ask how spatial orientation in terms of this particular, and particularly peculiar space, transforms the prophetic body of this atypical prophet Jonah.

For instance, Erickson quite intriguingly explores the metaphorical possibilities associated with the gender-bending fish as she highlights the presence of birth imagery in Jonah 2 that aptly captures the prophet's situation of being at the 'crossroads of life and death'. Both the belly of the fish (vv. 1–2) and the womb of Sheol (v. 3) are places of death, yet strangely they exhibit 'womblike features capable of offering comfort and protection', which Erickson poetically describes as Jonah not merely being 'entombed' but rather 'en-wombed' (2021, pp. 285–6).

We note in the previous section that the fish's belly is transformed to serve as an unexpected place of worship. But also, Jonah is transformed by this space. In terms of Ahmed's point that bodies take the shape of the space they inhabit, the tomb/womb of the big fish serves as a place of (re)orientation in which the prophetic body is transformed.[6] I propose that the following instances may be fruitfully explored in terms of the task at hand of *Queering the Prophet*.

First, in the tomb/womb of the fish, Jonah emerges as a *wounded body*, or one can say a *lamenting body*. Rhiannon Graybill has outlined how Jonah's body elsewhere in the book is subjected to violence – in chapter 1, Jonah is thrown overboard so that the sailors may 'come to realize the true power of God'; and in chapter 4, he is a 'body without shelter, exposed to scorching heat', and as also the prophet Jeremiah afflicted and 'rendered vulnerable by' the divine word (2016, p. 133). In chapter 2, though, we encounter most profoundly a prophetic body in pain as Jonah voices his suffering most graphically.

Expounding on the interpretative possibilities of the metaphor of a woman-in-labour in Jonah 2, Erickson offers the suggestive proposal that the pangs of childbirth are wreaking havoc on Jonah's body and causing him to cry out in anguish (2021, pp. 310–14). The metaphor of a woman in labour, which throughout the biblical prophets captures feelings of distress, helplessness and despair, functions as a powerful means to demonstrates the effects of suffering on the wounded prophet that in turn reflects an embodiment of a wounded people. Ironically, whereas the cries of women gripped in the pains of childbirth resound throughout the book of Jeremiah, this intimately female experience associated with the woman-in-labour metaphor is appropriated to express the feelings of vulnerability and anxiety of male warriors facing military defeat. Thus, even though the female experience of childbirth is instrumentalized in depicting the defeat of the nation, nowhere in the book of Jeremiah does this endless and futile process of being in labour without end result in the birth of a child that needs to be nursed and comforted (Dille 2004, p. 63; Bergmann 2007; Darr 1996).

Reminiscent of the traumatized prophet Jeremiah, who expresses his suffering and the suffering of his people in terms of the wounds on his body and psyche (see, for example, Jer. 8.22—9.2), Jonah expresses his anguish and pain in the form of lament as he draws on the Psalmic lament tradition to channel the anguish associated with a world in which nothing seems the right way up (Graybill 2016, pp. 129–30; cf. Claassens 2022, p. 2). Moreover, similar to Jeremiah, who is described by Graybill as a 'body in pain, but also in defiance', Jonah as a wounded, yet defying body impacts our understanding of his prophetic identity, that not only 'destabilizes masculinity' and 'undoes the body', but with 'this undoing opens new possibilities of being and becoming' (Graybill 2016, pp. 131, 141).

In this strange space in which lines between past, present and future are blurred, the prophetic body is thus able to find the words to voice how the bodies whom he represents have been shaped, or one should say scarred, by history. In terms of Ahmed's point that 'bodies take the shape of repetition', one finds that Jonah's prophetic identity is defined by this recurring act of lament – not only in chapter 2 but also in his challenge to God in chapter 4, which one could say, in Ahmed's words, orientates his 'body in some ways rather than others'.[7]

Also, the genderfluidity associated with the fish vessel in which Jonah finds himself may extend to the identity of Jonah as a lamenting body. Elsewhere, I show how the category of the lamenting prophet is fluid as the lines between the wailing women who are called to lament by a Lamenting God and the weeping prophet are blurred (Claassens 2012, pp. 30–35; Claassens 2010). And Graybill makes a compelling case in terms of how the female sound of keening and weeping attributed to the Weeping Prophet Jeremiah renders 'the male prophetic body as fluid opposes the normative ideal of the male body as self-contained, closed off, and without defect'.[8] Interestingly, the gendered space of a gender-bending fish in 'the watery deep' opens Jonah to take up his prophetic role. Graybill explores the 'association of water with rebirth' and the connection 'between fluidity and openness to new forms of being' as an avenue for contemplating a 'fluid prophetic masculinity' (2016, p. 134).

A second instance in which the prophetic body is shaped by the space through which he is moving regards the idea of thinking of Jonah as a *travelling body* or one could say *a migrant body*. Throughout the book of Jonah, the prophet constantly is turning, departing and arriving – by boat, by whale, by foot, ending up perched on a hill outside of the city of Nineveh, where he remains at the story's end. Much of this movement is involuntary as Jonah is hurled overboard, swallowed and then regurgitated by the whale. Jonah, though, exhibits a measure of agency, as evident in his decision to travel to Tarshish, and then towards the end of the book to set up a temporary structure outside the metropolis to which he had been called.

The fact that Jonah travels and eventually ends up in the queer space outside Nineveh, after spending time in an even queerer space of the big fish, impacts his identity as a prophet. Sitting on a hill outside of Nineveh, Jonah's gaze upon the metropolis demonstrates to what extent his construct of Nineveh, and what it represents, consumes his thoughts and emotions. Jonah's journey to this imperial epicentre comes with a history, what Ahmed describes as a 'background' that is '"unseen" in its "thereness"'[9] but which nevertheless shapes his arrival to this place where he sits on a hill, facing Nineveh, angry enough to die (2006, p. 37). The city, with its real and imagined inhabitants, serves as a strange object of fascination, but probably one that evokes feelings of hatred and revulsion in Jonah, which underscores the point made by Ahmed of how 'we are shaped by what we inherit' (2006, p. 124).

Nevertheless, in light of Ahmed's argument that voluntary, or more often than not, involuntary turns by the subject are responsible for new worlds coming into view, Jonah's distinct movements away from and then towards Nineveh culminate in facing the city and all that it represents. According to Ahmed, such turns offer the promise of new possibilities that she describes as 'the hope for new impressions, for new lines to emerge, new objects, or even new bodies ... to arrive in spaces where they are not already at home, where they are not "in place"' (2006, p. 62). Ahmed describes how these creative possibilities 'involve hard work'; that is, 'painstaking labor for bodies to inhabit spaces that do not extend their shape' (2006, p. 62).[10] With Jonah as a migrant body, arriving in the city of Nineveh and setting up lodging outside its walls, Ahmed's words concerning the impact of space on the (prophetic) body are quite fitting:

Having arrived, such bodies in turn might acquire new shapes. And spaces in turn acquire new bodies. So, yes, we should celebrate such arrivals. The 'new' is what is possible when what is behind us, our background, does not simply ground us or keep us in place, but allows us to move and allows us to follow something other than the lines that we have already taken. (Ahmed 2006, pp. 62–3)[11]

Queer biblical interpretation makes a difference in how we view Jonah, and how a queer orientation helps us to 'follow something other than the lines that we have already taken' (Ahmed 2006, p. 63). Perhaps, Jonah is not the only one shaped by his orientation towards Nineveh; Jonah's orientation may also shape us as readers as we are compelled to follow Jonah's gaze and consider how the collective takes shapes through the repetitive act of facing in a particular way and not another. As a lamenting body, recent postcolonial interpretations fruitfully invoke Jonah to serve as a prophetic witness against not only ancient but also contemporary manifestations of empire, so giving a whole new meaning to what is understood under Jonah's prophetic identity (Davidson 2016; 2018; Havea 2013; 2016; 2020; Ryu 2009). And as a migrant body, Jonah comes to represent future bodies on the move who offers an uncomfortable presence in a makeshift shelter outside of the metropole.

Graybill's intriguing interpretation of Jonah as the melancholic migrant whose refusal to be happy brings together these two reorientations concerning Jonah as prophet. The melancholic migrant may be a hallmark of the (queer) prophet who, in Ahmed's terms, utilizes unhappiness to 'perform its own claim for justice' by 'exposing injustice' (Ahmed 2006, p. 105).[12]

In this regard, the narrative ends with Jonah *not* leaving, but ultimately remaining connected in an uncomfortable, unhappy relationship to the city and all that it represents. In this way, the prophet, and we who have joined his gaze, are compelled to keep doing the hard work of embracing queer orientations which Ahmed describes as 'those [orientations] that don't line up, which by seeing the world "slantwise" allow other objects to come into view. A queer orientation might be one that does not overcome what is "off line", and hence *acts out of line with others*' (2006, p. 107; emphasis original).

## Queer effects

In this essay, I consider a few queer moments and queer turns in the book of Jonah that help us rethink the way the prophetic body is shaped by the queer spaces in which Jonah arrived, departed and arrives anew. Attention to Jonah as a queer prophetic body who as a lamenting and a migrant body can most definitely be said to be 'a body out of place' helps us in our quest to notice other 'bodies who do not or cannot follow the lines that are assumed to lead to happy endings'.[13]

Ahmed highlights numerous real-life consequences of what her *Queer Phenomenology* is proposing. For instance, recognizing how woman writers (philosophers like herself) quite often experience something of 'the "queer effect" ... created by bodies out of place'. Ahmed unequivocally states: 'Here I wish simply to say that when women write, when they take up space as writers, their bodies in turn acquire new shapes, even if the effect is no longer quite so queer' (2006, p. 61).

And in terms of her own experience as part of a lesbian couple, she shares an anecdote of how she and her girlfriend arrived at a romantic dinner with tables set for two, only to be struck as she entered the room by the fact that this space was exclusively filled with tables that were each occupied by a man and a woman, which quite viscerally showcased the extent to which the world is constructed to fit heterosexual bodies (Ahmed 2006, p. 82).

Finally, regarding her experience of the product of a white mother and brown father, Ahmed reflects on how often 'nonwhite bodies feel "out of place," like strangers' in "a sea of whiteness"' (2006, p. 133). As she writes: 'The effect of this "around whiteness" is the institutionalization of a certain "likeness," which makes nonwhite bodies uncomfortable and feel exposed, visible, and different when they take up this space.'

These bodies have all in common that they are bodies in pain, who have experienced, and all too often continue to experience, the trauma of not fitting, not belonging, not being recognized, respected and valued, shared by many women in a man's world, members of the LGBTIQA+ community in a heterosexual and often homophobic world, and non-white bodies in white spaces.

One important queer effect of embracing a queer orientation is that fellow travellers, misfits and wounded bodies may find one another to form an unlikely community, united by the common task of reading against the grain, challenging hegemonic systems of all kinds and interrogating white, male, heteronormative privilege (Williams 2006, p. 535). Individually and collectively in this volume, and I, on the journey of writing yet another commentary on Jonah, explore new lines, new possibilities for reading, but perhaps more importantly, for living. As Ahmed describes this laborious, persistent work of inhabiting queer spaces: 'The work of inhabitance involves orientation devices; ways of extending bodies into spaces that create new folds or new contours of what we would call livable or inhabitable space' (2006, p. 11).

## Notes

1 Sara Ahmed considers how various bodies in terms of gender, race and sexual orientation are forced to abide within narrow confines, as she describes it, 'pressed into lines' determined by heteronormative norms (2006, p. 17). See also Rhiannon Graybill, who argues that 'queer' encompass multiple meanings that extend to 'identity politics, nonheteronormative sexualities, and the troubling of normativities of all kinds (including those beyond the sexual)' (2016, p. 123).

2 Ahmed's reflection on how bodies fit or do not fit is quite personal as evident in, for instance, her reflection on having a white mother and brown father: 'I walk between you. Both of you are connected with me. I walk between you but I want to be on one side. I close my eyes and wish he would disappear. How would I appear without him? Would I be white like my mother? I feel guilt at my murderous fantasy, but the thought of her white body made me tremble with hope. Maybe I would seem like her, if only he would go away' (2006, p. 144).

3 Several scholars maintain that Nineveh served for Jonah's Persian Period readers as a symbol of another foreign empire, either representing the Babylonian empire, which continues to 'haunt the story of Jonah', casting a 'spectral shadow across Jonah's narrative', or the Persian empire, which at the time exerted control of Yehud (Downs, p. 40). See also the notion of Nineveh as a 'third-space' rather than 'first-space element', according to which Nineveh as 'a historical city ... had been wiped from the map at the time Jonah was composed', and hence rather serves as 'a symbol for wickedness' (Rees 2016).

4 Amy Erickson notes that the reference to being swallowed by a male fish evokes connotations of 'stomach, innards, bowels'. However, the reference to Jonah praying from the belly of a female fish 'tips the range toward meaning of womb' (Erickson 2021, pp. 310–11). Compare, though, Lena-Sofia Tiemeyer's careful exposition of the various text-critical, redaction-critical, narratological and Midrashic suggestions pertaining to the gendered ambiguity of the fish, followed by her proposal of 'an archaic lengthened nominal form', which counters the suggestion that the fish's biological sex had been changed (Tiemeyer 2017b, p. 323).

5 Claassens 2022; see also Claassens 2023.

6 Sherwood argues that the prophet within this transformed belly is able to change 'his identity and becomes a mythological superhero' who is focused on catching the Leviathan, which in the rabbinic tradition is to be served at 'the messianic feast of the righteous' (1998, p. 65). See also Tiemeyer 2017a, p. 52.

7 Ahmed makes this argument in light of the repetitive action associated with work that shape bodies 'in some ways rather than other' (2006, p. 57).

8 Graybill argues that Jeremiah's 'body and voice resemble the body and voice of the hysteric, displaying a curious crossing over of sound, flesh, and meaning' (2016, p. 139).

9 Ahmed reflects on those backgrounds of what are behind and what have happened before, contemplating on who and what 'shape an individual's arrival into the world' (2006, p. 38).

10 Ahmed writes that 'unanticipated arrivals point[s] not just to the future but to the past, which also cannot simply be reached in the present. Objects ... keep histories alive that cannot be reached, even if the "point" of the objects is that they can be reached' (2006, p. 152).

11 See also Ahmed's point of 'migration as a continuous process of disorientation and reorientation, with bodies moving away and arriving to inhabit a new space' (2006, p. 11).

12 As Graybill writes: 'Jonah resists being a prophet; he refuses to reorient his desires. Instead of the open or transformed body, he offers a body of refusal – and yet this too may be a queer body... The refusal, including the refusal of happiness, is a key prophetic stance' (2016, p. 138). See also Graybill 2019, in which she works out more comprehensively the notion of the practice of unhappiness as an essential part of the prophetic endeavour.

13 Graybill argues that: 'As an alternative, the body as troubled, wounded, transformed, and above all queer opens the possibility for embodiment as flux and assemblage. Queer suggests both resistance and refusal; it also hints at a reconfiguration of bodies and pleasures that is not bound to a logic of lack' (2016, p. 124).

# References

Ahmed, Sara, 2006, *Queer Phenomenology: Orientations, Objects, Others*, Durham, NC: Duke University Press.

Ahmed, Sara, 2010, *The Pursuit of Happiness*, Durham, NC: Duke University Press.

Bergmann, Claudia, 2007, 'We Have Seen the Enemy, and He is Only a "She": The Portrayal of Warriors as Women', *The Catholic Biblical Quarterly* 69/4, pp. 651–72.

Bolin, Thomas M., 1997, *Freedom Beyond Forgiveness: The Book of Jonah Re-examined*, Sheffield: Sheffield Academic Press.

Burke, Sean D., 2011, 'Queering Early Christian Discourse: The Ethiopian Eunuch' in Theresa J. Hornsby and Ken Stone (eds), *Bible Trouble: Queer Reading at the Boundaries of Biblical Scholarship*, Semeia Studies 67, Atlanta, GA: SBL Press, pp. 175–90.

Claassens, L. Juliana, 2010, 'Calling the Keeners: The Image of the Wailing Woman as Symbol of Survival in a Traumatized World', *JFSR* 26/1, pp. 63–78.

Claassens, L. Juliana, 2012, *Mourner, Mother, Midwife: Reimagining God's Liberating Presence*, Louisville, KY: Westminster John Knox Press.

Claassens, L. Juliana, 2022, 'Finding Words in the Belly of Sheol: Reading Jonah's Lament in Contexts of Individual and Collective Trauma', *Religions* 13/91, https://doi.org/10.3390/rel13020091.

Claassens, L. Juliana, 2023, 'Facing the Colonizer that Remains: Jonah as a Symbolic Trauma Narrative', *Catholic Biblical Quarterly* 85/1, pp. 36–52.

Darr, Katharine Pfisterer, 1996, '"No Strength to Deliver": A Contextual Analysis of Hezekiah's Proverb in Isaiah 37:3b' in M. Sweeney and R. Melugin (eds), *New Visions of Isaiah*. Journal for the Study of the Old Testament Supplemental Series, 214, Sheffield: JSOT Press, pp. 219–56.

Davidson, Steed Vernyl, 2016, 'Postcolonial Readings of the Prophets' in Carolyn J. Sharp (ed.), *The Oxford Handbook of the Prophets*, Oxford: Oxford University Press, pp. 507–26.

Davidson, Steed Vernyl, 2018, 'Jonah' in Hemchand Gossai (ed.), *Postcolonial Commentary and the Old Testament*, London: Bloomsbury T&T Clark, pp. 290–312.

Dille, Sarah, J., 2004, *Mixing Metaphors: God as Mother and Father in Deutero-Isaiah*, The Library of Hebrew Bible/Old Testament Studies, 398, London: T&T Clark.

Downs, David J., 2009, 'The Specter of Exile in the Story of Jonah', *Horizons in Biblical Theology* 31/1, pp. 27–44.

Erickson, Amy, 2021, *Jonah: Introduction and Commentary*, Illuminations, Grand Rapids, MI: William B. Eerdmans.

Graybill, Rhiannon, 2016, *Are We Not Men? Unstable Masculinity in the Hebrew Prophets*, Oxford: Oxford University Press.

Graybill, Rhiannon, 2019, 'Prophecy and the Problem of Happiness: The Case of Jonah' in Fiona C. Black and Jennifer L. Koosed (eds), *Reading with Feeling: Affect Theory and the Bible*, Semeia Studies. Atlanta, GA: SBL Press, pp. 95–112.

Havea, Jione, 2013, 'Adjusting Jonah', *International Review of Mission* 102/1, pp. 44–55.

Havea, Jione, 2016, 'Tossing Jonah Again: Sea of Readings', *Bible & Critical Theory* 12/1, pp. 1–3.

Havea, Jione, 2020, *Jonah*, Earth Bible Commentary, London: Bloomsbury T&T Clark.

Hendel, Ronald, 2019, 'Myth and Mimesis in the Psalm of Jonah' in Ilana Pardes and Ophir Münz-Manor (eds), *Psalms in/on Jerusalem*, Berlin: De Gruyter, pp. 1–10.

Pyper, Hugh S., 2007, 'Swallowed by a Song: Jonah and the Jonah-Psalm Through the Looking-Glass' in Robert Rezetko, Timothy H. Lim and W. Brian Aucker (eds), *Reflection and Refraction: Studies in*

*Biblical Historiography in Honour of A. Graeme Auld*, Leiden: Brill, pp. 337–58.

Rees, Anthony, 2016, 'Getting Up and Going Down Towards a Spatial Poetics of Jonah', *The Bible & Critical Theory* 12/1, pp. 40–48.

Ryu, Chesung Justin, 2009, 'Silence as Resistance: A Postcolonial Reading of the Silence of Jonah in Jonah 4.1–11', *JSOT* 34/2, pp. 195–218.

Sherwood, Yvonne, 1998, 'Cross-Currents in the Book of Jonah: Some Jewish and Cultural Midrashim on a Traditional Text', *Biblical Interpretation* 6/1, pp. 49–79.

Tiemeyer, Lena-Sofia, 2017a, 'Jonah and his Fish: The Monstrification of God's Servant in Early Jewish and Christian Reception History' in Zohar Hadromi-Allouche (ed.), *Fallen Animals: Art, Religion, Literature*, Lanham, MD: Lexington Books, pp. 47–70.

Tiemeyer, Lena-Sofia, 2017b, 'A New Look at the Biological Sex/Grammatical Gender of Jonah's Fish', *Vetus Testamentum* 67/2, pp. 307–23.

Tiemeyer, Lena-Sofia, 2021, *Jonah Through the Centuries*, Wiley Blackwell Bible Commentaries. Hoboken, NJ: Wiley.

Williams, Jennifer, 2006, 'Queer Readings of the Prophets' in Carolyn Sharp (ed.), *Oxford Handbook to the Prophets*, Oxford: Oxford University Press, 2006, pp. 527–45.

# 5

# Queering Memories of Nineveh as 'Great City' in the Book of Jonah: Challenging Presuppositions of Power in Post-exilic Yehud

## HENDRIK L. BOSMAN

## Introduction

Lord Acton, as an erudite researcher of history, wrote a letter to Bishop Creighton in April 1887 in which he famously remarked: 'Power tends to corrupt, and absolute power corrupts absolutely' (1907, p. 504). Less appreciated is his further suggestion that 'Great men are almost always bad men, even when they exercise influence and not authority.' This train of thought stimulated my interest in the impact or influence of perceived greatness on power and authority, and it also posed the challenge to make use of queer theory to interpret the prophetic critique of power relations underlying the references to Nineveh as a 'great city'. The corrupting potential of power requires the critique that queer theory can provide to open up new alternatives to dominant or 'normal' interpretative frames of understanding.

This contribution focuses on the references to Nineveh as a 'great city' in the book of Jonah, reaching a climax with the reference in Jonah 3.3 as a 'great city before God', framed by references in the introductory mention in Jonah 1.2 and in the enigmatic conclusion at the end of chapter 4 (Jonah 4.11). The 'greatness' of Nineveh is interpreted against the background of ancient cities as seats of power and theological reflection in the book of Jonah as post-exilic prophetic literature – ambiguous reflection that entailed the subtle critique of 'normal' power relations in Yehud and thereafter.

This contribution takes up Michael Warner's observation that 'queer' gets a 'critical edge by defining itself against the normal rather than the heterosexual' (1993, p. xxvi). Related to this is David Halperin's insistence that 'queer is by definition whatever is at odds with the normal, the legitimate, the dominant' (1995, p. 62). This understanding of 'queer theory' is undergirded by Michel Foucault's 1978 understanding of power that Kent Brintnall described as 'an operation that creates interiority, and thereby justifies a normalizing body of evaluative institutional practices' (Brintnall 2021). Queer theory is not exclusively about a critique of the presuppositions related to sex and gender (however important these might be) – it is also concerned with the critique of power relations that support preconceptions undergirding what a society considers to be 'normal' or orthodox.

Making use of queer theory enables one to read against the grain of texts and its dominant interpretations. Lena-Sofia Tiemeyer points out in her reception-historical commentary on Jonah that over millennia, some readers destabilize overt meaning by queering the 'normal' understanding of a text's 'message' – queering in this sense has been around for a long while (Tiemeyer 2021)! This contribution will argue that the title 'great city' of Nineveh represents a memory of Assyrian imperialism that provides the queering space to face up to the ambiguous presentation of divine mercy and retribution.

Interpreting references to Nineveh in Jonah as memories presupposes the research by Maurice Halbwachs that memories are shaped by social frameworks and are the result of mnemonic recollections influenced, among others, by conceptualized space (1980, pp. 156–7 and 1992, pp. 38–43). The way Nineveh is conceptualized as space features in the 'queering' discussion of Jonah 1.2; 3.2–3 and 4.11.

In this regard one is well served to take into consideration how the French sociologist Pierre Nora in his study of the role of memory in the construction of the French past coined the phrase 'site of memory' (1989, pp. 7–25). This referred to any constructed space, place, event, figure and even text that evokes images of the past that undergird the ongoing process of identity negotiation in society. As Paris, as a 'site of memory', was important for Nora, one can at least consider the importance of Nineveh for the redaction of the book of Jonah and early Jewish identity formation when Nineveh traditions were appropriated for audiences in subsequent post-exilic imperialistic contexts. Nineveh as 'great city' can be considered as 'normal' as far as ancient Near Eastern empires go, but as at odds with 'normal' when it becomes an ambiguous site of memory that illustrates the paradoxical potential of merciful or retributive divine intervention.

## Cities in the ancient Near East as background for Nineveh as 'great city'

Research on cities and urbanization in the ancient Near East informs the queering of the greatness of Nineveh. This data safeguards this discussion from falling into the trap of anachronistic interpretation. Ancient Near Eastern cities like Jericho and Megiddo were established more than 5,000 years ago (Benjamin 2000, p. 258), but Avraham Faust still considers the definition of 'cities' and 'villages' to be a 'complex endeavour' (2013, pp. 203–4). This complexity is not alleviated by the long history of urbanization in the Fertile Crescent and is despite the comments made by Gosta Ählstrom, who drew attention to modern scholarship's 'tell-minded' focus on the excavation of towns and cities with less appreciation for rural and semi-nomadic settlements (1982, p. 25).

According to Faust, urban settlements such as cities 'served as political and economic centres' as they functioned as 'centres of tax collection' and 'places of refuge in times of need' (2013, p. 204). Don Benjamin defines cities in the ancient Near East 'both by architectural design' ('a settlement where people live physically close together ... surrounded by a wall') and by 'economic structure' ('a centralized system for producing and distributing goods and services') (2000, p. 258). A city or town in the ancient Near East entail 'more than the sum of its buildings' because it can be interpreted from cultural, economic, political, religious and social perspectives (De Geus 2003, p. 1).

Different types of cities have been identified by archaeological excavations in Syro-Palestine: capital cities like Samaria or Jerusalem; administrative and regional centres like Hazor and Megiddo; and a proliferation of smaller towns and hamlets. While ongoing warfare during the Assyrian and Babylonian empires 'brought about large-scale destruction' of cities, urbanization during the Persian Empire 'concentrated on the Coastal Plain' and 'large-scale urbanization re-emerged only in the Hellenistic period' (Faust 2013, pp. 206–7). Should this circumstantial archaeological evidence about significant Hellenistic urbanization influence our diachronic contextualizing of Jonah – that is, when would priestly scribes consider it relevant to make use of urban symbolism, such as the reference to the destroyed Nineveh as a 'great city' that potentially qualified for merciful divine intervention?

The Assyrian Empire provided the backdrop of significant urban development in the ancient Near East when the role and function of a city changed 'from an independent center' to 'the tool of (the) territorial empire builder', when 'the basis of power shifted from an urban centered economic organization, with its emphasis on agriculture and trade, to military conquest of and exaction of tribute from subject peoples' (Frick 1997, p. 17). Therefore, a shift of power developed in the Iron Age ancient Near East when cities became the conduits of imperial power – a trend that continued in the Persian, Hellenistic and Roman Empires (Frick 1997, p. 17). The 'great city' of Nineveh as conduit of imperial power was different from older cities in the ANE (most of them being city states), but as imperial city became the precursor of subsequent imperial cities like Babylon and Susa – that is, it became the 'normal' imperial city. On the other hand, one could also argue that the reference to 'great' sets it apart from other cities and therefore may not be 'normal'.

Indeed, as will be evident in the way Nineveh functions in the book of Jonah, the memory of Nineveh in Jonah is one that is *not* a normal city.

The size of cities in the ancient Near East differed from region to region. In Southern Mesopotamia cities covered areas of around 400 hectares, while in Northern Mesopotamia cities did not exceed 100 hectares – in comparison, Nineveh comprised around 750 hectares, which is almost double the size of a 'normal' Mesopotamian city of that period (Frick 1997, p. 14). Charles Halton compared modern translations of Jonah 3.3 with 'ancient textual and archaeological evidence concerning the size of Nineveh' and concluded that every attempt at a literal rendering of 3.3 failed and opted for reading it as 'a figure of speech' that 'conveys the author's intention of representing Nineveh as a very large city' (2008, p. 193).

In his discussion of 'City Symbolism and Personification in the OT', Andrew Dearman points out that according to the Genesis narrative (4.17), Cain was the first city-builder; while Nimrod, the mighty hunter, 'is credited with building several cities in Assyria and Babylonia, including Nineveh (10.8–12)' (2006, pp. 675–6). Dearman assumes that 'larger cities from Mesopotamia certainly impressed the Israelites as powerful and aggressive, just the thing a renowned hunter would build, and his descendants would occupy' (2006, p. 676).

The 'greatness' of cities in the ANE was complex and multi-faceted because it entailed numerous aspects besides its physical size. Nineveh was indeed one of the largest cities in the ANE and the link with the mighty Nimrod as mythological founder warranted 'great' as an apt descriptor for this city. Above all, Nineveh was a conduit of imperial power that controlled the political destiny and religious practices of its subjugated countries and peoples. Nineveh was a deviation from urban life, as imperial city that represented a new form of urbanization in contrast to the existing city states of the ANE. The 'great city' of Nineveh as eventual capital of Assyria became the figurehead of an empire notorious for its 'merciless conquest' of surrounding nations in the ancient Near East. As an empire, the Assyrians implemented that forced large-scale resettlement of deported people to be 'conscripted to forced labor on one of the multiple building projects occurring throughout the empire' (De La Torre 2007, p. 11). Nineveh was also a symbol for violence and cruelty aimed at the northern kingdom of Israel when the population was deported and Samaria was destroyed (722 BCE), as well as the southern kingdom of Judah when Jerusalem was besieged, and the kingdom became an Assyrian vassal state during the reign of Esarhaddon (680–669 BCE). The imperial practices as the city represent departures from the normal, queer practices at a time when smaller cities and less violence were normal.

## Shifts in the interpretation of the book of Jonah

Although the focus is on the 'great city' of Nineveh, existing research on the book of Jonah that is appreciative of Christian and Jewish interpretations reveal dissenting trends in Jonah. Queering Jonah does not come as a sudden bolt of hermeneutical lightning, but is the continuation of longstanding dissent. In her research on the reception of Jonah in Western culture, Yvonne Sherwood (1998 and 2000) not only describes but also challenges several 'normal' interpretative trends through the ages.; among others the parallel between Jonah and Jesus, and the extent of God's inclusive grace and mercy. During the latter half of the twentieth century, attention was given to deconstructive elements that undermined the goals 'normal' interpretation set out to achieve. Recent Jonah research pays attention to the popularity of ironic and satirical interpretations that highlighted Jonah as a disobedient prophet, the YHWH-worshipping sailors, the rescue or salvation of the evil Nineveh, a God whose mind can change, the grotesque scenario when Jonah is saved by a big fish who unceremoniously regurgitates or vomits him back onto dry land and life.[1] The book features odd presentations of God. Sherwood also describes how Jewish interpreters (Rabbi Ishmael, Rashi, Abravanel etc.), as examples of interpretations from the margins of society, critique the role God plays in the book of Jonah by posing critical questions like: 'Is God siding with our enemies?', 'Is God a good god?' and 'Why should mercy be expressed to cruelly?' (2000, pp. 118–19).

Further, the literary presentation of Nineveh sets it apart from other cities in biblical literature. Mary Mills shows how the 'city of Nineveh is treated as a person who can be held responsible, as a moral agent, for the effect of its policies' (2012, p. 121). She agrees with Simon Parker that 'all discussions of urban formation can be said to depend on relations of power' (Parker 2004, p. 120; Mills 2012, p. 138). According to Mills, the author of Jonah uses a 'rhetorical style' that 'constantly engages the reader with paradox', resulting in the volatile signification of meaning, well-illustrated by the ambiguous depiction of the 'great city' of Nineveh as an oppressive and penitent space (2012, pp. 141–2). Steed Vernyl Davidson engages Jonah from a 'postcolonial optic' that displays the ambiguity of the city (2019, p. 290). He considers the 'destruction of the imperial city of Nineveh by both divine order and agency' as 'the central plot device in the book of Jonah', and according to his postcolonial interpretation of Jonah he identifies several 'features of exceptionalism' that 'situate the book within imperialist discourses' (Davidson 2019, pp. 291, 301). As part of his discussion of 'Spaces of exception', he points out that references to Nineveh being a 'great' imperial city (Jonah 1.2 etc.) 'immediately sets the city apart from the norm' and they are combined with descriptions of Nineveh as 'a degenerate space, with its insufficiently discerning residents (Jonah 4.4)' which implies 'that it functions as a marginal rather than a central space' (Davidson 2019, pp. 295–9).

In a Jonah commentary focused on its text and reception, Amy Erickson concurs with Sherwood by pointing out how Jewish interpreters tend to be more appreciative of Jonah's point of view and more critical about the 'normal' role ascribed to God and this results in 'queering' humour 'that is self-reflective and self-critical, but also targets the powerful … typical of diaspora humor, which often has a cathartic function' (2021, pp. 40–41). Contrasting features come to the fore in the description of YHWH's role and presence in the Jonah narrative: on the one hand, 'The character of God is sovereign over all creatures, nations, and realms of the cosmos'; on the other hand, 'he cannot get Jonah to bend his will' (Erickson 2021, p. 42). Erickson indicates that the depictions of the prophet, Nineveh and God in Jonah are much more complex than the impression given by 'normal' interpretations. Jonah is more than a disobedient prophet given a second chance to pronounce judgment on the 'great' Nineveh and the saving of Nineveh is not just the result of divine mercy and compassion.

In their work on Jonah, Steven McKenzie, Rhiannon Graybill and John Kaltner focused on the compositional layers of the book of Jonah, and in agreement with Thomas Krüger and James Nogalski, identify an older prophetic narrative in which Jonah responds obediently to his divine commission (embedded in 1.1–2; 3.3–5; 3.8b–9; 4.5–8; 4.10–11). According to this suggested compositional interpretation of the book of Jonah, the oldest part of the prophetic narrative 'originated in the Persian period' and 'illustrated ... the principle of reciprocal repentance laid out in Jer. 18:7', according to which it was 'normal' to expect that the repentance of the city and all its inhabitants resulted in the repentance of the Lord – not to sack but to save Nineveh (McKenzie, Graybill and Kaltner 2020, p. 102). A subsequent 'revision of the story in the Hellenistic period' is proposed when 'key themes like the element of hyperbole' (that is, the 'great city' of Nineveh) were added (2020, p. 103). In other words, the queer Jonah becomes straight through redactional activity in the Hellenistic period.

Juliana Claassens creates new pathways for thinking about queering the book of Jonah and the city of Nineveh by utilizing 'theoretical perspectives concerning postcolonial trauma theory' in the context of ancient and modern manifestations of colonialism. In terms of her 'postcolonial trauma framework', she demonstrates how place serves as 'the locus of many painful memories wrought by colonialism ... Nineveh, the epicentre of so many traumatic memories' (Claassens 2021, pp. 578 and 581). Queer interpretation, in conjunction with also feminist and postcolonial interpretation, is interested in exploring the effect of power on vulnerable bodies, and how 'the expression of self is "socially contingent" and dependent on a particular place with particular associations.'

The ongoing description of Nineveh as 'great city' seems to be a good example of a spatial locus of trauma that haunted Israelite and early Jewish memories for centuries. Jonah research seems to be more in agreement about 'what Jonah is *not* about (i.e. universal salvation)', but no consensus seems to be on the scholarly horizon 'on what the book *is* about' (Erickson 2021, p. 220; emphasis original). Although the relatively small book of Jonah received a lot of scholarly attention, this research survey has pointed out both the persistence of 'normal' interpretations and that new pathways have been developed that challenge 'normal' interpretations of the prophetic book and that queer theory opens new horizons of sense-making. The following discussion of Nineveh as 'great city' explores some of these new horizons by 'queering' the traditional ('normal') interpretation of the book of Jonah, continuing the age-old reading against the grain or 'normal' interpretations of Jonah.

## Memories of Nineveh as 'great city' in the book of Jonah

The fact that Nineveh was destroyed by the Babylonians in 612 BCE and that the vocabulary in the book seems to reflect 'Aramaic influences' and a 'dependence on the Exodus narrative and certain Psalms' suggests a dating during the Persian Empire or later, when Nineveh functioned as a symbol in the post-exilic memories of Jewish faith communities in Yehud and the Diaspora (Rees 2016, p. 43). The 'greatness' of Nineveh can be understood in terms of the lingering traumatic memories of an oppressive and violent imperial city that despite its pre-exilic destruction continued to haunt the post-exilic faith communities that were subjugated by successive empires.

## Remembering the 'great city' in Jonah

The significance of Nineveh as a 'great city' in the book of Jonah can be detected in Jonah 1.2, 3.2–3 and 4.11 with the same 'three-word combination' (נִינְוֵה הָעִיר הַגְּדוֹלָה) – this must be interpreted within the broader context of the 14 times that the adjective *gadôl* ('big', 'great' or 'important') appears in the book as a whole (Stuart 2014, p. 390).[2]

The first reference to Nineveh in Jonah 1.2, which forms part of the first episode of the book, probably evoked ambiguous memories: on the one hand, Nineveh was remembered as 'a city of crime, utterly treacherous, full of violence' – that is, a 'city of bloodshed' (Nahum 3.1) and condemned for its arrogance (Zeph. 2.13–15); but on the other hand, according to the Table of Nations (Gen. 10.8–12), it was the first city to be established after the Flood, by the mighty hunter Nimrod (Sasson 2008, pp. 69–70).[3] Although Nineveh was inhabited over several millennia, it only reached its 'full glory' as the Assyrian capital during the reign of Sennacherib (704–681 BCE) and was destroyed by the 'combined Babylonian and Median force' in 612 BCE (Sasson 2008, p. 70). Besides the obvious political importance of Nineveh, it can also be kept in mind that it was strategically placed on the intersection of north–south and east–west trade routes (Sieges 2016).

The significance of a city being referred to as 'great' is further indicated by the fact that in the Old Testament only Jerusalem was also referred to as a 'great city' as part of the prophecy of its destruction (Jer. 22.8), and Gibeon when its 'greatness' installed fear (Josh. 10.2); it was also used for other Assyrian cities like Calah (Gen. 10.2). A similar depiction of Nineveh as 'the large city' (τῇ πόλει τῇ μεγάλῃ) can be found in the late apocryphal Judith 1.1, which suggests that lingering memories about Nineveh as 'great city' seemed to persist in the post-exilic period.

The impressive size of Nineveh is mentioned as part of an introductory summary of Jonah's mission, not only to highlight its size, but also its historical importance, which was related to the magnitude of its evil (Simon 1999, p. 4). 'Great' is therefore highly ambiguous since the significance of Nineveh seems to be determined by its evil and notoriety.

The second reference to Nineveh as 'great city' is found in the first episode of the second half of the book of Jonah (3.1–3b), in which Jonah's commission to go to Nineveh is renewed (Youngblood 2019, p. 42). On the surface the differences between Jonah 1.2 and 3.2–3 might be considered minor, but closer scrutiny indicates it to be 'consequential' (Erickson 2021, p. 367).

The subsequent phrase עִיר־גְּדוֹלָה לֵאלֹהִים is important for this discussion and can be interpreted in different ways (Tucker 2006, p. 65): an idiomatic reference to the divine name (אלהים) can function as a superlative and thus be translated as 'an exceedingly great city'; while more literal renderings would be 'a great city to God' or 'a great city to the gods' or 'a great city belonging to God' (Tucker 2006, pp. 65–6). Trible appreciates the diverging ways in which this phrase can be interpreted: Nineveh making an impression on God ('great *before* God'), suggesting divine ownership ('great *to* God'), suggesting divine favour ('great *because of* God') or as a divine residence ('great *for* God') (2017, p. 670). Regardless of the exact meaning of the phrase, 'it specifies and highlights the greatness of Nineveh' – albeit in an ambiguous manner (Vermeulen 2017, pp. 235–6; Erickson 2021, p. 357).[4] Here the ambiguity concerning Nineveh as 'great city' spills over to include the underlying power relationship with God.

Verse 3 concludes with 'a journey of three days' (מַהֲלַךְ שְׁלֹשֶׁת יָמִים) that provides additional background information about the 'greatness' of Nineveh. The term 'journey' or 'walk' (מַהֲלַךְ) 'is not a standard linear measure' and is rather vague and can only be used as a rough measurement (Sasson 2008, p. 227). Despite its vagueness it supports and elaborates the initial description of Nineveh as a 'great city'. Almost all of the ancient references to Nineveh, like Herodotus, Diodorus, Strabo and Aristotle, agree about the impressive size of this 'great city' (Halton 2008, pp. 196–8).

In sum, the 'comments about Nineveh's proportions' are 'mutually reinforcing' by both pointing out 'the city's prominence in God's scheme' and by acknowledging 'its physical size' (Sasson 2008, p. 227). The ambiguity in Jonah 3.2–3 allows the description of Nineveh as a 'great city', that refers 'to both the actual size of the place and its symbolic pendant – the city's importance and power' (Vermeulen 2017, p. 235). Unmistakable ambiguity in texts, as indicated above, should be acknowledged, and not be ignored or underplayed to pay lip service to existing 'normal' interpretations of a text.

The final reference to the 'greatness' of Nineveh is found in the last verse of the concluding episode in the book of Jonah (4.5–11), for which there is no parallel episode in the first half, and according to the supposed 'logic of staircase parallelism' the theological thrust of the book becomes more apparent in this final episode (Youngblood 2019, p. 55).

Most of modern scholarship interprets the last verse of the book of Jonah as a rhetorical question, 'And should I not be concerned about Nineveh' (וַאֲנִי אָחוּס עַל־נִינְוֵה) and this traditional or 'normal' understanding of Jonah's ending is argued in the following way: Verse 11 starts with an emphatic pronoun 'I' (אֲנִי), in contrast with the emphatic 'you' (אתה) in 4.10, combined by a disjunctive *waw* that is used to indicate contrast with the preceding verse 10 (Tucker 2006, p. 103). This is followed by the negative (לֹא) and the Qal *yiqtol*, and although there is no interrogative present, the context as well as the disjunctive *waw* point in the direction of it being understood as a rhetorical question (Wolff 1977, p. 134). The rhetorical question employs an a fortiori argument (what applies for the lesser, even more applies for the greater):[5] if Jonah was concerned or upset about the withering of the plant in verse 10, why should God not be concerned in verse 11 with the 'greater Nineveh'? It is important to note that both verses 10 and 11 make use of the verb חוס, but in diverging and ambiguous ways.

In Jonah 4.11, Nineveh is again referred to as 'the great city' (הָעִיר הַגְּדוֹלָה) and this time its size or 'greatness' is illustrated by a reference to its numerous inhabitants: 'in which there are more than one hundred and twenty thousand people' (אֲשֶׁר יֶשׁ־בָּהּ הַרְבֵּה מִשְׁתֵּים־עֶשְׂרֵה רִבּוֹ אָדָם). Sasson observes that the inhabitants of Nineveh are referred to with the collective noun 'human being' (אָדָם), and this corresponds with Jonah 3.7–8, where it is also combines with the collective reference to 'animals' (וּבְהֵמָה) mentioned in the last clause (2008, p. 215).

One must acknowledge that the book of Jonah ends in Jonah 4.11 either with an unanswered rhetorical question to Jonah posed by YHWH that implies a merciful response to Nineveh, or a statement of fact that God will not take pity on Nineveh (Erickson 2021, pp. 406–9). It seems as if God has the last say, because no response by Jonah is recorded. How does this silence of Jonah influence our overall understanding of the book?[6]

The lack of response of Jonah at the end of the book creates the opportunity for subsequent readers to relate the ambiguity of the greatness of Nineveh with the ambiguity of God's response to the penitent 'great city'. In the next section, it will be shown how awareness of such ambiguities can already be traced in some deuterocanonical Jewish literature, including a Jewish festival liturgy. A selection of these interpretations will be showcased in order to demonstrate how ambiguity surrounding the city of Nineveh may be utilized as a fertile source for queering normal and dominant power relations.

## Nineveh's greatness in Tobit, Judith and Yom Kippur

Most scholars date the final form of the book of Jonah in the Persian and Hellenistic periods (McKenzie, Graybill and Kaltner 2020). The date suggests that inclusion of the deuterocanonical literature of the post-exilic era that co-existed with the finalizing of Jonah adds an understanding of Nineveh as 'great city'. The book of Tobit narrates Tobit's captivity in Nineveh by the Assyrians, where he experiences the horrors of living in exile among Gentiles and 'Nineveh represents the imperial captor' in the first chapter; while the last chapter describes Tobit's joy when he hears about the capture and destruction of Nineveh for which he praises God for 'all he had done to people of Nineveh and Assyria' (Dick 2016, p. 46). The framing function of Nineveh in the book of Tobit as quintessential imperial 'great city' that deserved to be destroyed probably represents the 'normal' understanding of Nineveh that prevailed in post-exilic times and was queered by the book of Jonah.

The book of Judith contains a diptych structure that resembles the symmetry between the first two and last two chapters of Jonah. More important than establishing corresponding literary structures of Jonah and Judith is their similarity of the juxtaposition of power relations – fearing Nebuchadnezzar or God as Lord. If Jonah is not only about the fate of the 'great city' of Nineveh, but also about the power relations with God, then Judith provides an illuminating sounding board for the queer interpretation of Nineveh in Jonah.

The use of Jonah during the Yom Kippur afternoon liturgy must also be considered (b.Meg.31a) because it illustrates the post-exilic Jewish liturgical appropriation of enigmatic Jonah and the fate of Nineveh. Yom Kippur provides further momentum to the 'normal' interpretation of the evil but repentant city of Nineveh that is saved due to the grace and mercy of the Lord. The festival also queers the exclusiveness among some Jews in the Diaspora – if Nineveh could be saved, who was beyond God's forgiveness? The penitent 'great city' of Nineveh, the figurehead of hubristic imperialism, becomes the 'model of repentance' on the 'holiest day of the Jewish Year, Yom Kippur' (Trible 2017, p. 686).

The short reception history of the early reinterpretation of Nineveh as 'great city' indicates what the 'normal' attitude towards Nineveh as symbol of violent oppression entailed (Tobit), as well as an appreciation of the queering of Nineveh reflected in the change from being a symbol of imperial power and violence to an illustration of total and unconditional penitence (Yom Kippur). Resonance with deuterocanonical literature also suggests ongoing critical reflection concerned with the power relationship between empire and God (Judith). This concurs with the research on cities by Ash Amin and Nigel Thrift that cities influence the definition of 'who or what is normal' and that 'symbolic cities' (such as Nineveh in post-exilic texts) provide a critique on power relations, not only with empire but also with God (2002, pp. 122–3).

The ambiguity of the 'great city' of Nineveh is continued by deuterocanonical literature and is further illustrated by Jewish Yom Kippur liturgy – providing additional sources for queering the interpretation of the book of Jonah.

## Queering the 'great city' of Nineveh

The repeated reference to Nineveh as a 'great city' occurs at the beginning (1.2), in the middle (3.2–3) and at the end (4.11) of Jonah. The 'greatness' of Nineveh plays a pivotal literary function by framing the book in 1.2 and 4.11. Combined with a hyperbolic reference to its 'greatness before God' in the centre of the book in Jonah 3.2–3, these references to 'greatness' are enhanced by a quantitative reference to its huge surface area in Jonah 3.3 and a qualitative reference to its substantial human and animal population in Jonah 4.11 (Tiemeyer 2021, p. 24).[7]

Cities in the time of the writing of Jonah became significant on a symbolic level and were perceived as 'the embodiment of good and evil, as representing progress or decline, and as being the site of human alienation or human salvation' (Frick 1997, p. 18). Claassens cautions Jonah interpreters not to fall into 'the trap of demonizing the evil city'; if Nineveh is simply 'a symbol of all empires to come', then 'the complexity and multiplicity of Nineveh is lost' (2021, p. 582). The ambiguity of the ending in Jonah 4.11 enhances the complexity of the fate of the 'great city' of Nineveh by blurring the distinction between past, present and future – a destroyed city can still be saved … or not; a merciful God can save a repentant enemy nation … or not!

However imposing the 'great city' of Nineveh might have been in the ancient Near East, as a 'site of memory' it was much more than a physical space and its primary significance in Jonah is symbolic or metaphoric in nature (Nora 1998, p. 632). It seems as if Jonah, Nahum and Zephaniah recorded different and diverging memories about Nineveh that shared its symbolic connection with evil and violence but differed with regards to its significance in depicting an ambiguous rendition of YHWH.

How can one relate the repeated references to Nineveh as

'great city' with the theological thrust of the book as reflected in the last verse of chapter 4? Even though the majority of Jonah research still accepts the 'normal' presupposition that 'benign theological universalism' is the most important undergirding theological trend in the book, recent scholarship has increasingly emphasized the supposition that YHWH is 'the only and most powerful deity in the cosmos' and that his dominion includes the 'great city' of Nineveh (Bolin 2010, pp. 108–9). This divine dominion over the 'great city' of Nineveh is, however, capricious and Jonah cannot be cited as an unqualified illustration for the mercy and grace of God.

This shift in presupposition from interpreting the book of Jonah as an illustration of divine grace and mercy, to an example of YHWH's capricious universal dominion and rulership over all – including the 'great city' of Nineveh – opens future scholarly debate to questioning power relations in more ways than one. A different interpretation not only challenges the power exuded by empires like Assyria or Persia (as personified by the 'great city' Nineveh), but it also cuts deeper to challenge the power relations with YHWH – 'did not Yahweh act in much the same was as an imperialist nation toward these gentiles in using unlimited power to get them to do what he wanted?' (Timmer 2009, p. 20). The power relations reflected in Jonah 4.11 entail 'that God decides, as he pleases, upon the final spatial position of Nineveh' – to be sacked or saved (Vermeulen 2022, p. 243).

Queering 'the great city' of Nineveh in Jonah not only brings the perennial impact of empire on HB/OT literature into focus, but also queers the 'normal' power relations between YHWH and the nations and with the post-exilic Jewish communities. Conflicting memories about Nineveh and the fate of its inhabitants form the background to the ambiguous ending in Jonah 4.11 that constitutes not only an ending, but its open-endedness stimulates ongoing reflection on the power relations between YHWH and faith communities. This open-endedness about the impact of memories of Nineveh is illustrated by how Nineveh was perceived by later apocryphal books like Tobit and Judith.

The ambiguity of the references to the 'great city' of Nineveh should not be avoided but rather be embraced because it allows the 'normal' (orthodox or traditional?) interpretation to coexist with critical and often even subversive interpretations. Thus, the resulting dialectic can provide stimuli for the open-endedness of biblical interpretation that is required for ongoing appropriations in the centre as well as on the margins of societies (Sherwood 1998, p. 62).

The queering of Nineveh memories in Jonah reveals much more than the way in which information of a violent past is recalled: a queer engagement with the political power relations within empires and the ongoing challenge how to respond to the ambiguous relationship with YHWH who can sack or save a 'great city' like Nineveh at will. In agreement with Davidson this queering investigation of the power exerted by Nineveh and God comes to the unsettling conclusion that 'divine violence in its imperialist representations is indistinguishable from the violence of empire, despite claims of moral superiority' (2019, p. 308). Queer theory challenges the dominant, the traditional and the normal canonized by mainstream biblical studies and theological-ethical reflection – this critique allows scholarship to move beyond just regurgitating existing exegetical consensus and to expose existing power relations in politics and religion.

## Conclusion

This contribution queers Jonah as prophet and Nineveh as an evil, imperialist and violent city. In doing so, queering of the power relations with YHWH in post-exilic imperial contexts takes place. Due to the premeditated ambiguity of Nineveh as 'great city' in Jonah, the 'normal' Christian emphasis on the grace and mercy of God that saved the repentant inhabitants of Nineveh, is queered by the Jewish critique of God that saved an evil Nineveh, that would eventually destroy the Northern Kingdom and devastate much of the Southern Kingdom.

To conclude, a paraphrase of the quotation by Lord Acton mentioned in the introductory paragraph: 'Great cities (like

Nineveh) are often bad, especially when they exercise influence through their painful memories of violent oppression, despite having lost their imperial authority and power.' The 'great city' of Nineveh became a lens to consider and queer the exercise of divine power, which could both sack and save. This lens is the result of the ambiguous references to Nineveh as sacked and saved 'great city' that create a queer space that invites the further queering of our understanding of God as being potentially both merciful and retributive.

Nineveh as queer space goes beyond the realms of ambiguity and paradox because it defies some fundamental principles of Aristotelian logic: the principle of non-contradiction and the law of the excluded middle or third. Queering opens new horizons of interpretation for the understanding of divine power and human greatness, providing new glimpses of constructive and appropriate alternatives to what is considered to be 'normal' by the dominant and the powerful.

## Notes

1 More than four decades ago, Brevard Childs (1979, pp. 419–20) identified two major trends in the history of the interpretation of the book of Jonah. The first, more Jewish trend is focused on 'some aspect of unfulfilled prophecy' or even false prophecy due to the 'lack of fulfilment of the prophecy against the nations'. The second, more Christian interpretative trend 'sees the point of the book to lie in the attempt to extend the message of salvation to the Gentiles against the resistance of the Jews'.

2 According to Kevin Youngblood, the book of Jonah divides in two halves (1.1—2.11 and 3.1—4.11), each with the same introductory line 'YHWH's word came to Jonah' (וַיְהִי דְבַר־יְהֹוָה אֶל־יוֹנָה) (2019, p. 31). Each half is divided into episodes that begin with the same verb 'and it happened' (וַיְהִי) that functions as one of the most important discourse markers in the book of Jonah.

3 Phyllis Trible summarizes the diverging depictions of Nineveh by the prophets as follows: 'Zephaniah and Nahum describe the historical Nineveh; Jonah depicts the legendary Nineveh' (2017, p. 647). This contribution argues that the 'memorized Nineveh' had a lingering influence on post-exilic theological reflection among early Jewish priestly scribes.

4 It might be telling that the ancient translations, except for the Vulgate ('civitas magna Dei'), take לֵאלֹהִים literally (Sasson 2008, p. 227).

5 Sherwood points out that this type of argumentation was referred to as 'a *qal ve homer* (literally, a little and large), a microscopic example that enables one to see a macro-cosmic truth' (1998, p. 72).

6 See Chesung Ryu, who makes the telling point that the silence of Jonah can be interpreted 'as resistance on the part of the weak over against the rhetoric of the strong, which ignores unbalanced power structures in human relationships in the name of universalism' (2009, p. 195).

7 The hyperbolic use of Nineveh as 'great city' in the book of Jonah forms part of a larger trend that is not only illustrated by the references to a 'great wind' and a 'mighty storm' (1.4), 'great storm' (1.12), 'large fish' (1.17) etc., but also by hyperbolic verbal expressions like 'the LORD hurled a great wind' (1.4), the fish 'spewed/vomited Jonah out' (2.10) and the worm 'that attacked the bush' in 4.7 (Sherwood 1998, p. 49).

# References

Acton, John D., 1907, 'Letter to Bishop Mandell Creighton, April 5 1887' in J. N. Figis and B. V. Lawrence (eds), *Historical Essays and Studies*, London: Macmillan.

Ählstrom, Gosta W., 1982, *Royal Administration and National Religion in Ancient Palestine*, Leiden: Brill.

Amin, Ash and Nigel Thrift, 2002, *Cities: Reimagining the Urban*, Malden: Polity.

Benjamin, Don C., 2000, 'City' in Daniel N. Freedman (ed.), *Eerdmans Dictionary of the Bible*, Grand Rapids, MI: Eerdmans, pp. 258–60.

Bolin, Thomas M., 2010, 'Jonah 4, 11 and the Problem of Exegetical Anachronism', *SJOT* 24/1, pp. 99–109.

Brintnall, Kent L., 2021, 'Once Upon a Queer Theory', *Religion Compass* 15/3, e12388.

Childs, Brevard S., 1979, *Introduction to the Old Testament as Scripture*, London: SCM Press.

Claassens, L. Juliana, 2021, 'Surfing with Jonah: Reading Jonah as a Postcolonial Narrative', *JSOT* 45/4, pp. 576–87.

Davidson, Steed V., 2019, 'Jonah' in Hemchand Gossai (ed.), *Postcolonial Commentary and the Old Testament*, London: T&T Clark, pp. 290–312.

Dearman, J. Andrew, 2006, 'City' in Katherine D. Sakenfeld (ed.), *The New Interpreter's Dictionary of the Bible*, A – C Volume 1, Nashville, TN: Abingdon Press, pp. 671–7.

De Geus, C. H. J., 2003, *Towns in Ancient Israel and the Southern Levant*, Palestina Antiqua 10, Leuven: Peeters.

De La Torre, Miguel A., 2007, *Liberating Jonah: Forming an Ethics of Reconciliation*, Maryknoll, NY: Orbis Books.

Dick, Michael, 'Tales of Two Cities (in the Second-Century BCE): Jerusalem and Nineveh', *JSP* 26/1, pp. 32–48.

Erickson, Amy, 2021, *Jonah: Introduction and Commentary*, Illuminations, Grand Rapids, MI: Eerdmans.

Faust, Avraham, 2013, 'Cities, Villages and Towns, Bronze and Iron Age' in Daniel M. Master (ed.), *The Oxford Encyclopedia of the Bible and Archaeology* Volume 1, Oxford: Oxford University Press, pp. 203–11.

Foucault, Michel, 1978, *History of Sexuality: An Introduction*, New York: Vintage Books.

Frick, Frank S., 1997, 'Cities: An Overview' in Eric M. Masters (ed.), *The Oxford Encyclopedia of Archaeology in the Near East* Volume 2, New York: Oxford University Press, pp. 14–19.

Halbwachs, Maurice, 1980, *The Collective Memory*, New York: Harper & Row.

Halbwachs, Maurice, 1992, *On Collective Memory*, Chicago, IL: Chicago University Press.

Halperin, David, 1995, *Saint Foucault: A Gay Hagiography*, New York: Oxford University Press.

Halton, Charles, 2008, 'How Big was Nineveh? Literal versus Figurative Interpretation of City Size', *Bulletin for Biblical Research* 18/2, pp. 193–207.

McKenzie, Steven L., Rhiannon Graybill and John Kaltner, 2020, 'Underwater Archaeology: The Compositional Layers of the Book of Jonah', *Vetus Testamentum* 70/1, pp. 83–103.

Mills, Mary E., 2012, *Urban Imagination in Biblical Prophecy*, LHBOT 560, London: T&T Clark.

Nogalski, James D., 1993, *Redactional Processes in the Book of the Twelve*, BZAW 218, Berlin: De Gruyter.

Nora, Pierre, 1989, 'Between Memory and History: Les lieux de memoire', *Representations* 26, pp. 7–25.

Nora, Pierre, 1998, *Realms of Memory: The Construction of the French*, Volume III *Symbols*, New York: Columbia University Press.

Parker, Simon, 2004, *Urban Theory and Urban Experience: Encountering the City*, New York: Routledge.

Rees, Anthony, 2016, 'Getting Up and Going Down: Towards a Spatial Poetics of Jonah', *The Bible and Critical Theory* 12/1, pp. 40–48.

Ryu, Chesung J., 2009, 'Silence as Resistance: A Postcolonial Reading of the Silence of Jonah in Jonah 4:1–11', *JSOT* 34/2, pp. 195–218.

Sasson, Jack M., 2008, *Jonah: A New Translation with Introduction,*

*Commentary and Interpretation*, Volume 24B, Anchor Yale Bible, New Haven, CT: Yale University Press.

Sherwood, Yvonne, 1998, 'Cross-Currents in the Book of Jonah: Some Jewish and Cultural Midrashim on a Traditional Text', *Biblical Interpretation* 6/1, pp. 49–79.

Sherwood, Yvonne, 2000, *A Biblical Text and its Aftermath: The Survival of Jonah in the Western Culture*, Cambridge: Cambridge University Press.

Sieges, Anna, 2016, 'Nineveh' in John D. Barry et al. (eds), *The Lexham Bible Dictionary*, Bellingham, WA: Lexham Press [LOGOS edition].

Simon, Uriel, 1999, *The JPS Bible Commentary: Jonah*, Philadelphia, PA: Jewish Publication Society.

Stuart, Douglas K., 2014, 'The Great City of Nineveh (Jon. 1:2)', *Bibliotheca Sacra* 171/684 (2014), pp. 387–400.

Tiemeyer, Lena-Sofia, 2021, *Jonah Through the Centuries*, Wiley Blackwell Commentaries. Hoboken, NJ: Wiley.

Timmer, Daniel C., 2009, 'The Intertextual Israelite Jonah Face l'Empire: The Post-Colonial Significance of the Book's Contents and Purported Neoassyrian Context', *Journal of Hebrew Scriptures* 9, p. 20.

Trible, Phyllis, 2017, 'The Book of Jonah' in *The New Interpreter's Bible Commentary* Volume 5, Nashville, TN: Abingdon Press, pp. 631–86.

Tucker, W. Dennis, 2006, *Jonah: A Handbook on the Hebrew Text*, Baylor Handbook on the Bible, Waco, TX: Baylor University Press.

Vermeulen, Karolien, 2017, 'Save or Sack the City: The Fate of Jonah's Nineveh from a Spatial Perspective', *JSOT* 42/2, pp. 233–46.

Warner, Michael, 1993, 'Introduction' in *Fear of a Queer Planet: Queer Politics and Social Theory*, Minneapolis, MN: University of Minnesota Press.

Wolff, Hans W., 1977, *Dodekapropheton 3 Obadja und Jona*, BKAT XIV/3. Neukirchen-Vluyn: Neukirchener Verlag.

Youngblood, Kevin J., 2019, *Jonah: God's Scandalous Mercy*, 2nd edn, ZECOT, Grand Rapids, MI: Zondervan.

# 6

# Queering the Straight Jonah –
# A Reception-Exegetical Exploration

## LENA-SOFIA TIEMEYER

## Introduction

Jonah is ישר (*yasar*)![1] This Hebrew adjective can mean straight, right, honest, straightforward, direct and upright. First, Jonah's world view is straight. Something is either right or wrong – there are no shades of grey for Jonah. There should be justice and divine retribution. When people sin, they ought to be punished, and the punishment should fit the crime. In the case of Nineveh, when a city has sinned as grievously as Nineveh has done, a mere 40 days of repentance is no reason to let them escape their just deserts!

Second, Jonah's personality is straight to the point of being rude and rebellious. When God tells him to go to Nineveh, he blatantly refuses because he wants to compromise neither his integrity nor his reputation. There is no point in going since God obviously plans to forgive the Ninevites anyway. Jonah has no desire to become a laughing stock in Israel due to, from his perspective, a failed prophecy.

Third, Jonah's communication with God is straight. When he is faced with the fact that he is the source of the storm, he tells the sailors straightaway to toss him overboard. Death is preferable to life in a world where he cannot depend on God having the ability to be unmerciful. In some later retellings, as in the Jewish–Hellenistic sermon *On Jonah* 14.3 and in Ibn Kathīr's *Tafsīr al-Qur'ān al-'Aẓīm* (commentary to Q21:87, but commenting on Q37:141), Jonah even jumps off the boat to expedite the matter. Jonah's lack of willingness to find a middle way comes to the forefront in Jonah 4, where he tells a rather perplexed God that he would prefer to die rather than live in a world where he cannot trust God to punish the wicked in a judicially satisfactory manner.

So Jonah is straight; he is not queer in any sense of the word. He would have been affronted by the thought. His way is not that of the trickster or the underdog, like Jacob before him (see e.g. Gen. 25.29–34; 27.5–30; 30.29–43). He refuses to dissemble, and he does not want to cajole those around him to do his bidding. Jonah speaks his mind without caring who is being hurt in the progress. His way is also not that of the gender-bending mediator, like Jonathan before him (see e.g. 1 Sam. 19.4–6; 20.28–34; 23.16–17). Jonah refuses to forego his aggressive masculinity to allow others to prosper. He stands upright in his conviction that his way, and his way alone, is the only straight way forward.

So given my belief in the inherent straightness of Jonah, what do I mean when I nonetheless call Jonah queer? In this essay, I explore the reception history of the book of Jonah through two fundamentally different lenses, namely *queering* and *post-truth*. These two reading strategies, albeit in different ways and for different reasons, share as their goal to destabilize, subvert and to a certain extent also to delegitimize the plain meaning of the text.

Beginning with the adjective 'queer' and the related verb 'queering', I follow a broad definition here, where the concept denotes something that is ambiguous, that crosses boundaries and that questions what is generally accepted. The concept of queering also stands for reading a text against its grain, with the goal of bringing out what is hidden in a text rather than remaining satisfied with its surface meaning. Queer readings of texts challenge norms and problematize what is often considered obvious.

Given this definition, I maintain that interpreters, for the last 2,000 years, have often queered the character of Jonah and the message of book bearing his name. They have read Jonah against its grain, either to make it conform to prevalent theological views or to destabilize those same views. As a result, Jonah, both character and book, are assigned views, often in a most cavalier manner, that may have caused their originators to turn in their graves.

Turning to the concept of post-truth, it was defined in 2016 by the Oxford Dictionary as the act of 'relating to or denoting circumstances in which objective facts are less influential in shaping public opinion than appeals to emotion and personal belief' (https://www.oxfordlearnersdictionaries.com/definition/english/post-truth). Objective truth is no longer essential; what is important is our personal beliefs about something. Prodding the issue further, Vittorio Bufacchi attempts a further clarification of the notion (Bufacchi 2021). He demonstrates that post-truth is not a *lie*, insofar as a lie recognizes that there is such a thing as truth. Post-truth honours truth although it denies it. In contrast, post-truth undermines the concept of truth, and thus makes it impossible to have a conversation about whether something is true or not. Post-truth is, furthermore, not the same as *bullshitting*. Bullshitting ignores truth and is disrespectful of it, but still recognizes it when it sees it. In contrast, post-truth seeks to delegitimize truth. To cite Bufacchi, post-truth is 'a deliberate strategy aimed at creating an environment where objective facts are less influential in shaping public opinion, where theoretical frameworks are undermined in order to make it impossible for someone to make sense of a certain event, phenomenon, or experience, and where scientific truth is delegitimized' (Bufacchi 2021, p. 350).

In this essay, I argue that Jewish, Christian and Muslim interpreters, through the ages, have all, each in their own way, been involved in creating post-true statements about the book of Jonah. They have deliberately delegitimized its plain meaning and sought to subvert the actual claims that the book of Jonah makes. More explicitly, they have used interpretative strategies to create and bolster interpretations of the book of Jonah to serve to shape public opinion to suit their own polemical needs.

After looking at these two perspectives together, the queering, which may be viewed as a desirable trait, and the post-truth, which may be viewed as a non-desirable trait, this essay finally highlights that both approaches draw their inspirations from extant details in the text. These readings are convincing (at least to some readers) because they are based on nuances that are veiled, yet present in the book of Jonah. Put succinctly, although the reviewed Jewish, Christian and Muslim readings appear to deny the plain sense of Jonah's message, they concurrently pick up voices in the texts that a straight reading may dismiss too quickly as either irrelevant or otherwise of secondary import. The book of Jonah *does* contain dissenting voices, and the act of reading the book against its grain brings them out into the open, ready to be used by a wide range of readers and for a variety of more or less edifying purposes.

In what follows I explore three sets of interpretations of the book of Jonah. I begin to show how many Christian readings have subverted the book with the aim of undermining the Jewish community. Next, I demonstrate how many Jewish interpreters have responded in kind for the purpose of casting doubts on Christian dogma. Finally, I touch upon how Islamic readings have subverted Jonah with a view to align Mohammad's flight from and return to Mecca with that of his biblical predecessor. All these interpretations are based on details that *are present* in the text. Yet, as I show, they are nonetheless subversive insofar as these details are being read against the grain, blown out of proportion or otherwise twisted to fit the interpreters' polemical purposes.

As test cases, I explore four motifs in Jonah: the reasons for Jonah's flight from God; the sailors' act of tossing Jonah overboard; the character of the fish; and the Ninevites' repentance. In order to make my points, I generalize my findings to some degree. In the end, I reveal the large brushstrokes; there are exceptions to all the points below.

## Christian subversions of the book of Jonah

Christian polemical readings of the book of Jonah serve two main objectives. They seek to assure the readers that Jonah was a narrow-minded Jew who did not wish Gentiles to experience

God's grace. In tandem, they wish to demonstrate that Jonah is a type for Christ who, like Jesus, died and was resurrected. These two mutually conflicting aims result in a range of subversive readings. Some interpretations are firmly anchored in the biblical text, while others require strenuous mental gymnastics to be attained and remain largely unconvincing to the open-minded and unbiased reader.

## The case of Jonah's flight from God

The biblical text claims that Jonah's initial refusal to obey God's command to go to Nineveh and foretell its doom (1.2) was triggered by the prophet's objection to God's habitual compassion. Jonah, being a straight person, flees (1.3) because he disagrees with what he considers to be God's slack approach to justice. Jonah admits that God is a 'gracious and compassionate God, slow to anger and abounding in love, a God who changes his mind concerning planned evil' (4.2). Jonah's understanding of God's underlying motives for sending him to Nineveh, expressed in Jonah 4.2, is fully in line with the ancient Near Eastern understanding of prophecy. The goal of prophecy was not its fulfilment; it was its cancellation (Tiemeyer 2005). In other words, the prediction of Nineveh's disaster served as the essential impetus for bringing about Nineveh's repentance, which was God's goal in the first place. Jonah, however, disagreed about the appropriateness of this goal. In his view, a righteous God should punish the Neo-Assyrians for their atrocious acts of violence committed against the nations around them, not hold out a hand in reconciliation.

In many respects, Christian polemical readings of Jonah, which portray him as a recalcitrant and grudging prophet who does not wish Gentiles to partake of God's grace, are firmly anchored in the biblical text. Many commentators state explicitly that Jonah's view vis-à-vis God's mercy is unacceptable in its harshness. Luther, regarding Jonah as a regrettable representative of Jews in general, states sharply that Jonah begrudged the Gentiles the privilege of becoming Christians. Speculating further, Luther argues that Jonah would have deplored the notion that Judaism was unnecessary and their laws useless – according to Luther, the logical conclusion of the Ninevites' salvation – as he would have understood it to deprecate and disparage his fellow countrymen (Luther, German commentary, Jonah 4.2). These same sentiments are also present in the earlier, patristic commentaries of the Church Fathers. Cyril of Alexandria, for instance, states that 'humanly speaking, [Jonah] was mean-spirited [...] His attitude was unstable, unworthy of a saintly mind' (commentary on Jonah 4.3).

At the same time, these Christian commentators ignore the political aspects that are intrinsic to the Jonah narrative. Given the Neo-Assyrian atrocities against the subjugated nations, the biblical Jonah's reluctance to extend God's grace to them is a valid viewpoint. Christian interpreters thus misrepresent the prophet insofar as they fail to consider the historical nuances of the text. Jonah is not a narrow-minded Jew who denies Gentiles the right to salvation; he is a citizen of a small and vulnerable nation that is fighting for its right to exist in the shadow of a cruel superpower.

## The case of the sailors' act of tossing Jonah overboard

The biblical narrative offers a nuanced description of the Gentile sailors as sympathetic people who hesitate before committing murder. After having learnt that Jonah is responsible for their dire situation (v. 10), they do not immediately throw him overboard but ask Jonah to advise them what to do (v. 11). Jonah, however, pushes the responsibility back to the sailors by suggesting that they toss him into the sea (v. 12): it is up to them to decide whether or not to commit murder, because Jonah is certainly not going to commit suicide! The sailors do not rise to the bait, however, but instead, as the decent men that they are, try to save Jonah (v. 13). In the end, though, they turn out to be neither better nor worse than most people. To save their own skins, they sacrifice Jonah (vv. 14–15).

Christian readings of this passage need to interpret it against the grain to uphold the common typological understanding of Jonah, which has its roots in the reference in Matthew 12.39–41 (as well as Luke 11.29–31) to the 'sign of the prophet Jonah'.

> He answered, 'A wicked and adulterous generation asks for a miraculous sign! But none will be given it except the sign of the prophet Jonah. For as Jonah was three days and three nights in the belly of a huge fish, so the Son of Man will be three days and three nights in the heart of the earth. The men of Nineveh will stand up at the judgment with this generation and condemn it; for they repented at the preaching of Jonah, and now something greater than Jonah is here'. (Matt. 12.39–41 NIV)

This rather opaque statement has given rise to the three-part typology that:

1. Jonah being tossed into the sea by the sailors is a precursor for Jesus' crucifixion (Jonah 1.15);
2. Jonah's three days inside the belly of the fish is a precursor for Jesus' death (Jonah 2.1b);
3. Jonah being vomited out of by the fish is a precursor for Jesus' resurrection (Jonah 2.10) (see further Chow 1995, 18–19).

For this typology to work, the sailors must either be praised to the skies or condemned to the darkest corners of hell. Beginning with those interpreters who inflate the sailors' virtue, Jerome writes:

> They refused to shed blood, preferring rather to die than kill. O how changed are they now! The people that had served God (Deut. 10:12) saying, 'crucify him, crucify him' (Luke 23:21). (Jerome, Commentary on Jonah 1:13)

Thus, the Gentile sailors, in contrast to the Jews at the time of Jesus, refuse to kill Jonah/Jesus.

A significantly smaller group of Christian retellings, yet equally anti-Jewish in their outlook, depict the sailors' act of throwing Jonah over board in Jonah 1.13 as that of brutal Jewish men prone to violence and hatred. A medieval painting in Härkeberga Church (Sweden) epitomizes this interpretative line. This painting, done by medieval German-Swedish painter Albrekt Målare (latinized as Albertus Pictor) (1440/45–1509), depicts the sailors as cruel men with grotesque noses and conical hats, both aspects associated with European medieval Jewry (Melin 2009). This painting thus portrays the sailors as Jews, or rather what a person in the medieval age would have associated with Jewry (Friedman 1988, p. 128). The onlookers would, as a result, have interpreted Jonah 1.13 as a precursor to the passion narrative: the sailors/Jews killed Jonah/Jesus.

In both cases, the Christian interpreters misrepresent the biblical text to make it serve their own polemical needs. The first reading has stronger ties to the biblical text. The biblical sailors were unremarkable men who, at least initially, held the moral high ground, even though they later, when push came to shove, chose to save their own lives. In contrast, the second reading is a glaring triumph of post-truth, whereby the illiterate churchgoers are effectively being told the blatant falsehood that the sailors were Jews rather than, as the biblical text indisputably states, Gentiles.

## The case of the fish

Our third example relates to the fish in Jonah 2. The text states unequivocally that *God* appointed the fish to swallow Jonah (2.1). Once inside the fish, Jonah prays and offers thanksgiving. In the final form of the book, Jonah's song of praise aptly captures the sense that the fish has just saved his life. In 2.3 [Eng. 2.2], Jonah praises God for saving him 'from the belly of Sheol'. A contextual reading suggests that the fish is the saviour while 'the belly of Sheol' is the netherworld where Jonah would have ended up had he drowned. Jonah cries out to God before the fish came along. When the fish comes along, he is saved. Put succinctly, Jonah is not in the belly of the netherworld (בטן שאול) precisely because he is in the womb of the fish (מעי הדגה).

Christian readings, beginning already in the aforementioned Matthew 12.39–41, delegitimize this contextual reading and instead turn not only the fish but also Jonah's time inside it into hell. This interpretative tradition, which has its roots in the LXX translation of the Hebrew term דג as κῆτος (Jonah 1.17; 2.1; and 2.10), gradually gains ground due to the polemical need to align Jonah's time in the fish with Jesus' time in the realm of the dead between Good Friday and Easter Sunday. We can thus observe how Christian interpretations of the fish downgrade God's faithful servant, a process that culminates in medieval times when Jonah's fish is conflated with the Leviathan and depicted as the gateway to hell. We see the fish at its most despicable low in 'The Whale', an Old English poem preserved in the tenth-century Exeter Book (Exeter Cathedral Library MS 3501, folio 96b–97b). In this poem, the mouth of hell is compared to a whale's mouth, and the whale is understood as the servant of the Devil or even as the Devil himself. The fish is described as a cunning monster that sinks seafarers and lures fish into its mouth to be devoured. In this retelling, which probably owes its imagination partly to the Leviathan and partly to Jonah's fish, the fish thus serves simultaneously as a symbol of hell itself and as the Devil personified, who entices unwary sinners towards destruction (Schmidt 1995, pp. 62–3; Eng. transl. Thorpe 1842, pp. 360–64).

Turning to Christian art, there is ample evidence that the fish signifies hell. In particular, it is common to depict the entrance to hell as a giant set of jaws. A painting from 1736 by Daniel Blavér and Annika Jönsdotter Daggren, found in Ödeshög church, Sweden, for example, features the archangel Michael, who separates the 'sheep' from the 'goats'. The latter group (on the right) are entering hell through the mouth of a sea creature, who is probably none other than Jonah's fish.

Taken together, this Christian character assassination of the fish is an illuminating example of post-truth, whereby someone's reputation can be lost despite clear evidence that the charges lack a solid foundation.

LENA-SOFIA TIEMEYER

## The case of the people of Nineveh

Our final example constitutes the repentance of the people of
Nineveh. Unless God is a gullible fool, the fact that he was
convinced by the Ninevites' repentance suggests that it was real.
God saw how the Ninevites stopped doing what was evil and,
as a result, decided not to set in motion his planned punishment
(3.10).

This reading suited the Church Fathers eminently well. After
all, from their perspective, what is there not to like? A Gentile
city repents, and God is compassionate. This endearing picture
could be used to preach God's grace to repentant sinners all
over the world. Unfortunately, however, the church did not
stop there but went beyond the biblical text and turned the
Ninevites' repentance into a Jew-bashing weapon (Urbach
1949, pp. 118–22; Golka 1986, pp. 51–61). In his *Dialogue
with Trypho*, Justin Martyr offers a scathing comparison:

> And though all the men of your nation knew the incidents in
> the life of Jonah, and though Christ said amongst you that
> He would give the sign of Jonah, exhorting you to repent of
> your wicked deeds at least after He rose again from the dead,
> and to mourn before God as did the Ninevites, in order that
> your nation and city might not be taken and destroyed, as
> they have been destroyed; yet you not only have not repented,
> after you learned that He rose from the dead, but, as I said
> before you have sent chosen and ordained men throughout all
> the world to proclaim that a godless and lawless heresy had
> sprung from one Jesus, a Galilean deceiver, whom we cruci-
> fied, but his disciples stole him by night from the tomb, where
> he was laid when unfastened from the cross, and now deceive
> men by asserting that he has risen from the dead and ascended
> to heaven. (Justin Martyr, Dialogue with Trypho, ch. 108).

Justin Martyr is, however, not alone in expressing this kind of
anti-Jewish sentiments. We find similar statements in a wide
array of patristic writings, among them Jerome's commentary
to Jonah 3.5, Cyril of Alexandria's commentary to Jonah 3.5,

and in a long metrical homily called *The Repentance of Nineveh* penned by Ephraem the Syrian.

In this manner, building on the foundation of the biblical text, Christian exegetes went where the biblical text did not *explicitly* go, namely, to compare the Ninevites with the Israelites. Even so, the biblical narrative may implicitly encourage this kind of comparison to jolt its intended readership; that is, people in post-monarchic Yehud (see Tiemeyer 2017), to adopt a more universalistic outlook. There is, however, no doubt that the biblical text does not support the patristic anti-Jewish vitriol. As such, this is yet another example of post-truth, where lack of textual evidence constitutes no barrier for creating a reading which serves the reader's own polemical interests and appeals to feelings rather than to facts.

## Jewish subversions of the book of Jonah

Turning to Jewish subversions of the book of Jonah, we observe an essentially defensive twofold stance. First, the Jewish interpreters need to rehabilitate Jonah by refuting the Christian claim that Jonah is a narrow-minded Jew. Instead, according to many Jewish readings, Jonah acts altruistically on behalf of Israel. Second, they have to problematize the idea that Jonah, in some form or shape, serves as a precursor of Christ. Yet to accomplish these goals, a fair amount of violence needs to be applied to the biblical text. This endeavour, in turn, results in a new set of subversive interpretations of the book of Jonah.

### The case of Jonah's flight from God

Jewish commentators are involved in their fair share of post-truth by turning the sour and largely unpalatable prophet into an altruistic hero. A few Jewish exegetes understand Jonah's flight against the background of the Neo-Assyrian (seen from Jonah's perspective still) future destruction of the Northern Kingdom of Israel. This interpretation is informed by the reference to Jonah ben Amittai in 2 Kings 14.25, according to which Jonah was a historical prophet who was active during the reign of Jeroboam II (eighth century BCE). Isaac ben Judah Abarbanel, for example, states that:

> Jonah did not want to go to Nineveh for he knew of the future difficulties which would befall the [ten] tribes of [the Northern Kingdom of] Israel. Therefore, he closed his soul to God's call for the purpose that the nations of Assyria and Nineveh its capital would be destroyed. (Abarbanel, Rabbinic Bible, Commentary on Jonah 2:3).

In other words, Jonah (being a prophet) knows already prior to the fact that Assyria will threaten and later also destroy the Northern Kingdom. Therefore, by refusing to prophesy (lest he should encourage the Ninevites to repent), Jonah seeks to ensure Nineveh's destruction and concurrently to safeguard Israel's survival. Thus, rather than being a grudging and grumpy man, Jonah is a sacrificial hero who is willing to die in the watery abyss to save his people (see further Tiemeyer 2017). This interpretation receives support not only from its canonical context, but also from a dialogical reading of Jonah and Nahum, where the latter predicts the God-ordained fall of Nineveh. Even so, its portrayal of Jonah is nonetheless highly subversive. Rather than focusing on the overt message of Jonah, it picks up the faint resistant traces extant in the biblical text and brings them out into the open.

### The case of the sailors' act of tossing Jonah overboard

Jewish interpreters are likewise responsible for twisting the portrayal of the sailors to suit their own polemical needs to refute the aforementioned Christian anti-Jewish polemic. This is done in one of two mutually exclusive ways that correspond to the Christian dual lines of interpretation: the sailors either become Jews or Christians. Beginning with the former trajectory, chapter 10 of *Pirqe de Rabbi Eliezer*, a Jewish midrash that is traditionally attributed to the tanna Rabbi Eliezer ben Hyrcanus but probably not written prior to the eighth century CE), transforms the sailors into Jewish converts. Having seen God's salvation of Jonah through the fish, they abandon their idolatry, return to Yafo, go up to Jerusalem and allow themselves to be circumcised.[2]

The latter trajectory is represented well by the twentieth-century novel *The Strange Nation of Rafael Mendes*, which is inspired by the Jonah narrative. The Jewish Brazilian author Moacyr Scliar portrays the sailors as outspoken Jew-haters who actively wish to throw the Christ-killer (that is, the Jews) overboard. The Gentile sailors are thus conceived through the lens of 2,000 years of Christian persecution of Jews. In sum, as in the Christian polemics, the sailors either ascend into heroic converts, albeit this time to Jewish proselytes, or descend into brutal villains. Neither tradition allows them to stay the middling men that the biblical text presents.

## The case of the fish

In the same way as their Christian peers, Jewish exegetes also transform the fish to suit their own needs. We noted earlier that the fish's downward spiral towards death and hell had already begun in the LXX. It is also attested in several other Hellenistic Jewish texts, among them 3 Macc. 6.8; *Genesis Rabbah* 5.5; the *Hellenistic Synagogal Prayers*; and the Jerusalem Talmud (*j.berakhot. 9.1*).

Yet once the Christian interpreters had adopted this 'monstrous' line of exegesis, many Jewish interpreters began to swerve in a different direction, namely towards rehabilitating the fish beyond its wildest dreams. The aforementioned *Pirqe de Rabbi Eliezer* (ch. 10), for example, picks up the hitherto lone voice of the Jewish-Hellenistic sermon *On Jonah* (presumably written between 25 BCE and 50 CE in Alexandria), wherein the fish, like an ancient Nautilus, carries Jonah in relative comfort on a sight-seeing tour of the wonders of the great deep:

The belly of the huge fish became the house of the drowning prophet, its eyes the mirror of the external visible things, and the movement of its flippers similar to a king's chariot. O prophet, you were given great honour when you moved at a chariot's speed, just as when the huge fish swam toward you! Did any ruler ever have the opportunity to look as deep into the world's abyss as you? Invisible things have become visible to you! To whom among humans were the ends of the earth seen as clearly as to you, and [to whom] was the abyss of the sea shown as a view? For whom else have the crafts ever rendered such a perfect machine possible, so that you are there and observe everything, but no one sees you, the observer? (*On Jonah* 17:1–4).

The fish is furthermore not a creature who just *happens* to pass by. On the contrary, God has already appointed him to this task on the fifth day of creation!

In this context, we should not forget the widespread and delightful rabbinic habit of queering not only the grammatical but also the biological gender of the fish, an interpretation advocated by none other than Rashi himself (*Rabbinic Bible*, Commentary to Jonah 2:1). This exegetical move is triggered by the alleged change between a masculine singular form of the term 'fish' in 2.1, 11 (*dag*) and its apparent feminine singular form in the intermittent 2.2 (*dagah*). The little-known *Midrash of the Repentance of Jonah the Prophet* (MRJP) epitomizes this change, as attested in only three manuscripts. This midrash describes how Jonah was swallowed by three fish. Following MS Warsaw 258 (as cited in Kadari 2016, pp. 111–13), Jonah is first swallowed by a male fish (*dag*). Being too comfortable there, the male fish spits him out and he is swallowed by a female fish (*dagah*). While there, Jonah's living quarters turn out to be highly uncomfortable, given that the female fish is full of little baby fish. This discomfort, in turn, makes Jonah turn to God in prayer. The midrash concludes by having God command the *dagah* to spew out Jonah. Right before Jonah's return to dry land, however, God summoned a male fish (*dag*), bigger than all the others, which swallowed Jonah *and* the female fish.

Taken together, this final manoeuvre 'explains' how Jonah is being spat out of a male fish in Jonah 2.11. Despite the evident attraction of this wonderfully queer interpretation, however, I maintain that this gender-bending of the originally straight male fish is a misunderstanding of an enclitic *he* attached to some pausal forms (Tiemeyer 2016).

## The case of the people of Nineveh

The rabbis' rejoinder to the anti-Jewish patristic interpretation of the Ninevites' repentance did not take long. To respond to the Christian accusations, triggered by the comparison made between the Israelites and the Ninevites, the Rabbis needed to destabilize the surface meaning of the text. Put succinctly, the Jewish interpreters needed to uncover the Ninevites' insincerity and cruelty. This aim was accomplished by a three-way strategy.

First, by drawing on both the book of Nahum and general knowledge of world history, Jewish scholars highlighted Nineveh's factual destruction in 612 BCE by Babylonian and Median forces. If Nineveh was destroyed so soon after Jonah visited the city, so the argument goes, whatever remorse the Ninevites may have felt was clearly short-lived (see e.g. *PRE* 43).

Second, by appealing to common sense, the Rabbis managed to turn the reference to fasting animals in Jonah 3.7–8 into a sign of the Ninevites' inherent cruelty and insincerity. No truly repentant sinner would force innocent animals to starve. The Babylonian Talmud, for example, states the people of Nineveh began to bargain with God, saying that unless God had mercy on them, they would not have mercy on the animals: 'Let them be covered with sackcloth, both man and beast' (Jonah 3.8).

What did they do?

They set beasts by themselves and children by themselves and said before him, 'Lord of the world, if you don't have mercy on us, we shall not have mercy on these'. (b.Tan. 2:1–11; see also y.Tan. 2:1, Pesiqta deRab Kahana xxiv: xi)

Third, inspired by the phrase 'and they called out mightily to God' in Jonah 3.8, a few Jewish interpreters maintain that the people of Nineveh remained cruel even in their so-called repentance. Rashi, for example, taking the adverbial statement *beḥozkah* (בחזקה) to mean 'with force', argues that the men of Nineveh separated children from their mothers 'with force' and stated to God that 'if you do not show us mercy, we will not show mercy to these hostages' (Rashi, *Commentary to Jonah* 3:8).

Together, these readings manage, at least to the open-minded, to cast doubt upon the plain sense of the text. Yes, it is possible – although overall rather unlikely – that God was fooled by the Ninevites' dishonest performance of repentance.

## Muslim subversions of the book of Jonah

Before drawing to a close, I briefly mention the Muslim subversions of the book of Jonah. To make a long story short, Jonah appears six times in the Qur'an (Sura 4:163; 6:86; 10:98 [Yunus]; 21:87–88; 37:139–48; 68:48–50). These references are opaque and difficult to forge together into a coherent and cohesive narrative. Most likely, the original readers were familiar with the biblical narrative about Jonah and thus able to interpret the extant elusive Qur'anic references in this light. As time went by, however, the biblical narrative faded from memory, and the Qur'anic fragments became the building blocks for creating new and alternative Jonah narratives with a sequence of events that differs drastically from the original biblical one. (To use a modern equivalence, it is as if the box of the jigsaw puzzle has been lost, with the result that the pieces are put together to form a different picture than the one that was originally intended.) This modified narrative, in turn, was subsequently interpreted by Islamic traditions (*hadīth*) and Qur'anic exegesis (*tafsīr*), whereby more details were gradually added and thus caused the Islamic Jonah traditions to evolve even further.

A common outline runs as follows: God sends Jonah to Nineveh to preach a message, but the people of Nineveh refuse to listen to him. As a result, Jonah leaves Nineveh and boards a ship. A storm commences, the sailors cast lots and, realizing that Jonah is the cause of the storm, throw him into the sea. A gigantic fish then swallows Jonah. Once inside the fish, Jonah repents and glorifies God, and the fish spits him out. As Jonah suffers great physical discomfort from having been inside a fish, God provides a gourd to offer shade, and the archangel Gabriel gives him clothes. The story ends with Jonah returning to Nineveh and successfully bringing the people to repentance (e.g. Al-Kisai, Al-Ṭabarī, Al-Tha'labī, see further Tiemeyer 2021, pp. 7–8).

This new Jonah story is a striking example of post-truth. In this case, the rewriting of the biblical narrative legitimizes Muhammad's conquest of Mecca in the eyes of the public. Just as Muhammad and his followers encounter opposition from the people in Mecca, so Jonah's first mission to Nineveh fails due to the hostility of the city. Further, just as Muhammad, after his interlude in Medina, returns to and seizes control of Mecca, so also Jonah returns and converts the people of Nineveh. At the same time, although Muhammad, like Jonah (Surah 68), feels rejected by those to whom he is sent to preach, he should not emulate Jonah's enraged departure but instead be patient and see that God would sort things out.

## Conclusion

To conclude, post-truth is not a new thing. On the contrary, following Bufacchi, post-truth has been around since the time of Cicero and the Roman Republic. Politicians and people in power have resorted to lies, bullshit and, when convenient, they have even appealed to post-truth accounts in their attempt to sway public opinion. Likewise, queering is not a novel reading strategy. Instead, people through the ages have read the texts before them against their grain. To make texts applicable to situations that bear little resemblance to those experienced by their original authors, interpreters have destabilized their overt surface meaning and problematized their message. In this way, the texts have been allowed to generate a wide array of new meanings.

Speaking more specifically about the Bible, the notion of subverting and delegitimizing the biblical narratives, not only to shape public opinion but also to bring out into the open their inherent ambiguity and unstable character, is as old as biblical exegesis. Expressed more positively, the reading strategies that we observe in this essay, Jewish, Christian and Muslim alike, ultimately result in the queering of the straight prophet: the conformist Jonah and the book bearing his name, are given roles and viewpoints that they would never have dreamt of having. At the same time, there *are* aspects of the text that allow for these queer retellings. The plasticity of the text enables the book of Jonah to mean many different things, and this range of meaning(s) stem from meetings between text and reader. Readers have filled, and indeed continue to fill, the textual gaps and to assign motives to the characters in accordance with their own convictions and for the sake of communicating their own message to their own audiences.

## Notes

1 Much of the material in this article appears throughout my commentary *Jonah Through the Centuries*, albeit often in a different form. There is also significant overlap with my article 'The Book of Jonah in Jewish–Christian Debate', *Taiwan Baptist Christian Seminary Journal* 17 (2019), pp. 9–39.

2 The rationale behind this interpretation is twofold. First, the term 'sacrifice' in v. 16 is reinterpreted to refer to the blood of the covenant shed during circumcision. Second, as sacrifices can only be offered in the temple, and as only Jews can offer sacrifices, the sailors, almost by default, *must have* converted to Judaism.

# References

## Primary sources

Abarbanel, Rabbinic Bible, Commentary on Jonah. For an English translation, see Steven Bob, 2013, *Go to Nineveh: Medieval Jewish Commentaries to the Book of Jonah, Translated and Explained*, Eugene, OR: Pickwick Publications.

Cyril of Alexandria, 2008, 'Commentary of Jonah' in Robert C. Hill (trans.), *Saint Cyril of Alexandria: Commentary on the Twelve Prophets*, Vol. 2, Fathers of the Church 116, Washington DC: Catholic University America Press.

Ephraem the Syrian, 1853, *The Repentance of Nineveh*, Henry Burgess (trans.), London: Robert B. Blackader. For the full text in English translation and with a commentary by Henry Burgess, see https://books.google.co.uk/books/about/The_repentance_of_Nineveh_a_metrical_hom.html?id=GcICAAAAQAAJ&redir_esc=y.

Jerome, 2014, *Commentary on Jonah*, in Robin MacGregor (trans.) and John Litteral (ed.), *Ancient Bible Commentary in English*, Ashland, KY: Litteral's Christian Library Publications.

Justin Martyr, 1885, *Dialogue with Trypho* (chapter 108) in Alexander Roberts and James Donaldson (trans.), *The Ante-Nicene Fathers*, volume 1, Buffalo, NY: Christian Literature Publishing Company. Accessed via http://www.earlychristianwritings.com/text/justinmartyr-dialoguetrypho.html, accessed 7.06.2023.

Al-Kisai, Muhammad Ibn Allah, 1997, *Tales of the Prophets*, W. M. Thackston (trans.), Chicago, IL: Kazi Publications.

Luther, Martin, 1974, *Jonah, Habakkuk*, H. C. Oswald (ed.), Luther's Work 19, St Louis, MO: Concordia Publishing House. The lectures on Jonah were originally printed in 1525.

*On Jonah*, Aram Muradyan and Gohar Topchyan (trans.), 2013, 'Pseudo-Philo, On Samson and On Jonah' in Louis H. Feldman, James L. Kugel and Lawrence H. Schiffman (eds), *Outside the Bible: Ancient Jewish Writings Related to Scripture*, 3 Volumes, Philadelphia, PA: Jewish Publication Society / Lincoln, NE: University of Nebraska Press.

*Pirqe de Rabbi Eliezer*, Gerald Friedlander (trans.), 1916, *Pirqe de Rabbi Eliezer* (The chapters of Rabbi Eliezer the Great) according to the Text of the Manuscript Belonging to Abraham Epstein of Vienna, London: Kegan Paul, Trench, Trubner & Co. / New York: Bloch.

Rashi, Rabbinic Bible, Commentary on Jonah. For an English translation, see Steven Bob, 2013, *Go to Nineveh: Medieval Jewish Commentaries to the Book of Jonah, Translated and Explained*, Eugene, OR: Pickwick Publications.

Al-Ṭabarī, 1987, *History of al-Ṭabarī*, Moshe Perlmann (trans.), *The Ancient Kingdoms*, Albany, NY: State University of New York Press.

Al-Tha'labī, 'Kadari, 2002, *Lives of the Prophets*, William M. Brinner (trans.), Leiden: Brill, pp. 681–8.

Scliar, Moacyr, 1987, *The Strange Nation of Rafael Mendes*, Eloah F. Giacomelli (trans.), New York: Ballantine Books.

## Secondary literature

Bufacchi, Vittorio, 2021, 'Truth, Lies and Tweets: A Consensus Theory of Post-Truth', *Philosophy and Social Criticism* 47/3, pp. 347–61.

Chow, Simon, 1995, *The Sign of Jonah Reconsidered: A Study of its Meaning in the Gospel Tradition*. Coniectanea Biblica New Testament Series 27, Stockholm: Almqvist & Wiksell International.

Friedman, John B., 1988, 'Bald Jonah and the Exegesis of IV Kings 2.23', *Traditio: Studies in Ancient and Medieval History, Thought, and Religion* 44, pp. 125–44.

Golka, Friedemann W., 1986, 'Jonaexegese und Antijudaismus', *Kirche und Israel* 1 (1986), pp. 51–61.

Kadari, Tamar, 2016, 'Aggadic Motifs in the Story of Jonah: A Study of Interaction Between Religions' in Alberdina Houtman, Tamar Kadari, Marcel Poorthuis and Vered Tohar (eds), *Religious Stories in Transformation: Conflict, Revision and Reception*, Jewish and Christian Perspectives Series 31, Leiden and Boston, MA: Brill, pp. 107–25.

Melin, Pia (ed.), 2009, *Albertus Pictor: Målare av sin tid*. Volume 1: Bilder i urval samt studier och analyser. Stockholm: Kungl. Vitterhets historie och antikvitets akademien.

Schmidt, Gary D., 1995, *The Iconography of the Mouth of Hell: Eighth-Century Britain to the Fifteenth Century*, Selinsgrove, PA: Susquehanna University Press / London: Associated University Presses.

Tiemeyer, Lena-Sofia, 2005, 'Prophecy as a Way of Cancelling Prophecy: The Strategic Uses of Foreknowledge', *Zeitschrift für die alttestamentliche Wissenschaft* 117/3, pp. 329–50.

Tiemeyer, Lena-Sofia, 2016, 'A New Look at the Biological Sex/Grammatical Gender of Jonah's Fish', *Vetus Testamentum* 67/2, pp. 307–23.

Tiemeyer, Lena-Sofia, 2017, '"Peace for our Time": Reading Jonah in Dialogue with Abravanel in the Book of the Twelve', *Journal of Hebrew Scriptures* 17, Article 6, DOI: 10.5508/jhs.2017.v17.a6.

Tiemeyer, Lena-Sofia, 2019, 'The Book of Jonah in Jewish–Christian Debate', *Taiwan Baptist Christian Seminary Journal* 17, pp. 9–39.

Tiemeyer, Lena-Sofia, 2021, *Jonah Through the Centuries*, Wiley Blackwell Bible Commentaries, London: Wiley.

Urbach, Ephraim, 1949, 'The Repentance of the People of Nineveh and the Jewish–Christian Dispute', *Tarbiẓ* 29, pp. 118–22 (Hebrew).

# 7

## Would Vishnu Save Jonah's Poor Fishie? A Transtextual Query

### JIONE HAVEA

## Introduction

God appointed a 'slender plant' (*qiqayon*)[1] to provide relief over an angry Jonah – he was so angry that he wanted to die[2] – after he exited from Nineveh (Jonah 4.6). The next day, God appointed a worm to attack the plant – so severely, that the plant withered (4.7) and perished (4.10). The (mythologized) plant sprouted one night, and it was gone the next day. Thanks to God, the lifetime of the plant was as slender as its body. The plant had no chance to recover in the harsh conditions of the (narrativized) outback.

The Qur'an 'crosses into' the Hebrew Bible narrative and relocates the slender plant from the outback to the seashore (Surah 37.145–146). As in the Hebrew narrative, in the Qur'an Jonah was swallowed by a fish. In the Qur'an, Jonah (Yunus) would have remained in the belly of the fish till the Day of Resurrection if he had not been blameworthy and devoted to Allah (37.142–144). For his past merits (instead of being the result of a prayer that he offered from the belly of the fish, in the Hebrew Bible), Allah threw Jonah on to the shore. But this was not the sandy kind of shore that i am familiar with in the coral islands of Pasifika (for Pacific, Oceania). Rather, it was a 'wide bare tract of land' (37.145) familiar to the people of the desert.

I imagine that Jonah would have landed with a thud, and he would have felt pain and may have even been injured from his landing, in addition to the effects of having been whirled in the filthy pool in the belly of the big fish. Jonah was whirled, and mangled, but he was not washed clean.

Seeing that Jonah was ill, Allah caused a gourd plant (*yaqteen*: a creeper) to grow over him (37.146). The plant would have given Jonah shade and food, and importantly – place, time and opportunity to catch his breath, and to heal and recover. The Qur'an thus relocates the plant (to the seashore) and repurposes it (for healing). Moreover, the Qur'an 'heals' the Hebrew narrative: there is no worm to attack the plant in the Qur'an, and so the plant did not have to wither and die. Put another way, the Qur'an saves the plant from the sultry wind and baking sun of the Hebrew Bible.

The Qur'an 'crosses into' the Hebrew Bible, as well as 'crosses out' some of the details in the Hebrew Bible narrative. For example, the Qur'an does not name or describe the spatial size (three days' walk, in the Hebrew Bible) of the nation ('city', in the Hebrew Bible) into which Jonah went. Rather, the Qur'an sizes the nation according to the number of people – 'a hundred thousand people or more'. The Hebrew Bible sees land-space, but the Qur'an sees nation-people. Also, the Qur'an crosses out any reference to Jonah having preached in/to the unnamed nation.[3] The Hebrew Bible gives Jonah a message of five Hebrew words to deliver, but the Qur'an gives Jonah no message or words. The silencing of Jonah in the Qur'an puts the people in better light: they do not need to be preached at/ against. Without Jonah saying anything, the people believed, and Allah let them enjoy life for a while (37.147–148).[4]

Between the Qur'an and the Hebrew Bible, *crossing into* and *crossing out* – a double crossing of sort – are common, expected and somewhat accepted. Such double crossings are part and parcel of cross-scriptural events.

## Transtextual reading

I coined 'transtextuality' for the *crossing into* and *crossing out* described above (Havea 2003),[5] which are both scriptural (in texts) and hermeneutical (in readings). First, transtextuality is part and parcel of the scriptures in the faith communities to which i belong. Crossing into and crossing out are evident in both the Hebrew (e.g. different versions in Judges and Joshua on the complete, partial, or failed invasion of Canaan) and the Christian (such as Matthew's appropriation of Mark and other sources) scriptures.[6] Second, transtextuality is what we, readers of scriptures, do. We cross into, between, across and over scriptures, and the readings that we offer – including our so-called faithful readings – also cross out some of the details in the scriptural texts that we read.[7]

My conceiving of transtextuality was influenced by my mentors and conversation partners, who in the late 1980s and early 1990s encouraged literary, narrative and intertextual reading … pushing back at, and being transgressive upon, formalist practices and mindsets.[8] And i received warm encouragements among readers who look like me, and who continue to influence my reading even nowadays.[9] These transgressive readers and their comrades encouraged interdisciplinary and cross-cultural reading, and i draw special attention to Itumeleng Mosala because in his 1989 work *Biblical Hermeneutics and Black Theology in South Africa*, he crossed the divides between biblical studies, theology, politics and economics – divides that many in the Euro-American academic circles taught me to enforce. In other words, Mosala and others do what i call transtextual reading, but to their own beats and timings.

In my musings around the slender plant above, i offer a snapshot of what a transtextual reading could look like. That snapshot is easy to draw because both scriptural texts address the same characters, Jonah and the slender plant, and because my drive was not to determine which text was literarily original or authentic (read: the primary concern of dominant biblical criticisms).[10] On the other hand, my transtextual reading noted where the Qur'an crosses into as well as crosses out the Hebrew

Bible narrative, and i left room for readers to draw their own transtextual conclusions.

Going further than the snapshot offered above, i add here that transtextual reading is not limited to written or scripted texts. One may even argue that a reading is not transtextual enough until one also reads non-scripted texts (or non-traditional scriptures). One may accordingly also transtextually engage (some) oral, drawn, or performed text(s).

## Queer reading

The 'crossing out' feature of transtextual reading places it under the shadows of queer reading. In return, the openness to sensual and sexual exploration in queer reading could be lubrication for the wheels of transtextuality.[11] I am appealing here to Stephen D. Moore's understanding of 'queer' as:

> a supple cipher both for what *stands over against* the normal and the natural to oppose, and thereby define, them, and what *inheres within* the normal and the natural to subvert, and indeed pervert, them – this opposition and subversion privileging, but by no means being confined to, the mercurial sphere of the sexual. (Moore 2001, p. 18, emphasis original; see also Althaus-Reid and Isherwood 2007; Stone 2001)

My transtextual reading of the slender plant above does not touch the 'mercurial sphere of the sexual' or engage with a non-scripted text. But there is opportunity for queering through the work 'Yunus [Jonah] and the Whale' (*c*.1314 CE) by Rashid al-Din, which also comes from the Qur'an's Arab world.[12]

The Qur'an trans-ported the slender plant from the desert to the beach, to become a slender beach plant – and in the artwork by Rashid al-Din (Figure 1), Yunus (Jonah) is naked, sitting under a slender beach plant with wide leaves, opening flowers, hooking vines and two big fruits. Yunus covers himself with the leaves and touches one of the fruits with his left hand. Touching the fruit suggests that he wants to eat it, which anyone who

Figure 1: Rashid al-Din, 'Yunus and the Whale' (*c.*1314 CE).
Copyright The University of Edinburgh. Free use.

has been at sea would understand. Or did he just want to feel the round bottom of the fruit, and to pull it close enough so that he could inhale its gourd-y-ness? The artwork by Rashid al-Din is queer, teasing readers with its opening flowers and big, round, hanging fruits. The teases are in the reading, and i do not pretend that they were intended by the artist or original to the text; in light of the distinction made above, the teases are hermeneutical rather than scriptural.

My transtextual reading engages another textual form – artwork (which is scriptural in oral cultures). The queer elements in the transtextual reading above arise from the interweaving of the Hebrew and Qur'anic texts with the artwork, also from the Arab world. In the shadows of queer reading, the above reading teases readers into the spheres of the sensual and sexual. Put differently, the teases tempt readers to get physical.

## Cross-scriptural reading

Transtextual reading is effective for cross-scriptural reading. Because of the shared narratives and traditions between the so-called Abrahamic faiths, it is easy to make a case for reading their scriptures transtextually. But there are non-Abrahamic scriptures, some of which (e.g. Mesopotamian and Hindu Vedas) are more ancient, and one of the challenges for cross-scriptural readers in Abrahamic circles is to engage non-Abrahamic scriptures.

There is space for this query in traditional – literary and historical – biblical criticisms. The similarities between the flood story in Genesis and the Gilgamesh epic is evidence that the Hebrew scriptures crossed into Mesopotamian scriptures. And the imaginary Q document of synoptic Gospels scholars is evidence that Matthew and Luke crossed into other scriptures outside of Mark. The above examples are based on one scripture crossing into another scripture. But could one also do cross-scriptural reading of scriptures that do not *cross into* each other's paths? What stops readers from cross-reading scriptures that are strangers to each other?[13]

I push my transtextual reading further in the following section by engaging scriptural texts that neither the Hebrew nor the Qur'anic narratives of Jonah cross into. Put directly, these scriptures do not cross into (the paths of) each other but juxtaposing them prompts a transtextual reading. The ploy for undertaking such a reading stands squarely on the reader; it is hermeneutical rather than scriptural. The transtextual exercise is therefore, and also, an outing of the power of readers and the politics of reading.

In the following transtextual cross-scriptural reading, i follow the lead of Archie Chi Chung Lee (1993; 2002)[14] of Hong Kong and i also appeal to the simple fact that i live alongside Muslims and Hindus. I don't read Jonah in Palestine, Assyria or Babylon, but in a world peopled by Muslims and Hindus, with their customs, clothes, scents, foods, scriptures etcetera. And so i shift from the slender plant to the 'poor fishie'.

## Poor fishie

My Earth Bible reading looks for healing on behalf of Jonah, and i foreground one of the Pasifika native insights: that after the fish vomited, it would have died. In that work, i did not consider another option for the big fish until i was reminded of our daughter's concern on her first fishing trip – at four years old, she was adamant that the 'poor fishie' that she caught did not have to die – and her mother telling me that one of Vishnu's avatars was a fish. Hence the new twists in this reflection, beginning with our daughter's question: does the poor fishie have to die? Raising this question in the context of the Qur'an's repositioning of the slender plant invites a second question: did the slender desert plant of the Hebrew scriptures have to die? Both questions transgress the control of the biblical and Qur'anic texts, and they bring me to the Hindu Vedas.

### Vishnu

When there are problems, the Gods incarnate in some avatar to re-establish order. This kind of incarnational theology is also affirmed in the *Bhagavad Gita* – which consists of conversations between Prince Arjuna with Krishna, his charioteer and guru: 'Whenever there is a decline in righteousness and an increase in unrighteousness, O Arjun, at that time I manifest Myself on earth' (4.7). When dharma (duty, law, righteousness) is observed, there is righteousness; but when dharma is not observed, there is unrighteousness – the latter is the state of adharma (or unrighteousness). To re-establish dharma, the Gods incarnate in an avatar(s) and come to re-establish order/ dharma. For this reason, Lord Vishnu – one of the supreme deities of Hinduism, who is venerated as Mukunda (the giver of moksha) – has ten avatars/incarnations (*Dashavatara*), the first two of whom are creatures of the sea.

There are many traditions in the Hindu world, and the eighth and ninth avatars differ from tradition to tradition, and from place to place, but the other eight remain the same. Briefly, the ten avatars of Vishnu are:

1  Matsya: a big fish that came to save the creation from the great flood;
2  Kurma: a giant tortoise that carried the mountain Madrachala;
3  Varaha: a wild boar, which came to bring the earth back when Hiranyaksha (the adversary) pulled it down to the bottom of the sea;
4  Narasimha: who was half human and half lion;
5  Vamana: who was very short (dwarf-like);
6  Parashurama: warrior avatar who carried an axe;
7  Rama: the prince who went to Lanka to rescue Sita;
8  Krishna, a popular hero in many legends – in some traditions this avatar is Balarama, the older brother of Krishna;
9  Buddha, or sometimes Krishna, Vithoba (Goa, Maharastra), Jagannath (Odisha);
10  Kalki: who comes on a white horse at the end, when adharma prevails, and thus marks the beginning of another cycle of existence.

The first three avatars relate to the ocean, and for this trans-textual reading I explore how the first two avatars – which are water creatures – might help with the questions for the poor fishie and the slender plant.

## Matsya

Matsya is a big fish that came to save the creation from the great flood. The legend starts with Manu, the progenitor of the human race, one day finding a little fish in his hands as he performs his water-offering. The little fish asks (read: dares) Manu if he was wealthy enough to provide home and hospitality for … a little fish. Manu agrees and shows off his wealth, by providing an elaborate home for the little fish.

But the fish keeps growing and growing, and threatens to be larger than Manu's wealth. So Manu releases the fish to the sea, and in the process Manu learns that the fish was Vishnu! Vishnu tells Manu that the world will be destroyed by fires and floods, and instructs Manu to gather all the creatures of the world into a boat that has been built by the gods. Noah was not the only mythological human that had access to a big boat.

When the deluge came, Vishnu appears as a great big fish with a horn – that avatar is named Matsya. Manu ties the boat to Matsya, and the big fish takes the boat and its cargo to safety. At one level, the story of Matsya is about a big fish providing rescue, rather than destruction and death as in the story of Jonah's big fish.

At another level, the story of Matsya is about a fish tricking the first human person. At this transgressive level, i realize that i have been tricked by Jonah's fish. I expected it to die but birth and death are not properties of legends, myths and avatars. Avatars are not born, and they do not die. They manifest for a purpose, then they disappear. In that connection, the big fish that saved Jonah did not have to die.

In the presence of Vishnu, the poor fishie did not have to die. Reincarnation is not about beginning or end but about recovering dharma and transforming adharma. At this cross-scriptural juncture, i stand corrected!

## Kurma

Kurma is a giant tortoise whose legend relates to the churning of the ocean to extract the nectar of immortality – Amrita. Vishnu instructed the divine beings (devas) and demigods (asuras) to churn the ocean in order to release Amrita – the nectar of immortal life. This milk will give humans immortality.

For a churning pole, the devas and asuras used the mountain Madrachala; and they used the serpent Vasuki for their churning-string. To assist the churning process, Vishnu came as a giant tortoise to carry the mountain, and the devas and asuras would pull the serpent like they were in a rope-pulling game. When the Amrita was released the devas and asuras fought over it, and the story turned bad, but my focus here is on Kurma – a giant turtle that lifted a mountain so that the devas and asuras could churn the ocean.

Kurma's role was to facilitate the task of churning the sea. The Qur'anic slender beach plant served a similar function – to facilitate Jonah's recovery by giving him shade and food so that he may rest, heal and recover, before he goes in to churn Nineveh up. The slender plant did not die in the Qur'an, but lives on with a critical question upon the biblical narrative: did the poor slender desert plant in the Hebrew narrative have to die?

In the presence of Vishnu, the poor plant did not have to die. Herewith is a critique of the biblical narrative's inclination to deliver death and destruction, which are evidence of adharma and unrighteousness in the Vedas.

## Yunus

To reiterate, the Qur'an shifts the slender plant from providing relief to the angry Jonah looking over Nineveh to the beach, where it provides relief for a fishy traveller who needs care after being vomited on to shore.[15] The Qur'an uproots the Hebrew Bible plant and replants it at the beach – my kind of place. The Qur'an encourages me to queer the narrative.

If i was a die-hard historical and literary critic, i would reject the Qur'anic version. But in a transtextual reading, the Qur'an shows that the Masoretic text does not control the narrative. This is an example of one scripture crossing into and transgressing another scripture, and accordingly keeps the text open for readers with transgressive and queering eyes.

## Talanoa[16]

In this cross-scriptural reading the Qur'an provides transtextual space for reimaging the biblical narrative, and the Vedas (through two of Vishnu's avatars) invites reimagining the biblical and Qur'anic narratives. In closing, i confess to the obvious – the cross-scriptural insights proposed here are products of reading. Readers do not control the texts, but we can churn them. And Jonah is a great narrative for this kind of reading. Jonah is mythological and cynical, and i find healing in reading it accordingly. I confess my readings, my crossings, my transgressions; and i celebrate that i too do not control the texts.

In closing, i return to Rashid al-Din's image of the Qur'an's slender beach plant: my transtextual reading sees the text flowering, and dares to touch the fruits of the text, and i leave them opening and hanging for other readers to do what they like to do with such inviting flowers and titillating fruits.

## Notes

1 See Steed Vernyl Davidson's essay in this collection.

2 Jonah was angry because the whole of Nineveh – including animals – had repented, and consequently God spared them and their city.

3 In this Surah, which places Jonah in the same light as other messengers like Moses and Elijah, 'preaching' is not a key characteristic of being a messenger.

4 I offer another reading of the Qur'anic (sub-)version in Havea 2020.

5 I used 'trans' to convey the double-crossing motions of *crossing* (between texts, between subjects, between ideas, between authorities, between locations etc.) and *transgressing* (of textual, methodological and ideological positions) – crossing of limits, and transgressing of ideologies and positionalities. The main controversies in my 2003 invitation were two: (1) *crossing*: i argue that unrelated texts that lie together under the same covers of the bible may be read across from one text to, and around, the other texts – that is, texts do not have to be related, or relatable, for one to read them transtextually; and (2) *transgressing*: i insist that the meanings of biblical texts are outside the control of texts, of textuality and of readers. Thinking that meanings are contained within and by texts, and thinking that one can control textual meanings, are i-llusions because texts and meanings are e-lusive. See also Aichele 2001.

6 In my experience, the gatekeepers of traditional ways of biblical criticism are more anxious with intra- and inter-scriptural crossing into (or between) and crossing out than the sacred texts are. Borrowing, appropriating, subverting and transgressing take place in, and at the crossing of, scriptures.

7 *Elusions of Control* is also a call for readers to own our i-llusions and the limits of our reading practices. Put another way, readers should

not be too anxious about needing to use the correct method, to draw the correct textual relations, or to find the correct meanings. My version of transtextual reading (in the late 1990s) affirms that reading is a crossing and transgressive exercise – transgressive upon the text, transgressive upon biblical traditions, transgressive upon the institutions of biblical criticism, etcetera, etcetera.

8 I am indebted to my mentors and their works: Fewell 1992; Gunn and Fewell 1993; Jobling 1986.

9 I humbly acknowledge the following elders and their works: Miranda 1974; Mosala 1989; Sugirtharajah 1991; Felder 1991; Segovia and Tolbert 1995; Foskett and Kuan 2006.

10 In the case of the Jonah narrative, with its fantastic events in the sea and on land, historical credibility is difficult to establish.

11 Althaus-Reid 2005, p. 11: 'I have said elsewhere that theology is a sexual act, and therefore to reflect on the theologian, her vocation, role and risks means to take seriously the changing geographies of Christian kneelings, and confessionary movements, and how they relate to positions of affection in Christian theology. In this way, queering who the theologian is, and what is her role and vocation is a reflection on locations, closely linked to the locale's events and spaces made of our concrete and sensual actions.'

12 Rashid al-Din, 'Yunus (Jonah) and the Whale', available at https://collections.ed.ac.uk/calendars/record/19410 (accessed 13.08.2022).

13 These questions expect that readers could manage the obsessions and illusions of traditional biblical criticisms.

14 On the flood narrative, see Lee 2010.

15 The Qur'an gives the slender beach tree a different function. I explain the wisdom of this shift in my Earth Bible commentary (2020, pp. 66–7). Yunus would have been worn out from being mangled in the belly of the fish, and it makes good sense that there is a plant at the beach for him to rest under and recover, before he goes into the city. Hence the relocation of the slender plant to the beach invites caring for Yunus.

16 The term 'talanoa' (in many but not all of the Pasifika languages) refers to three events: story, telling, conversation. Here, it invites rereading the stories (Jonah, plant, fish), retelling the stories, and ongoing conversations around the stories and the retelling. In the spirit of transtextuality, i challenge readers not to trap the stories, retellings and conversations.

# References

Aichele, George, 2001, *The Control of Biblical Meaning: Canon as Semiotic Mechanism*, Harrisburg, PA: Trinity International.

Althaus-Reid, Marcella, 2005, *The Queer God*, London and New York: Routledge.

Althaus-Reid, Marcella and Lisa Isherwood, 2007, 'Thinking Theology and Queer Theory', *Feminist Theology* 15/3, pp. 302–14.

Felder, Cain Hope (ed.), 1991, *Stony the Road We Trod: African American Biblical Interpretation*, Minneapolis, MN: Fortress Press.

Fewell, Danna Nolan (ed.), 1992, *Reading Between Texts: Intertextuality and the Hebrew Bible*, Louisville, KY: Westminster John Knox Press.

Foskett, Mary F. and Jeffrey Kah-Jin Kuan (eds), 2006, *Ways of Being, Ways of Reading*, St Louis, MO: Chalice.

Gunn, David M. and Danna Nolan Fewell, 1993, *Narrative in the Hebrew Bible*, Oxford: Oxford University Press.

Havea, Jione, 2003, *Elusions of Control: Biblical Law on the Words of Women*, Atlanta, GA: SBL.

Havea, Jione, 2020, *Jonah: Earth Bible Commentary*, New York: Bloomsbury.

Jobling, David, 1986, *The Sense of Biblical Narrative: Structural Analyses in the Hebrew Bible*, Sheffield: JSOT.

Lee, Archie Chi Chung, 1993, 'Biblical Interpretation in Asian Perspective', *Asia Journal of Theology* 7/1, pp. 35–9.

Lee, Archie Chi Chung, 2002, 'Cross-textual Interpretation and its Implications for Biblical Studies' in Fernando F. Segovia and Mary Ann Tolbert (eds), *Teaching the Bible: Discourses and Politics of Biblical Pedagogy*, Maryknoll, NY: Orbis Books, pp. 247–54.

Lee, Archie Chi Chung, 2010, 'When the Flood Narrative of Genesis meets its Counterpart in China: Reception and Challenge in Cross-Textual Reading' in Athalya Brenner, Archie Lee and Gale Yee (eds), *Genesis: Text @ Contexts*, Minneapolis, MN: Fortress Press, pp. 81–97.

Miranda, José, 1974, *Marx and the Bible: A Critique of the Philosophy of Oppression*, Maryknoll, NY: Orbis Books.

Moore, Stephen D., 2001, *God's Beauty Parlor and other Queer Spaces in and around the Bible*, Stanford, CA: Stanford University Press.

Mosala, Itumeleng J., 1989, *Biblical Hermeneutics and Black Theology in South Africa*, Grand Rapids, MI: Eerdmans.

Segovia, Fernando and Mary Ann Tolbert (eds), 1995, *Reading from This Place*, Minneapolis, MN: Fortress Press.

Stone, Ken, 2001, 'Homosexuality and the Bible or Queer Reading? A Response to Martti Nissinen', *Theology & Sexuality* 14, pp. 107–18.

Sugirtharajah, R. S. (ed.), 1991, *Voices from the Margin: Interpreting the Bible in the Third World*, Maryknoll, NY: Orbis Books.

# PART 2

# Becoming Queer Prophets

# 8

# Queering the Prophetic Process: From Jonah to the Ujamaa Centre's CBS on Galatians

GERALD WEST, CHARLENE VAN DER
WALT, SITHEMBISO ZWANE, CRYSTAL
HALL, SIZWESAMAJOBE (SIZWE) SITHOLE
AND TRACEY SIBISI

## Introduction

Local shack dwellers in Amawoti, KwaZulu-Natal, South Africa, commented that 'Jesus is tricky, and God is undemocratic' when reading Matthew's version of the 'kin-dom of God' (Philpott 1993). What the book of Jonah makes clear is that the prophet, like others of this co-opted class, is undemocratic too. The prophetic 'I' of Jonah matches the Godly 'I' of Yahweh (Jonah 1.1–2), though perhaps the regular use of Elohim (Gods) and the presence of multiple gods (Elohim) (1.5–9) disrupts any stable understanding of 'God/god'. More worrying is the prophetic 'I', which is sustained and stable. Even when there are prospects of prophetic caucusing, first with 'the sailors' (1.8–9), and later with 'the men [people] of Nineveh' (3.5), Jonah remains resolutely individualistic. Both the sailors and 'the least' people of Nineveh (3.5) (and their cattle (3.7; 4.11)) offer Jonah, if he is truly interested in justice, an opportunity to do theology from below, from the margins, even the margins of empire. Yet Jonah refuses these opportunities and remains committed to his own individual understanding of a singular God and his own personal understanding of justice.

At this point in our essay we turn from Jonah, unable to find in him resources for an inclusive and collaborative liberatory praxis. However, Jonah remains on the margins of our reflections, as a reminder of his lack of prophetic participatory process, a process we will elaborate as part of our own Ujamaa Centre prophetic praxis. Jonah's marginal presence in the genre that his book represents prompts us to turn to the work of our colleague Itumeleng Mosala on the prophet Micah, drawing on similar work by Robert Coote (Coote 1981). Mosala insists that the prophetic voice is always co-opted, 'eloquent in its silence on the ideological struggle waged by the oppressed and exploited class of monarchical Israel', which the prophet purports to represent (Mosala 1989, p. 120). 'Micah itself,' says Mosala, 'as is true of most of the Bible, offers no certain starting point for a theology of liberation' (Mosala 1989, p. 121).

However, Mosala does offer a way into working with a Bible that is 'a ruling-class document', for 'enough contradictions within Micah [as in any biblical book] enable eyes hermeneutically trained in the struggle for liberation today to observe the kindred struggles of the expressed and exploited of the biblical communities in the very absence of those struggles in the text' (Mosala 1989, p. 121). A hermeneutic of queer appropriation requires, therefore, both an LGBTIQA+ predominant presence and an analysis of textual production (for a fuller analysis see West 2020a), recognizing from the outset that biblical texts are intrinsically sites of contestation and that there must be collaboration with queer eyes in order to observe kindred struggles in a text such as Galatians. Here too Jonah interrupts our reflections, as we wonder, with the essays in the first part of this volume, how unlikely texts like Galatians and Jonah might be used for queer purposes.

A turn to contemporary sites of contestation and struggle is central to the praxis of the Ujamaa Centre for Community Development and Research (Ujamaa Centre). Since our inception in 1989, we have always begun with contemporary reality as it is represented by organized formations of the poor and marginalized. While our formative work took shape within the struggle against apartheid racial capitalism, other systems of oppression have been engaged. This essay reflects on a particular project within our work within the heteropatriarchal system.

We provide an analysis of how our work with Pietermaritzburg Gay and Lesbian Network, now the Uthingo Network, began in 2013, and of how we work extensively with Genesis 19 and 18 (in that order) (West, Zwane and Van der Walt 2021). In that article, we briefly mention a three-stage training process funded by the Arcus Foundation in which we work with pairings of local LGBTIQA+ activists and church leaders from five African countries (South Africa, Kenya, Tanzania, Mozambique and the Democratic Republic of Congo). Here we analyse this process in more detail, focusing on how we use a Pauline biblical text, Galatians, as a site of struggle for discerning with regional LGBTIQA+ groups a queer presence within its textual absence.

## Queer collaboration

The Ujamaa Centre worked with the Arcus Foundation (together with the Chicago Consultation) in three Africa-wide and inter-religious workshops focused on sexuality in general and queer sexuality in particular (Chicago Consultation 2015; Gunda and Naughton 2017, pp. viii–x). Following the trajectory of these workshops, which brought religious leaders (from the church and mosque) and queer people of faith (both Christian and Muslim) together for collaborative social analysis, Bible study, testimony and reflection, the Ujamaa Centre proposed a more focused project within Southern and Eastern Africa. Our Arcus Foundation proposal begins as follows:

> The Ujamaa Centre's vision is: 'Building a society in which religion enables a just and inclusive life for all'. Our commitment is to work from the lived realities and epistemological perspective of the excluded and marginalized, specifically LGBTQ Africans.

From this perspective it is clear that the major religions of our Southern and Eastern African region, Christianity and Islam, align themselves with indigenous forms of religio-cultural patriarchy, forming a cultural-religious hybrid that condemns and excludes LGBTQ African Christians and Muslims.[1]

This proposal centred around collaborative participation, bringing together paired participation, including two LGBTIQA+ activists and two affirming religious leaders, from each of three Southern and Eastern African sites, South Africa, Kenya and Tanzania. In addition, there was paired participation, but with only one activist and one church leader, from both Mozambique and the Democratic Republic of the Congo (DRC). This regional spread allowed us to do Contextual Bible Study (CBS) work within each of four lingua francas, English, Portuguese, French and KiSwahili, and through these languages to access a host of local indigenous African languages.

We planned for three workshops, beginning with South Africa, then Kenya, then Tanzania. In each case we worked closely with local LGBTIQA+ organizations and theological education institutions in arranging and facilitating the workshops. Our workshops were structured so that the core group of paired participants could work intensively together, forging relationships and resources from workshop to workshop. Each workshop also offered space and time to participants from the locality, enabling local activists, church leaders and theological students to join the core participants. The project was conceived as being increasingly inclusive of the religious diversity in these five contexts. However, the first phase, reflected on here, focused on African Christianity. CBS was the focal resource for these inclusive opportunities, resulting in small-group work which included both the core group and the local participants.

Each workshop followed the same format: See–Judge–Act. This cyclical movement is fundamental to Ujamaa Centre CBS praxis (West, Zwane and Van der Walt 2021, pp. 5–6). Each workshop began with 'Seeing' the lived realities of LGBTIQA+ in each of the five contexts. Each successive workshop deepened the analysis of the dominant heteropatriarchal systems in each of these African post colonies, recognizing and analysing both the indigenous and colonial contributions to this toxic system. Socio-sexual analysis then led into the Judge phase of each workshop, where we used CBS to construct a heterotopic space (West 2015), an invented space (Zwane 2020), a safe and sacred space within which to discern (Judge) redemptive prophetic voices within the biblical text. Our workshops always concluded with allocating substantive time to 'Acting', planning actions that we would do between workshops and report on in the subsequent workshop. Among the actions we planned was the translation of the CBS we had used together into other languages for use within local community groups in each of our five contexts.

The Covid-19 pandemic, which has exacerbated violence against the LGBTIQA+ community (Reid and Ritholtz 2020; Sánchez et al. 2020; Pae 2021; Oginni, Okanlawon and Ogunbajo 2021), meant that the final workshop in the series, in Tanzania, had to be postponed. This essay, therefore, concentrates on a CBS that was integral to the South African workshop (April 2019) and the Kenyan workshop (November 2019).

## From Genesis to Galatians

As indicated, one CBS we used, with regular revisions, was on Genesis 19—18 (West, Zwane and Van der Walt 2021, pp. 11–12), given the reality of how this text is being used against the LGBTIQA+ community. The dominant heteropatriarchal reception of particular biblical texts and the effects of such receptions on the LGBTIQA+ community has guided which biblical texts the Ujamaa Centre works with. In various collaborative workshops in the KwaZulu-Natal region of South Africa with the Uthingo Network (Rainbow Network). Colleagues from the Uthingo Network asked us to work on Genesis 19; they also asked us to work on Pauline texts.

Instead of engaging directly with homophobic readings of well-worn Pauline texts, we suggested to our Uthingo Network colleagues that we work with a potentially inclusive Pauline text, Galatians 3.28: 'There is neither Jew nor Greek, there is neither slave nor free, there is neither male nor female; for you are all one in Christ Jesus.' There was considerable excitement at this suggestion, and so the process began of constructing a viable CBS on this text.

The Ujamaa Centre does not do proof-text CBS, so it was important that we engage fully with the socio-historical and literary-narrative detail of this text. One of the problems we encountered in constructing CBS resources on Pauline texts is their genre. The letter genre of the Bible is a difficult genre for ordinary readers of the Bible, given their didactic orientation. The Pauline letter constructs a theological didactic argument which is often difficult to follow, devoid as it is of a narrative frame. More than 30 years of work with CBS demonstrate the egalitarian opportunities of narrative text. Ordinary readers, given sufficient time (which is why CBS is a protracted process), have no difficultly in discerning narrative detail, whether of character, plot, spatial and temporal setting and so on. (For a good example of this process see West and Zwane 2020.) Our experience with Pauline letters made it clear that we had to find a way of providing the theological argument with a narrative frame in order to assure an egalitarian reading process.

We turned to Crystal Hall, who had become an Ujamaa Centre associate, for assistance. At the time (2014), she was doing PhD work at Union Theological Seminary on Paul, with a focus on Galatians, and was familiar with and a practitioner of CBS type work in her activist work with the United Workers, a human rights organization in Baltimore, USA. She offered us the following resources with which to begin crafting a CBS on Galatians.

In resisting the 'I' of Paul, it is important to acknowledge the tremendous damage inflicted on the queer community in the name of Paul, especially the 'clobber passage' of Romans 1.26–27.[2] 'Paul' is a deeply ambiguous figure who on the one hand articulates a saving word of justice and grace, and on the other condemns and excludes, especially women, the enslaved, children and the queer community.

In both the reception history, and the distinctions biblical scholars make among the authentic, disputed and pastoral letters,[3] there is a polyphony of 'Pauls'. To add to this complexity, modern scholars lay aside the predominant portrait of Paul as a Roman citizen with substantial privileges and a Jew who 'converted' to Christianity, although this concept still predominates in the pews and popular understanding.[4] Biblical scholars continue to hotly contest the question of who Paul is, and this essay limits itself to the Paul of Galatians, while acknowledging this larger context.

In the same way this essay resists the 'I' of Paul, it also acknowledges that there is not yet a stable understanding of what is meant by 'Church', nor is there anything recognizable as 'Christianity' before the second century CE at the earliest. Recent scholarship suggests that the early Church was really more accurately early 'Jesus movements' in the plural, significantly more heterodox and diverse in belief, texts and practices than reconstructions of a singular 'early Christianity' that make easy distinctions between orthodoxy and heresy would suggest (Vearncombe et al. 2021).

These caveats and context make the turn towards Galatians potentially more fruitful. As part of the authentic letters, the 'Paul' of Galatians is a Greek-speaking, Jewish Jesus follower in a pastoral relationship with the communities to whom he writes letters throughout the Mediterranean basin in the decades of the 50s and early 60s CE. The church is still overwhelmingly rooted in Judaism and wrestling with how to include people of other 'nations' ('Gentiles') within the body of Christ.[5] Paul works out this inclusion by writing that both Jews and all other nations (ethnic-cultural-economic-political-religious geographical groups) have a common faith ancestor in Abraham (Gal. 3.15–24). Through this inclusion in the same covenant promise, all nations are equally brought into right and just relationship with God and the 'Other' who is one's neighbour. Within in the context of CBS, it is especially important to communicate this context in narrative form.

As we describe above, one of the most egalitarian textual forms in CBS is narrative.[6] Regardless of education or specialized training, in the context of CBS a reader/listener can identify literary devices such as characters, setting and plot. Perhaps because of this accessibility, there is a tendency to use narrative texts in CBS curricula. For example, with the notable exceptions of passages from lament poetry in Job and the Psalms, the texts used in the Contextual Bible Study Manual produced by the Ujamaa Centre are drawn from Old Testament and Gospel narratives (Ujamaa Centre 2015; for some attempts at using Paul see Ujamaa Centre 2011). There are no texts from the Pauline corpus. This tendency to create accessibility through use of narrative texts raises the question of whether non-narrative texts can be equally accessible.

Pauline letters are decidedly non-narrative. Many use complex rhetorical strategies. It would be easy to assume CBS workshop participants would be more likely to connect their own experiences, often told in narrative form, to stories about Jesus than to the techniques Paul uses to construct his arguments. There are, however, compelling reasons to attempt making Pauline texts more approachable, such as bridging the gap between their socio-historical location and theological content with contemporary concerns. Based on the difficulties presented by the epistolary genre as largely non-narrative, one approach for engaging these texts is to 'supply' narratives implicit within the Pauline text from three sources, 'behind the text', 'on the text' and 'in front of the text' (West 1991).

One potential source of narrative is the back-story 'behind the text' – the text's socio-historical and literary contexts. Narrative elements such as setting and plot are typically not present within a Pauline passage excised from its context, but this back-story can be reconstructed in the context of a CBS workshop. The reconstruction might engage some of the following questions: What kind of relationship did Paul have with the church at Galatia? What prompted Paul to write this letter? Where is Galatia located and why might that matter? Reconstructing this back-story suggests both text and readers' context can supply narrative from 'behind the text'.

Another potential source of narrative is implicit within the logic of the Pauline text itself when read in its literary context. This logic is narrativized through a focus 'on the text'.[7] One way of narrativizing the text is Brigitte Kahl's application of semiotic theory to key passages in authentic Paul. Working with Greimas' semiotic theory, Kahl explains that 'The semiotic square represents the meaning or semantic inventory of a text (in the widest sense) through oppositional and complementary relationships between the terms or concepts present in it ... [and] thus provides a basic structure of signification' (Kahl 2010, p. 18). Also known colloquially as 'battle squares' or 'combat squares', these semiotic squares illustrate and 'narrativize' the tensions and conflicts within the structure of the text, for example, between 'good and bad, condemnation and salvation, blessing and curse' in Galatians 1.1–9 (Kahl 2010, p. 247). Each 'movement' and its corresponding semiotic square illustrate an 'event', and the progression through these events develops a kind of narrative arc of the text's internal logic, for example, as a 'battlefield, it seems, unfolds before our eyes in the first nine verses of Paul's Galatian letter' (Kahl 2010, p. 247).

A third potential source of narrative is the stories shared by the participants from their own experience as they connect to the biblical text – namely, the stories 'in front of the text'. As Bob Ekblad observes, 'Paul's letters present a special challenge because, unlike narrative texts, they lack characters, places, and actions that can serve as launches for contextual readings. People's own lives must serve as the primary narrative, which can then be read in the light of Paul's theology' (2005, p. 179).[8] Although not text in the traditional sense, the 'texts' of people's lives are another potential source of narrative 'in front of the text', and are accorded a privileged place in CBS as the 'first text', or in the words of Carlos Mesters, the 'first book' (Mesters 1989, p. 128).

With these three approaches in mind, this CBS 'supplied' Pauline narrative by reconstructing the narrative back-story that informs Galatians 3.28 using the first approach, a combination of literary and socio-historical context. This reconstruction can be described as follows.

When Paul arrived among the Galatians, he was injured or ill in some way. How specifically the text does not say. The text indicates that he is physically vulnerable. The Galatians nursed

Paul back to health (Gal. 4.13–15). During this time among the Galatians Paul preached that both Jews and Gentiles, Jews and all other nations conquered by Rome, are justified, brought into right relationship with the God of Israel. They are brought into right relationship with this God and one another through faith in Jesus the Anointed One (Gal. 2.16).

Through sharing this good news, Paul founds the Jesus communities in Galatia. He gathers people together – not despite of, but because of, their differences – in the name of Jesus the Anointed. Paul then leaves them to continue his calling to preach the gospel to the nations elsewhere.

After Paul leaves, other Jewish Jesus-believing teachers arrive among the churches in Galatia preaching a different gospel, which Paul derides as not even a gospel (Gal. 1.6–7). These other teachers tell the Galatians that to be in right relationship with God they must be circumcised (Gal. 6.12). They must take on this male Jewish marker of identity and sign of the covenant God made with the Jewish people. These teachers tell the Galatians they must become like them in order to belong.

Paul learns what these other teachers are preaching, thinks they are absolutely wrong, and fires off this angry letter to the churches in Galatia to explain why. He argues that 'works of the law' like circumcision and Torah-observant table fellowship do not bring the believer into right relationship with God. Paul rejects how these teachers use circumcision to exclude people who are 'Other' from the church. He rejects the theology that you 'Others' (non-Jewish Jesus-believers) must become like 'Us' (Jewish Jesus-believers) to belong.

It is against this reconstructed narrative backdrop that Paul rejects the hierarchical structures of Greco-Roman society used to marginalize and exclude in Galatians 3.28. He rejects the view that Jews are superior to Greeks, that free people are superior to slaves, and that men are superior to women. He argues, rather, that all are one in Christ, that ethnic, legal and gendered distinctions do not matter.

What Paul offers instead is a counter vision from the margins of Greco-Roman society that through baptism all are one in Christ. He offers this counter 'from below' to the dominant narrative. If these distinctions have no power within the church, there is no need for the outsider 'Other' to become like the insider 'Us' in order to belong. Paul says, on the contrary, come as you are. The only thing needed to be in right relationship with God is faith in Jesus the Anointed.

## Constructing the CBS

With these resources we began our work on a CBS. The invitation from a local Anglican church to Gerald West to do a Lent series (in 2019) focusing on racial and gender inclusion provided an opportunity to use the emerging CBS. While it was hoped that participants would recognize a trajectory from race, class, and gender to sexuality, the first version of the Galatians CBS was not overt about sexuality. Significantly, the force of Paul's theological argument, within the narrative frame of Galatians, did prompt participants towards sexual inclusion, who suggested that the summons to ethnic, class and gender inclusion (3.28) should be extended to include sexual diversity, adding, in the words of one of the participants, the phrase 'there is neither gay nor straight'.

Given the positive reception of this initial CBS, we then revised the CBS to make it more explicit about sexuality, and offered it to the participants in our Arcus Foundation project, in both the first and second workshops. Here is the most recent revised version:[9]

1 Listen to a reading of Galatians 3.27–28. How has this text been understood in your church or community?

2 Now listen to a reading from Galatians 1.6—2.14. Here Paul begins to explain why he adopts a theology of inclusion. What stands out for you as you listen to this text from scripture?

3 Listen to a brief historical input about this letter.
   • While it is not clear precisely what geographical area 'Galatia' refers to, what is clear is that is Paul is writing at a time historically when there was not yet a distinction

between 'synagogue' and 'church'. Paul writes this letter as a Jew, who is trying to work out how to be in relationship with Gentile 'Greeks', who are different from 'Jews'.

- What is of particular relevance to this letter are Torah-related markers of Jewish identity, particularly circumcision and food purity laws. The Galatians are Other in relationship to the Jews because they are not circumcised and they do not observe kosher (the food requirements of the Jewish law).
- This means that, based on these identity markers and an interpretation of Torah (Genesis, Exodus, Leviticus, Numbers, and Deuteronomy) which is exclusive rather than inclusive, Jews and Galatians cannot be part of the same community or eat at the same table.
- Yet, says Paul, God has 'called' him (1.15) to proclaim 'the gospel of Christ' (1.7) rather than the 'different/heretical gospel' (1.6) which the Galatians are in danger of heeding.
- The 'gospel of Christ', according to Paul, is an inclusive gospel, inclusive of the Other, and so genuinely 'good news' for Jew and Gentile, slave and free, male and female. The letter to Galatians is a remarkable testimony to the need to 'do theology' in a changing context, written in the very early days of an emerging 'church'. Indeed, Galatians is one of the earliest of the New Testament writings in our Bibles.

4  In small groups, reread Galatians 1.6—2.14 again, following in your preferred translation, and paying particular attention to the narrative Paul is telling. (Take turns reading, dividing the text as follows: 1.6–12; 1.13–17; 1.18–24; 2.1–10; 2.11–14.)
- Why does Paul tell this story, spanning more than a decade?
- What is the theological shape of the story he tells?
- What is Paul's concern about what is happening to the theology of the Galatians?

5  When Paul goes to Jerusalem for the second time (2.1), he takes Titus with him. Reread Galatians 2.1–10.
- What do we know about Titus?

- Why is the presence of Titus so important to Paul's theological argument?
- How is Titus an example of 'the freedom we have in Christ Jesus' (2.4)? (See also 5.1a.)

6  Later, Paul confronts Cephas in Antioch (2.11). Reread Galatians 2.11–14.
   - What story does Paul tell of Cephas?
   - Why is Paul so angry with Cephas?
   - What do you think Paul means by 'If you, being a Jew, live like the Gentiles and not like the Jews, how is it that you compel the Gentiles to live like Jews?' (2.14)

7  Now read Galatians 3.27–28. This is Paul's summary of his theological argument. Read this scripture in a number of different translations.
   Paul's emphasis in his letter to the Galatians is on the relationship between Jew and Gentile (or Greek), so it is not surprising that he begins by stating: 'There is neither Jew nor Greek'.
   - How would you summarize Paul's theological argument with respect to Jew and Greek?

8  Paul does not stop with Jew/Greek opposition, but goes on to include the two other major hierarchical binaries that typified his time: 'There is neither Jew nor Greek, there is neither Slave nor Free, there is neither Male nor Female' (3.28).
   - How is Paul's careful theological argument with respect to the Jew/Greek opposition relevant to the oppositions Slave/Free and Male/Female?

9  In making his theological argument Paul uses the phrase: 'clothed yourselves with Christ' (3.27).
   - What is significant about his use of a 'clothing' metaphor?

10 What are the prevailing hierarchical binaries/oppositions with respect to sexuality that shape our world?

- What from Paul's theological argument can we take that would enable us (and our churches) to move beyond these sexual binaries/oppositions 'in Christ Jesus'?
- How can you share Paul's theology of inclusion with others in your church or community?

11 Despite the theological differences between James and Cephas and John on the one hand and Paul on the other hand, they agree on one thing: 'They only asked us to remember the poor – the very thing I also was eager to do' (2.10).
  - How does poverty intersect with gender and sexuality in our contexts?

This CBS is unusual in that it includes fairly extensive socio-historical input and framing (3). In earlier versions of the CBS we began with the input, then we shifted it after the initial reading, and in the most recent revision we have moved it after the second reading. We do this, however, deliberately, offering as it does a narrative frame for a queer understanding of the theological logic of Paul's argument. The CBS, in this revision, follows the shape of a typical CBS, beginning with present community receptions of the text (1 and 2). The socio-historical input is unusual so early in a CBS (3), but is placed here to situate the narrative emphasis of the following questions (4–9), and then to community re-appropriations of the reread text within the generative theme that generated the CBS (10–11).

Questions 4, 5 and 6 align the introductory historically reconstructed narrative frame (3) with these three respective narrative threads within the letter. The narrative frame (3) enables participants to recognize that the letter contains narrative elements, and questions 4, 5, and 6 each identify a particular narrative strand. In our limited experience with this CBS, participants had no difficulty in following the historically reconstructed narrative input (3), provided that it was read aloud slowly. We revised the input repeatedly, attempting to make it clear and understandable, and represent here (3) how we divided the input into accessible sections.

Participant attentive facilitation was crucial to this CBS, as it is with every CBS. Because we were using far more input (3) than is our practice, we also provided each participant with a printed version of the CBS. The PowerPoint slides were the focal point for the plenary group, creating a sense of common purpose, but we noted that some of the participants reread and referred to their printed version regularly. It was clear too that questions 4, 5 and 6, discussed in small groups, were crucial in offering a scaffolding with which to navigate the three interconnected narrative strands within the Pauline prose: the Paul strand (4), the Titus strand (5) and the Cephas strand (6). Participants were excited by the cumulative sense of evidently connected stories that these CBS questions generated.

Questions 7, 8 and 9, also discussed in small groups, offered resources in a question format to draw out Paul's theological argument. Again, participants had no difficulty in doing this. In one of the workshops a participant reported from their small group, in response to question 9, how 'he' had been constantly discriminated because of the clothes 'he' wore to church, yet Paul was making the argument that 'he' in Christ was clothed as everyone else in church!

Question 10 includes elements of See, Judge and Act in its three component parts, offering an opportunity to re-reflect on their lived realities, to summarize their understanding of Paul's theological argument and to plan for redemptive action in their contexts. We could have ended the CBS at this point, emphasizing as the CBS process does the movement towards transformative action. However, the Ujamaa Centre recognizes the intersectional nature of systems of domination and marginalization, and the centrality of economic systems to all forms of oppression, so question 11 is included. The Ujamaa Centre's inaugural reality was that of apartheid racial capitalism and we remain true to this heritage, recognizing the econo-patriarchal dimensions of heteropatriarchy (West 2020b, pp. 113–16). By including this question, we bore witness to and summoned the participants towards recognition of the intersections of systems of oppression.

## Participant reflections

In addition to feedback from the participants in our two work-shops, each of the core participants reported back to the core group in the Kenyan workshop about their own translation of the CBS (begun in the South African workshop) and their own facilitation of the CBS in their home contexts.

As co-participants in this CBS, with some of us facilitating and some of us participating fully in a small group, the Ujamaa Centre team reflected on whether the input (3) is necessary to the CBS. Could the CBS 'work' without this input? One of the core participants, who translated the CBS into a local Kenyan language, insisted that this input was crucial to the CBS as it facilitated 'actual engagement with the Bible', referring to questions 4–6. As already indicated, in our latest revision we relocated the input, placing it after participants have an opportunity to listen to and reflect on the focal text (Gal. 3.27–28) (1) and the larger introductory narrative text (Gal. 1.6—2.14) (2).

The core group, who had translated the CBS into lingua francas and local languages, made it clear that the translation exercise itself was useful, even though there were challenges. A concept like 'sexuality' was difficult to translate but the diffi-culty was itself an opportunity to grapple, with a local group, with local concepts and terms. One of the core participants from Mozambique explained how he incorporated translation of the CBS into the CBS process itself, inviting local partici-pants to translate with him.

There was consensus among the core participants that the CBS was a significant contribution in their activist and pastoral work. Rereading Paul in this way provided substantive theo-logical resources for change in their contexts, though some reported that it was easier to do this CBS within the queer community than with the church. One of the participants from Tanzania reported that one of the participants in his local com-munity, who was actually quite homophobic, has taken the CBS and is using it within another language group. In addi-tion, he used resources from this CBS to advocate on behalf of decriminalization. Another outcome of this CBS, common to CBS work among those who have been driven from their churches by homophobic stigmatization, was that three of the participants in the Mozambican workshops made the decision to return to church, empowered biblically and theology. As the colleagues from the Democratic Republic of the Congo put it, 'the overall perspective is that LGBTI people are cursed, and the sign of this is HIV. The CBS refuted this!'

Alongside this feedback we have had more extensive and detailed feedback from our South African participants and knowledge production collaborators. Through their engagement, they witnessed the power that CBS has in terms of affirming those that felt as though they have been excluded and pushed to the margins within the African faith context. Through the narration of the Bible in this setting, participants felt that they were given a chance to journey together as readers, and for the first time they felt that they were a part of the process in which they were allowed to interpret the text, instead of this being imposed of them. Through this process, LGBTIQA+ individuals were able to 'read the Bible in our context and from our own position. Rather than seeing this fact as a problem, we understand this to be a gift as it allows us to bring the embodied stories of our own lives in conversation with the stories of the Bible' (Davids et al. 2019, p. 35). This CBS enabled us to relate to both the stories in the text and the story behind the text.

As activists in the fields of LGBTIQA+ human rights and transgender awareness, our South African colleagues, Sizwe Sithole and Tracey Sibisi,[10] found that through the process of CBS the embodied reality of participants became central to the reading and interpretation of the Bible, enabling a significant impact for bodies that are 'often excluded, marginalised, and ultimately annihilated' (Sibisi and Van der Walt 2021, p. 68). The history of the Bible and the way it has been interpreted has made it clear that 'stories … can make the world, unmake it, and remake it in different forms. They can erase people, places, and events or add them in, elevate or downplay their importance, retell or reinterpret them' (Wilcox 2020, p. 1). CBS models, remakes and rewrites the bodies of queer individuals within biblical narratives in an affirmative way. The reading process brings queer bodies back to the centre of Christian faith and biblical interpretation, reading the text from their own context, drawing them from the margins to which they are said to belong. Through CBS those who are marginalized, othered, and discriminated against are given a voice through the understanding that the Bible does not speak, but is itself given a voice, and therefore has 'no single message or voice' (West 2021b, p. 132), which leaves room for a diversity of voices to be heard. The CBS process demonstrates the principles of a theology of inclusion, which has capacitated participants in these workshops to become queer ambassadors, who felt eager to draw closer to God and the church. Through its inclusive interpretative praxis, CBS becomes 'a soul winning' resource (for similar analysis of the impact of CBS on lived realities see West 2021a), drawing excluded others closer to the word of God, which has now revealed itself to be life affirming and relational.

The Bible must be read, as Jeremy Punt reminds us, within its social setting, because biblical texts were written from a particular context, and therefore contemporary context must not be 'superimposed' (2007, p. 247), and this is the gift that this particular CBS offers. For LGBTIQA+ individuals and traditional healers (for work on African traditional healers see Mkasi 2013), reading the Bible in relation to their context and from their own lived experiences empowered them to read the Bible, not as an abstract document, but as a guiding narrative in their current context. They could do so because the Bible was no longer seen as life-denying, because the CBS process de-centres the power of a single interpreter. This takes into consideration the fact that 'readers always bring their questions and or their concerns to the reading of the Bible' (West 2006, p. 131). Through this process CBS becomes a dynamic reflective surface that offers a starting point for important conversations about the reality that we find ourselves in, enabling participants to collectively lean into discomfort.

A foundational truth that members of the Ujamaa team often remind each other of is that 'change is not an event, it is a process'. CBS is never a one-off activity, it is embedded in ongoing processes and activities that labour for change. Through their engagement with LGBTIQA+ individuals and traditional healers, alongside this particular CBS, Sithole and Sibisi found that CBS compels or pushes people to talk about uncomfortable truths and realities that they may have not been ready yet to talk about (for ongoing reflection on navigating 'discomfort' in CBS processes and other pedagogical settings see Terblanche and Van der Walt 2019), creating a safe and sacred space through which the participants found 'a connection between the Bible and their lives' (West 2006, p. 132), which is also something that we noted within the Kenyan engagement. CBS enables important conversations that determine the agenda for further change-making.

The ongoing and evolving conversations of this project have also sparked a project aimed at defining and reclaiming vernacular queer terminologies and vocabulary. Although the momentum of this work was hampered by the Covid-19 pandemic, remarkably, people who endured so much hatred, pain and suffering found a voice to speak to their own lived reality and reclaim their sacred identity. Many shared how CBS brought back hope to them and for them and for the communities that they represent. This was the case among traditional African healers, Sangomas, among whom we worked.

'Depending on how safe the CBS workshop is, there is a communal owning of what has been articulated – this is both empowering and potentially transformative' (West 2006, p. 146). This is indeed the gift of CBS that was noted when a participant stated that 'as a Sangoma it is good to know that I can be saved as well. Our faith is within us, and you can't say because we are queer and have the gift of traditional healing we cannot go to church and worship God.' Another participant articulated a similar feeling:

A Sangoma can be saved. I say this because Elijah was a prophet, and he was able to talk to God. Like a Sangoma, we can see beyond the now and we can save the lives of others, and this is a gift from God, the difference is that I use tradition, herbs, and candles in accessing my calling.

Another shared as follows:

> Being gay, a Sangoma, and spiritual/Christian is double if not a triple stigma. As gay sangomas we really are faced with so much backlash, and it is heart breaking because we love church, but we also cannot abandon our spiritual gifts, so this kind of work is important to us, and we need it.

In sum, our participation in this and related CBS processes helped us collectively to disrupt the norms and blur the lines in terms of who is allowed to interpret the Bible and who is not. (For similar sentiments within the context of being HIV-positive see West and Zengele 2006).

## Queer corporate process

In his book, *Kenyan, Christian, Queer* (2012I), Adriaan van Klinken offers us the following subtitle: 'Religion, LGBT Activism, and Arts of Resistance in Africa', alluding to the title of James Scott's classic study of subaltern resistance to domination (Scott 1990), as van Klinken acknowledges (2021, pp. 188–91). What makes van Klinken's work 'queer' is not primarily the 'arts' of resistance he documents but that they are 'queer' – LGBTIQA+ – arts of resistance. The transgressive character of arts of resistance is a crucial component of queer arts of resistance (Van Klinken 2021, p. x), but without actual queer bodies these arts of resistance are not queer. We say this because queer CBS process is more than transgressive forms of Bible rereading. What makes this particular CBS process queer is that it is shaped by organized queer communities. The term 'corporate' is instructive, for it includes a sense of embodied incarnate collaboration. Queer bodies, queer lived experience, probe the biblical text differently, transgressively, summoning sacred scripture to speak inclusively and redemptively.

The ongoing work in this area done by the Ujamaa Centre aims to contribute and develop an Izitabane zingabantu Ubuntu theology (see for example Van der Walt and Davids 2022).

Izitabane zingabantu Ubuntu theology begins from the embodied contextual and situated reality of African Izitabane,[11] and broadly calls for an *embodied reclaiming* of all that is life-affirming within faith landscapes, *reimagining* community and the engagement with the sources of faith, and *remembering* our communal sacramental identity. Rather than talking 'about' LGBTIQA+ people within African faith communities, this work advocates for a process where we read 'with' each other and discover and celebrate the gifts of our unity and diversity as African people of faith.[12]

## Conclusion

Our essay reflects on the Ujamaa Centre's queer praxis, emphasizing how queer corporate collaboration summons Paul to be queerly inclusive. What is an absence in Paul's Galatians becomes present through the participation of queer eyes. Marcella Althaus-Reid queered liberation theology by reminding Latin American theology that sex workers were also workers (Althaus-Reid 2000), and Avaren Ipsen queered biblical studies by doing biblical interpretation with organized sex workers (Ipsen 2009). In this essay we suggest a literary pathway to queer Jonah and the prophetic process through a queering of Paul.

The case studies in van Klinken's research make it clear that 'religion is not only a source of homophobia in Africa but also a source of lgbt activism and queer politics' (2021, p. ix). Similarly, our collaborative process makes it clear that the Bible too is a site of LGBTIQA+ religious activism and LGBTIQA+ politics. As with the prophet Jonah and the apostle Paul, religious change is political. Van Klinken's work also demonstrates that, in the Kenyan context, 'The strategic use of highly public instead of hidden forms of [queer theological] resistance, and the explicit rather than disguised strategies of [queer] political action, indicates that the individuals and communities involved feel rather emboldened and empowered' (2021, p. 189). Contextual Bible Study has had a similar effect, on the paired groups who were integral to the project, including LGBTIQA+ activists and church leaders, but also on the regional participants from each locality who joined us in CBS. The CBS itself outed Paul, summoning his letter to Galatians to understand its own inclusive theology more fully. The CBS summons Jonah to a more inclusive participatory prophetic process and Galatians to a fuller understanding its own inclusive theology.

## Notes

1 We gratefully acknowledge our funding partnership with the Arcus Foundation. The quotation is from formal Arcus Foundation project documentation.

2 While not a focus of this essay, recent scholarship has significantly contested the idea that modern conceptions of 'homosexuality' as consenting, same-sex relationships between adults is relevant for the understanding the ancient Greco-Roman practice of pederasty, a 'power over' sexual relationship between adult men and boys. For a foundational rereading of 'homosexuality' see Martin 1995. For more recent scholarship on the history of translation of the word 'homosexual' in Romans 1 see Oxford and Baldock, forthcoming.

3 Biblical scholars divide the canonical Pauline corpus into three categories: authentic, disputed and pastoral. There is broad consensus that the historical Paul wrote the authentic letters (1 Thessalonians, 1 and 2 Corinthians, Philippians, Philemon and Romans) in the decades of the 50s and 60s CE. Biblical scholars debate whether 2 Thessalonians, Colossians and Ephesians were written by the historical Paul or a first-generation follower using the common practice in antiquity of pseudepigraphy. There is general scholarly consensus that a second-generation follower of Paul wrote the pastoral letters (1 and 2 Timothy, Titus) in the early second century CE. It is also important to note that there are significant divergences among the way Paul describes himself and events in his own letters versus the way the author portrays him and the same events in Luke-Acts.

4 The foundational shift away from traditional and Protestant interpretations of Paul as a 'Christian' began with Stendahl 1976. For a history of scholarship on the 'New Perspective' on Paul and more recent scholarly rereadings of Paul within Judaism see Zetterholm 2009.

5 For rereading *ethne* ('nations', 'Gentiles') in Galatians within its Roman imperial context see Lopez 2008. For Galatians as a whole within the same context see Kahl 2010.

6 The following five paragraphs are revised from Hall (forthcoming).

7 For scholarly engagements with the narrative logics implicit within Pauline texts, the foundational text remains Hays 2002. See also Longenecker 2002; Witherington 1994.

8 That Pauline texts lack characters, places and actions entirely is perhaps a bit of an exaggeration, especially as these elements can be constructed from the text itself.

9 We revised this CBS a few times, after the initial church-based version (2019), after the Arcus project version (2019) and after a workshop at Pilgrim Theological College in Melbourne, Australia (2022).

10 Sizwe Sithole is a PhD candidate in the School of Religion, Philosophy and Classics at the University of KwaZulu-Natal, Pietermaritzburg, South Africa; Tracey Sibisi is a PhD candidate in the Gender and Religion Program of the School of Religion, Philosophy and Classics at the University of KwaZulu-Natal, Pietermaritzburg, and a queer activist situated within the Uthingo Network in Pietermaritzburg, KwaZulu-Natal, South Africa.

11 Hanzline Davids, Abongile Matyila, Sizwe Sithole and Charlene van der Walt unpack the notion of Izitabane, arguing that 'appropriating the derogatory term Izitabane and (impossibly) coupling it with theology requires some attention before we move into a critical contextual reflection.' Briefly, 'Nasi lesizitabane or lezizitabane', which literally translates to 'here comes these homosexuals, lesbians or gays' are words we often hear being uttered to LGBTIQA+ people walking the streets in local townships. Isitabane (singular) or Izitabane (plural) is the Zulu word most frequently used in communal spaces to discriminate, undermine and shame LGBTIQA+ people. This word is applied to both gender non-conformance and same-sex desire and at times is used interchangeably with words such as Ungqingili (singular) or oNgqingili (plural), Inkonkoni (singular) or Izinkonkoni (plural).

The term Isitabane originates from conceptual engagements with intersexuality and articulates something of the understanding of intersex people as people who possess both sexual organs traditionally associated with being a female or male. The term is consequently often applied to gays, lesbians and transgender people and insinuates the notion of an individual possessing both sexual organs and someone that subsequently does not conform to the heteronormative orientation and gender identity. Despite the populist argument, especially from African leaders that so-called 'homosexuality' is a Western import, historical research has highlighted that in the Southern African context ubutabane relationships were well established and documented' (cited from Davids et al. 2019, p. 10).

12 For a more comprehensive engagement with the potential of Izitabane zingabantu Ubuntu theology for queer biblical interpretation see Van der Walt 2021.

# References

Althaus-Reid, Marcella, 2000, *Indecent Theology: Theological Perversions in Sex, Gender and Politics*, London and New York: Routledge.

Chicago Consultation, 2015, 'Statement of the Elmina Consultation', http://www.chicagoconsultation.org/?p=250, accessed 30.06.2023.

Coote, Robert B., 1981, *Amos among the Prophets: Composition and Theology*, Eugene, OR: Wipf & Stock.

Davids, Hanzline, M. Matyila, Sizwe Sithole and Charlene van der Walt, 2019, *Stabanisation: A Discussion Paper About Disrupting Backlash by Reclaiming LGBTI Voices in the African Church Landscape*, The Other Foundation, https://theotherfoundation.org/stabanisation/.

Ekblad, Bob, 2005, *Reading the Bible with the Damned*, Louisville, KY: Westminster John Knox Press.

Gunda, Masiiwa Ragies and Jim Naughton, 2017, *On Sexuality and Scripture: Essays, Bible Studies, and Personal Reflections by the Chicago Consultation, the Ujamaa Centre, and their Friends*, Pietermaritzburg and New York: Cluster Publications and Church Publishing, Inc.

Hall, Crystal L., forthcoming, 'Biblical Challenges to Housing Inequity: Toward a People's Theology of 1 Corinthians 1:18–31' in Matthew J. M. Coomber (ed.), *Companion to Bible and Economics: Engaging Bible in a Capitalist Era*, Eugene, OR: Cascade Books.

Hays, Richard B., 2002, *The Faith of Jesus Christ: The Narrative Substructure of Galatians 3:1–4:11*, Grand Rapids, MI: Eerdmans.

Ipsen, Avaren, 2009, *Sex Working and the Bible*, London: Equinox.

Kahl, Brigitte, 2010, *Galatians Re-imagined: Reading with the Eyes of the Vanquished*, Minneapolis, MN: Fortress Press.

Longenecker, Bruce W., 2002, *Narrative Dynamics in Paul: A Critical Assessment*, Louisville, KY: Westminster John Knox Press.

Lopez, Davina C., 2008, *The Apostle to the Conquered: Reimagining Paul's Mission*, Minneapolis, MN: Fortress Press.

Martin, Dale B., 1995, 'Heterosexism and the Interpretation of Romans 1:18–32', *Biblical Interpretation* 3/3, pp. 332–55.

Mesters, Carlos, 1989, *Defenseless Flower: A New Reading of the Bible*, Francis McDonagh (trans.), Maryknoll, NY: Orbis Books.

Mkasi, Lindiwe P., 2013, 'A Threat to Zulu Patriarchy and the Continuation of Community: A Queer Analysis of Same Sex Relationships Amongst Female Traditional Healers at Inanda and KwaNgcolosi', Masters thesis, University of KwaZulu-Natal.

Mosala, Itumeleng J., 1989, *Biblical Hermeneutics and Black Theology in South Africa*, Grand Rapids, MI: Eerdmans.

Oginni, Olakunle Ayokunmi, Kehinde Okanlawon and Adedotun Ogunbajo, 2021, 'A Commentary on COVID-19 and the LGBT Community in Nigeria: Risks and Resilience', *Psychology of Sexual Orientation and Gender Diversity* 8/2, DOI:10.1037/sgd0000476.

Oxford, Ed and Kathy Baldock, forthcoming, *Forging a Sacred Weapon: How the Bible Became Anti-gay*, Reno, NV: Nevada CanyonWalker Connections.

Pae, Keun-Joo Christine, 2021, 'Indecent Resurgence: God's Solidarity against the Gendered War on Covid' in Jione Havea (ed.), *Doing Theology in the New Normal: Global Perspectives*, London: SCM Press, pp. 179–95.

Philpott, Graham, 1993, *Jesus is Tricky and God is Undemocratic: The Kin-dom of God in Amawoti*, Pietermaritzburg: Cluster Publications.

Punt, Jeremy, 2007, 'The Bible and the Dignity of Human Sexuality: Compromised Sexual Selves and Violated Orientations', *Scriptura: Journal for Contextual Hermeneutics in Southern Africa* 95/1 (2007), pp. 241–52.

Reid, Graeme and Samuel Ritholtz, 2020, 'A Queer Approach to Understanding LGBT Vulnerability During the COVID-19 Pandemic', *Politics & Gender* 16/4, pp. 1101–9.

Sánchez, Odette R., Diama B. Vale, Larissa Rodrigues and Fernanda G. Surita, 2020, 'Violence Against Women During the COVID-19 pandemic: An integrative review', *International Journal of Gynecology & Obstetrics* 151/2, pp. 180–7.

Scott, James C., 1990, *Domination and the Arts of Resistance: Hidden Transcripts*, New Haven, CT and London: Yale University Press.

Sibisi, Tracey and Charlene van der Walt, 2021, 'Queering the Queer: Engaging Black Queer Christian bodies in African Faith Spaces', *African Journal of Gender and Religion* 27/2, pp. 67–91.

Stendahl, Krister, 1976, *Paul Among Jews and Gentiles: And Other Essays*, Minneapolis, MN: Fortress Press.

Terblanche, Judith and Charlene van der Walt, 2019, 'Leaning into Discomfort: Engaging Film as a Reflective Surface to Encourage Deliberative Encounters' in Chikumbutso Herbert Manthalu and Yusif Waghid (eds), *Education for Decoloniality and Decolonisation in Africa*, London: Palgrave Macmillan, pp. 203–24.

Ujamaa Centre, 2011, 'Economy matters', Ujamaa Centre, http://ujamaa.ukzn.ac.za/Libraries/manuals/Economy_matters_A_series_of_Ujamaa_Cent.sflb.ashx, accessed 7.06.2023.

Ujamaa Centre, 2015, 'Doing Contextual Bible Study: A Resource Manual', Ujamaa Centre, *University of KwaZulu-Natal*, http://ujamaa.ukzn.ac.za/RESOURCES_OF_UJAMAA/MANUAL_STUDIES.aspx, accessed 7.06.2023.

Van der Walt, Charlene, 2021, '"Better is Never Better for Everyone; It Always Means Worse for Some." Could there be Space in an African Women's Theology for those known as Izitabane?' in Lilian C. Siwila and Fundiswa Kobo (eds), *Religion, Patriarchy, and Empire: Festschrift in Honour of Mercy Amba Oduyoye*, Pietermaritzburg: Cluster Publications, pp. 389–414.

Van der Walt, Charlene and Hanzline R. Davids, 2022, 'Heteropatriarchy's Blame Game: Reading Genesis 37 with Izitabane during COVID 19', *Old Testament Essays* 35/1, pp. 32–50.

Van Klinken, Adriaan, 2021, *Kenyan, Christian, Queer: Religion, LGBT Activism, and Arts of Resistance in Africa*, University Park, PA: Pennsylvania State University Press.

Vearncombe, Erin K. et al., 2021, *After Jesus before Christianity: A Historical Exploration of the First Two Centuries of Jesus Movements*, New York: HarperOne.

West, Gerald O., 1991, 'The Relationship Between Different Modes of Reading (the Bible) and The Ordinary Reader', *Scriptura* S9, pp. 87–110.

West, Gerald O., 2006, 'Contextual Bible Reading: A South African Case Study', *Analecta Bruxellensia* 11, pp. 131–48.

West, Gerald O., 2015, 'The Biblical Text as a Heterotopic Intercultural Site: In Search of Redemptive Masculinities' in Hans De Wit and Janet Dyk (eds), *Bible and Transformation: the Promise of Intercultural Bible Reading*, Semeia Studies, Atlanta, GA: SBL Press, pp. 241–57.

West, Gerald O., 2020a, 'Towards an Inclusive and Collaborative African Biblical Hermeneutics of Reception and Production: A Distinctively South African Contribution', *Scriptura* 119/3, pp. 1–18.

West, Gerald O., 2020b, 'Trans-Textual and Trans-Sectoral Gender-Economic Reading of the Rape of Tamar (2 Sam 13) and the Expropriation of Naboth's Land (1 Kgs 21)' in Jin Young Choi and Joerg Rieger (eds), *Faith, Class, and Labor: Intersectional Approaches in a Global Context*, Eugene, OR: Pickwick Publications, pp. 105–21.

West, Gerald O., 2021a, 'Contextual Bible Study and/as Interpretive Resilience' in Ezra Chitando, Esther Mombo and Masiiwa Ragies Gunda (eds), *That All May Live: Essays in Honour of Nyambura J. Njoroge*, Bamberg: University of Bamberg Press, pp. 143–59.

West, Gerald O., 2021b, 'Phantsi Patriarchy, Talitha Cum! The Quest for Post-Patriarchal Biblical Resources' in Lilian C. Siwila and Fundiswa Kobo (eds), *Religion, Patriarchy and Empire: Festschrift in Honour of Mercy Amba Oduyoye*, Pietermaritzburg: Cluster Publications, pp. 123–45.

West, Gerald O. and Bongi Zengele, 2006, 'The Medicine of God's Word: What People Living With HIV and AIDS Want (And Get) From the Bible', *Journal of Theology for Southern Africa* 125, pp. 51–63.

West, Gerald O. and Sithembiso Zwane, 2020, 'Re-Reading 1 Kings 21:1–16 Between Community-Based Activism and University-Based Pedagogy', *Journal for Interdisciplinary Biblical Studies* 2/1, pp. 179–207.

West, Gerald O., Sithembiso Zwane and Charlene van der Walt, 2021, 'From Homosexuality to Hospitality; From Exclusion to Inclusion;

From Genesis 19 to Genesis 18', *Journal of Theology for Southern Africa* 168, pp. 5–19.

Wilcox, Melissa M., 2020, *Queer Religiosities: An Introduction to Queer and Transgender Studies in Religion*, Lanham, MD: Rowman & Littlefield Publishers.

Witherington, Ben III, 1994, *Paul's Narrative Thought World: The Tapestry of Tragedy and Triumph*, Louisville, KY: Westminster John Knox Press.

Zetterholm, Magnus, 2009, *Approaches to Paul: A Student's Guide to Recent Scholarship*, Minneapolis, MN: Fortress Press.

Zwane, Sithembiso S., 2020, 'Invited, Invigorated and Invented Spaces: A Trans-Development Approach' in Jin Young Choi and Joerg Rieger (eds), *Faith, Class, and Labor: Intersectional Approaches in a Global Context*, Eugene, OR: Pickwick Publications, pp. 212–33.

# 9

# On the Public Intellectual as Queer Prophet: Considering the Activism of Zethu Matebeni and Charlene van der Walt

## ASHWIN AFRIKANUS THYSSEN

## Introduction

In October 2021, the Gender Unit of the Faculty of Theology, Stellenbosch University, made public the call for papers for its upcoming conference in March 2022. This conference would, with acute socio-historical sensitivity, investigate what may be found in the theological sources while offering reflection on the world before us. Interestingly, weeks before the conference was to take place, its theme set the Reformed Afrikaans (Afrikaner) community ablaze. The validity and academic integrity of this conference (and its organizers) would be disputed in various Afrikaans newspapers (Eybers 2022; Klaasing 2022; Kerkbode 2022). Something about the theme, the conference's intention to offer a queering analysis, unsettled this Afrikaans community – its 'Calvinist' conservatism, its puritanical piety, the very heart of its identity.[1]

While the resistance against this conference serves as background, in this essay, I have no intention of responding to these queries. Rather, I focus my attention on why conservative groupings, such as this one, are unsettled by such queering work – truly, by the work of queer theology, theorists, activists and lgbtiqa+ people.[2] As such, I consider, first, the ways in which the public intellectual may be perceived as a queer prophet. Second, I discuss the work of two pioneering public intellectuals in South Africa: the queer theorist Zethu Matebeni and the queer theologian Charlene van der Walt. And third, I outline what the work of Matebeni and Van der Walt offers for South African society, especially its theological academy.

## Public intellectual as prophet

At the outset of this essay, it is pertinent to raise the question: Why consider the work of the public intellectual? The present is a time of seemingly opaque socio-political disintegration. Here, in South Africa where we are coming to terms with a maturing democracy, while being confronted with its faults and limitations. To answer this, I briefly draw on the work of two academics who may be considered the public intellectuals of their day: Antonio Gramsci and Sara Ahmed. I turn to these two scholars for the ways in which they present the work of the intellectual as being responsive to the demands of both the academy and society. Requiring this responsiveness and responsibility, on the part of the intellectual, Gramsci and Ahmed challenge our notion of the public intellectual.

### Organic intellectual

To make sense of Antonio Gramsci's notion of the organic intellectual, we first need to get to terms with his understanding of the intellectual. Gramsci categorically states:

> All [people] are intellectuals, one could therefore say: but not all [people] have in society the function of intellectuals ... Each [person], finally, outside [their] professional activity, carries on some form of intellectual activity, that is, [they are] a 'philosopher,' an artist, a [person] of taste, [they] partici-pate in a particular conception of the world, has a conscious line of moral conduct, and therefore contributes to sustain a

conception of the world or to modify it, that is, to bring into being new modes of thought. (2005, p. 51)

If all people are intellectuals, although not serving the 'function' of intellectual; what, then is the organic intellectual? Informed by Gramsci, Buchanan (2010) offers a helpful description of the organic intellectual: 'An intellectual or someone of professional standing who rises to that level from within a social class that does not normally produce intellectuals, and remains connected to that class.' Given that they are not shaped by the hegemonic class, one of the tasks of organic intellectuals, then, is to resist being 'the "deputies" of the dominant group – the function-aries, exercising important functions of political government and social hegemony' (Ramos 1982).

At present we are witnessing, albeit minimally, the entry into the academy of scholars who may rightly be identified as organic intellectuals – many, of course, self-identify using the term. These scholars are still connected with the hope of the class position they occupied prior to entering the privileges of the academic classes. In some sense, I argue, queer theorists and theologians may also be considered under the title 'organic intellectual' – by virtue of the fact that their presence in the academy is not normative, and often quite resisted. I, therefore, contend that Matebeni and Van der Walt are organic intellec-tuals, for the reasons set forth – they do not come from the class that normally produces intellectuals; and, more import-antly, they are actively transgressing the hegemonic (indeed heteronormative) dictates of the academy.

## Orientation

For the intellectual, which may also be considered the public intellectual by virtue of the societal impact of their work and ideas, space and spatiality play and important roles in the intel-lectual life. Here I argue for considering the organic intellectual as also a public intellectual precisely because her work has a characteristically public dimension; both the organic and public intellectual attends to address the challenges of a given time, in rather transgressive ways. For this reason, I consider it wise to draw on Sara Ahmed's queer phenomenology. Her notion of orientation and how that may influence our conception of the public intellectual, in and for our time, particularly intrigues me. Defining space, Ahmed writes,

> then becomes a question of 'turning,' of directions taken, which not only allow things to appear, but also enable us to find our way through the world by situating ourselves in relation to such things ... The concept of 'orientation' allows us then to rethink the phenomenality of space – that is, how space is dependent on bodily inhabitance. (2006, p. 6)

Grappling with spatiality therefore means coming to terms with the ways in which bodies occupy space, it requires an investigation into *which* bodies may reside and which are excluded.

As previously stated, we are witnessing those who are not its historically imagined populace – people of colour, women, queers, to name but a few – entering the academy. The organic intellectual – using Gramscian logic – is forced to come to terms with the ways in which her body is not the norm within the academic space, and the manifold forms of silences required of her. By considering our orientation to something, Ahmed notes we get to understand 'how we begin; how we proceed from "here"' (2006, p. 8). Part of the work of orientating the self requires the recognition of others, and the realities of othering.

These 'others', says Ahmed, are created as a result of the reproduction of whiteness (2006, p. 121). The West – who have made themselves the agents of whiteness – have 'come to embody distance. This embodiment of distance is what makes whiteness "proximate," as the "starting point" for orientation. Whiteness becomes what is "here," a line from which the world unfolds, which also makes what is "there" on "the other side."' Differently stated, whiteness estranges itself from other forms of existence, thereby rendering itself (most fallaciously) as the default, as the standard. Currently, I witness, that heteronormativity operates using the same logic in society and the academy

– in the hope of securing its sole legitimacy (presenting itself as the default). I argue that, in their work and activism, Matebeni and Van der Walt take seriously the ways in which orientation shapes not only people's lives but also forms societies; and for this reason, I think they are public intellectuals.

## But is the public intellectual a queer prophet?

Reflecting on the turn of the twentieth century, Eve Kosofsky Sedgwick writes:

> New, institutionalized taxonomic discourses – medical, legal, literary, psychological – centering on homo/heterosexual definition proliferated and crystallized with exceptional rapidity in the decades around the turn of the century ... Both the power relations between the genders and the relations of nationalism and imperialism, for instance, were in highly visible crisis. (1990, p. 2)

This zeitgeist, Sedgwick maintains, gave rise to the century of the sexual revolution, to the decade of Stonewall. That time would require, in the decades to come (and perhaps still today), an adequate interrogation for how gender and sexuality is allowed to exist in our societies – and, of course, globalization has not made this task any easier. In effect, then, the public intellectual would, since then, be required to grapple with the realities that discrimination based on gender and sexuality continue to render the lives of minorities (truly, those who are minoritized) precarious.

As queer theorist and queer theologian, I argue that Zethu Matebeni and Charlene van der Walt help us reimagine the public intellectual, in fact they are queering the notion. This is for three reasons. First, Matebeni and Van der Walt actively engage in grassroots organizations – their public intellectualism goes beyond just the public of the academy. Second, these scholars intentionally draw on their lived experience in the process of the development their scholarship, thereby inviting others to centre themselves as subjects (in a world that renders them objects). Third, their rootedness in the NGO sector and their drawing on lived experience is foundational to their academic projects. These three reasons, I posit, allow us to see Matebeni and Van der Walt as public intellectuals who are prophets, queering normative understandings and destabilizing dualistic modes of thought. In both their being organic intellectuals and their orientation to the world, Matebeni and Van der Walt highlight the demands required of the public intellectuals in our time.

## Contemporary 'queering' prophets in South Africa

Throughout the Hebrew Bible, God invites the prophets to analyse their contexts, calling them to respond to the words presented to Amos: 'What do you see?' (Amos 8.2; Jer. 1.11). In this second section, then, I present the work of Matebeni and Van der Walt as those queer prophets, because of their contributions as public intellectuals show us what they see. They, in my estimation, are prophets *of* and *for* our time. I provide a brief discussion of each scholar's work; particular attention is afforded to a seminal text in their respective body of works. To be sure, the intention is not to offer an exhaustive analysis of their activism; instead, the hope is to consider what Matebeni and Van der Walt are gesturing to – differently put, to consider what they are seeing.

### Zethu, what do you see?

In the South African lgbti+ community the name of Zethu Matebeni is, of course, quite familiar. If anything, it ranks with the name of Bev Ditsey. Matebeni is well known. But who is she? Who is this public intellectual? Zethu Matebeni, originally from Port Elizabeth, Eastern Cape, is a sociologist and writer, who pursued her educational formation at the University of the Witwatersrand. Throughout her career she has held academic posts at the University of the Western Cape and the University of Cape Town. While at the University of the Witwatersrand, she completed her doctoral dissertation, with the title 'Black Lesbian Sexualities and Identity in Johannesburg'. Introducing the contours of her doctoral study, Matebeni (2011) notes:

> This study ... reads the term lesbian as both a political and a theoretical project. It speaks to current concerns, which raise questions related to the politics of inclusion/exclusion, love, sexuality, identity politics, violence, style and urban space while sensitively giving agency to women's narratives.

Already in her doctorate Matebeni sheds light on the contribution she would make to academia. More tellingly, in her doctoral research she draws greatly on the work of grassroots activists – in this case, the formations OUT LGBT Wellbeing and *Uthingo* Women's Group (based in Johannesburg). In this work, Matebeni makes it quite clear that lesbian women should be recognized as those who 'occupy subject positions in which they determine the structures and meanings of their lives' (2011, p. 286). Differently put, lesbian women are more than just the victims of violence, but they are also actively surviving as subjects (amid conditions that render them precarious). Matebeni, therefore, calls into question the manner in which lesbian women are presented in the socio-political imagination of South Africa.

In 2021, because of her pioneering work, Matebeni was the recipient of the South African Research Chairs Initiative (SARChI), and invited to occupy the Chair in Sexualities, Genders and Queer Studies. Taking up this chair, meant that she would now do so from the University of Fort Hare, in Alice, Eastern Cape. It is helpful here to note the particular role the University of Fort Hare has played in South African history; it offered tertiary education to black people who were largely excluded from higher education. This chair, then, may be considered an advancing of the legacy of the institution's commitment to the Africanizing of education. At the time of her appointment in 2021, asked to reflect on the intersectional area of her research, Matebeni responded:

My approach to Queer Studies, a very western field of study, is from an African perspective. I put African people and African experiences at the forefront. In unpacking genders and sexualities from an African perspective, my interest has moved away from seeing these as un-African. Rather, diversity has become central and sits at the core of understanding sexualities and genders. Thus, the terms lesbian, gay, bisexual, transgender and intersex in my work have not only become limited, but redundant, although I still make use of them as a starting point. Through African paradigms, my work seeks to develop African Queer Studies by not only developing alternatives, but though exposing the hidden realities that have always made Africans diverse and dynamic in exploring sexualities and gender identities. (Wilson 2021)

From her work as an activist, engaged with *Uthingo* Women's Group and Free Gender (a black lesbian organization in Khayelitsha, Cape Town), as well as her academic work, I maintain that these confluence of activities highlights how Matebeni as public intellectual functions as a prophet. Still, it may be wise to raise the question to this prophet: Zethu Matebeni, what do you see? My reading of Matebeni's works sheds light on her close concern for the construction of queer subjectivity in society – that is, how lgbtiqa+ people lead their lives as persons.

As Matebeni's doctoral dissertation may suggest, she has a particular concern for lesbian women. Therefore, any consideration of lgbti+ subjectivities must address the forms of violence that are directed at lesbian women, particularly poor and working class black lesbian women. Here, I draw attention to one form of this violence, 'corrective rape' [homophobic rape]. Reflecting on the killing and raping of lesbian women, Matebeni writes:

As all women in South Africa, Black lesbians are similarly vulnerable to sexual violence. At the same time, they occupy a different space in society – as challenging, often openly rejecting, sexual, gender, and other cultural norms. While sexual violence towards women is generally aimed at abusing power over female bodies, we also understand that the added vulnerability of rejecting Black heteronormativity carried a heavy, and often deadly, penalty on Black female bodies. (2017, p. 32)

Matebeni's linking subjectivity to violence is as important as her linking it to spatiality. In an interview with Nadia Davids, Matebeni decries the ways in which the city of Cape Town is hailed the '*gay* capital' when this title only references 'a white, gay Cape Town, which is what you get from the Green Point, Sea Point side' (Davids and Matebeni 2017, p. 161). For too long, Matebeni and others contend, the experience of this liberatory Cape Town – a home to queers – has been the sole preserve of white middle-class gay cisgender men, much to the exclusion of all those who do not share in this set of identity markers. For Matebeni, a truly queer Cape Town (which asserts itself to be a capital) must take seriously the lgbtiqa+ people in Salt River, Athlone and Khayelitsha (Davids and Matebeni 2017, p. 161).[3] Participating in the activist formations in communities that are not at the centre of this 'gay Cape Town' (such as Free Gender in Khayelitsha), Matebeni challenges the inscribed dictates of spatiality in Cape Town, which continue to exclude poor and working class lgbtiqa+ people of colour.

In sum, then, I contend what Matebeni – the prophet – sees is a world in which lgbtiqa+ people, particularly black people, are able to lead lives of flourishing. This is not a flourishing that denies the violence of homo-, trans- and queerphobia; but recognizes that lgbtiqa+ are agents and not only victims. Further, by considering the sociality of Cape Town's spatiality, Matebeni also sees a cosmopolitan city that celebrates the rich diversity of sexual and gender minorities, who are not residing at the city's centre.

## Charlene, what do you see?

The second contemporary prophet worth our consideration is Charlene van der Walt; a familiar name among lgbti+ people of faith as well as activists. Arguably, she embodies the 'supposed' contradiction that Simon Nkoli did too – him being black and gay, and she being queer and Christian. A supposed contradiction, I say, because we know people are more than just one identity. But who is she, who is this public intellectual? Charlene van der Walt, originally from Johannesburg, is a Hebrew Bible scholar who pursued her theological training at Stellenbosch University. Her research foci are the following: 'contextual and intercultural bible reading, feminist and queer interpretation of the bible, [the] intersection [of] gender, health and theology, sexuality and queer studies' (Schoeman 2020). Even so, it is important to note that she is also a Minister of the Word and Sacrament in the Dutch Reformed Church, and this plays an influential role in her conception of activism.

Unsurprisingly, Bible reading and interpretation, then, occupy a central place in Van der Walt's work in the academy and in her activism. Foundational to her approach to reading the Bible (which hereafter I refer to as scripture) is uncovering the ways in which power and ideology play out. Introducing her doctoral dissertation, she writes: 'This study examines the role of power and ideology in a concrete intercultural conversation space which is established when individuals from diverse contexts meet one another to discuss Biblical texts' (2010, p. vii).

In this dissertation, she brilliantly draws on the insights of feminism and African hermeneutics, highlighting the collaborative promise they offer a reading community. For her project, quite interestingly, she generates a new methodological orientation; describing this, she writes:

> The theoretical points of departure [principles] of Feminism and African hermeneutics finds expression in the communal discussion space which exists when Bible interpreters, from diverse contexts, meet each other ... The communal space, as it develops from these points of departure [principles] of the African hermeneutic, provides a safe space in which the voice of the individual can be heard rightly. (2010, p. 60)

A communal reading, according to this argumentation, always takes seriously the contribution of the individual – recognizes their uniqueness and dignity. In other words, communal reading holds together the tension of appreciating the individual and affirming the group. A reading of her works suggests that she takes seriously the role scripture plays within faith communities. In fact, she consistently interrogates the power relations that inform this role. She proposes communal reading as a corrective to the reality that scripture continues to be used to marginalize and exclude those who are considered 'other'.

Some years after completing her doctorate, Van der Walt continued this project of communal Bible reading. She set out its agenda in the article 'Danger! *Ingozi*! *Gevaar*! Why Reading Alone Can be Bad for You'. In this article, she considers that an intercultural Bible reading space allows us to see the reader as 'no longer an individual or a single group, but multiple readers who are linked together' (Kessler quoted in Van der Walt 2016, p. 9). Communal reading, therefore, facilitates a space in which a diversity of skills may flourish, and thorough recognition afforded to their contextually embedded readings. Articulating her vision of communal reading, she opines:

> By allowing for the interaction among culturally diverse individuals, the intercultural Bible reading process theoretically becomes a safe space that promotes human dignity and facilitates social transformation … By reading Biblical text together the intercultural Bible reading space thus serves as a counter for harmful exclusivist interpretative practices. (2016, p. 11)

Still, she goes beyond this position. Resisting the temptation to read alone is not enough. The process of intercultural Bible reading, she notes, should result in the creation of a safe space in which flesh and blood Bible readers could encounter each other, in the hope of facilitating change (2012, p. 110). This hope of facilitating change is vivified by having difficult conversations.

In a chapter titled 'Having Difficult Conversations: Engaging Film as a Reflective Surface to Encourage Dynamic Intersectional Encounters', Van der Walt shares thoughts on teaching Stellenbosch University's Master of Theology Gender, Health, and Religion Core Module. For her, two aspects stand out as foundational for creating the space in which these master's students could engage in difficult conversations (Van der Walt 2019, p. 81). First, an acknowledgement that all participants have pre-existing embodied knowledge. Second, the invitation to participants to destabilize and deconstruct that which is the normative, calling into question the binaries and dualistic thinking. These two conditions, argues Van der Walt, enable participants to 'develop and grow within a diverse community of voices represented by those present in the class and by the richness of the theoretical voices introduced through reading and other content sharing methods' (2019, p. 82).

Van der Walt's role in the Ujamaa Centre for Community Development and Research demonstrates her commitment to both the liberating potential of scripture and the necessity of difficult conversations. West, Van der Walt and Kaoma best display this link of scripture to difficult conversations in the publication 'When Faith Does Violence'. For them we must address the fact that an unhealthy (perhaps even toxic) reading of the Bible informs the violence directed at lgbti+ people. This moment, they contend, requires going beyond 'decent theology' and instead doing theology 'in ways that include [lgbti+] Christians who have been othered, objectified and vilified as subjects is vital for the African churches if they need to move beyond a faith that does violence' (West, Van der Walt and Kaoma 2016, p. 7).

In short, I posit that Van der Walt – the prophet – sees a diverse community of Bible readers who are courageously setting out to engage in difficult conversations, paying attention to how the Bible is used to render the lives of some precarious (particularly those persons who are sexual and gender minorities). Communal reading Van der Walt sees as a cultural tool that enriches the community, which also contributes to the space to facilitate change (amid the violence that faith communities perpetuate).

## Unconcluding – pointing to the *not yet*

In rather profound ways, as public intellectuals – truly, those who are queer(*ing*) prophets – Matebeni and Van der Walt focus our attention on the pervasive violence that is endemic in our society. In her work Matebeni invites us to confront the violence of spatiality; to consider the ways in which identity markers (race, gender, sexuality) render the lives of certain individuals and communities precarious. And Van der Walt requests that we take seriously the ways in which our inter-pretation of scripture allows – and at times causes – violence; to imagine life-giving approaches to the Bible that do justice to the victims and survivors of violence. In both Matebeni and Van der Walt we encounter two public intellectuals who are both organic intellectuals (not being the normative scholar) and thinkers orientated towards those minoritized others.

Matebeni, Monro and Reddy write:

> to be queer in Africa is to be in effect constrained and regu-lated by the 'heterosexual matrix' (Butler 1999), 'the straight mind' (Wittig 1992), and the 'compulsory heterosexuality' (Rich 1980) that informs the hegemonic order of hetero-sexuality. (2018, p. 1)

This is the world in which Matebeni and Van der Walt make their contribution as queer prophets, as public intellectuals. Defining queer theory in relation to temporality, Esteban José Munoz helpfully writes:

> Queerness is not yet here. Queerness is an ideality. Put another way we are not yet queer. We may never touch queerness, but we can feel it as the warm illumination of a horizon imbued with potentiality. We have never been queer, yet queerness exists for us as an ideality that can be distilled from the past and used to imagine a future. The future is queerness's domain. Queerness is a structuring and educated mode of desiring that allows us to see and feel beyond the quagmire of the present. (2009, p. 1)

I return to the anecdote shared at the start of this essay. The resistance demonstrated by those who question the academic value of the Gender Unit's conference is rooted in the desire to continue the constraining and regulating power of the hetero-sexual matrix, to continue the status quo. Differently put, they resist because they know what Matebeni and Van der Walt see is a world in which the richness of the genders and sexualities are embraced and celebrated – in short, they are seeing the *not yet*. Yes, it is this *not yet* that continues to cause our detractors' immense discontent. It is this *not yet*, which Matebeni and Van der Walt witness to, that makes them queer prophets in and for our time.

## Notes

1 Giliomee 2003 offers a telling discussion about the Afrikaner iden-tity and the people.

2 lgbtiqa+ is here taken to include all persons who identify as gender and sexual minorities, which may include persons who are lesbian, gay, bisexual, transgender, intersex, and whose identities may not be captured by these terms. Following Adriaan van Klinken (2019, p. x). I prefer to use the term in lowercase to denote its fluid and deconstruc-tionist symbolism.

3 Green Point and Sea Point here refers to communities that are populated by white and middle-class persons; whereas the communities of Salt River, Athlone and Khayelitsha are populated by black, poor and working-class people. Quite often when Cape Town is noted to be gay, capital black and poor communities are excluded from this designation.

## References

Ahmed, Sara, 2006, *Queer Phenomenology: Orientations, Objects, Others*, Durham, NC: Duke University Press.

Buchanan, Ian, 2010, 'Organic Intellectual' in *A Dictionary of Critical Theory*, Oxford: Oxford University Press.

Butler, Judith, 1999, *Gender Trouble: Feminism and the Subversion of Identity*, New York: Routledge.

Davids, Nadia and Zethu Matebeni, 2017, 'Queer Politics and Intersec-tionality in South Africa', *Safundi* 18/2, pp. 161–7, DOI: 10.1080/ 17533171.2016.1270015.

Eybers, Johan, 2022, 'Queer-teologie by Maties 'n "krisis vir die kerk"', *Netwerk24*, https://www.netwerk24.com/netwerk24/nuus/aktueel/queer-teologie-by-maties-n-krisis-vir-die-kerk-20220220, accessed 15.03.2022.

Giliomee, Hermann, 2003, *The Afrikaners: Biography of a People*, London: Hurst.

Gramsci, Antonio, 2005, 'The Intellectuals' in S. P. Hier (ed.), *Contemporary Sociological Thought: Themes and Theories*, Toronto: Canadian Scholars' Press Inc.

Kerkbode, 2022, 'Uiteenlopende sienings oor Jona-konferensie', 24 February 2022. Available online at https://kerkbode.christians.co.za/2022/02/24/uiteenlopende-sienings-oor-jona-konferensie/, accessed 7.06.2023.

Klaasing, Henrietta, 2022, 'Stellenbosse-konferensie laat vrae', *Netwerk24*, https://www.netwerk24.com/netwerk24/stemme/gesels-saam/stellenbosse-konferensie-laat-vrae-20220221, accessed 16.03.2022.

Matebeni, Zethu, 2011, *Exploring Black Lesbian Sexualities and Identities in Johannesburg*, Johannesburg: University of the Witwatersrand.

Matebeni, Zethu, 2017, 'Southern Perspectives on Gender Relations and Sexualities: A Queer Intervention', *Revista de Antropologia* 60/3, pp. 26–44.

Muñoz, José Esteban, 2009, *Cruising Utopia: The Then and There of Queer Futurity*, New York: New York University Press.

Matebeni, Zethu, Surya Monro and Vasu Reddy, 2018, 'Introduction' in Zethu Matebeni, Surya Monro and Vasu Reddy (eds), *Queer in Africa: LGBTQI Identities, Citizenship, and Activism*, Abingdon: Routledge.

Ramos, Valeriano Jr, 1982, 'The Concepts of Ideology, Hegemony, and Organic Intellectuals in Gramsci's Marxism', *Theoretical Review* 27 (March-April), trans. and ed. Paul Saba, https://www.marxists.org/history/erol/periodicals/theoretical-review/1982301.htm, accessed 16.03.2022.

Rich, Adrienne, 1980, 'Compulsory Heterosexuality and Lesbian Existence', *Signs* 5/4, pp. 631–60.

Schoeman, Leroux, 2020, 'Profiel: Die Prof in die Ongemakstoel', *Kerkbode*, https://kerkbode.christians.co.za/2020/07/28/die-prof-in-die-ongemakstoel/, accessed 15.03.2022.

Sedgwick, Eve Kosofsky, 1990, *Epistemology of the Closet*, Oakland, CA: University of California Press.

Van der Walt, Charlene, 2010, 'Ideologie en Mag in Bybelinterpretasie: Op Weg na 'n Kommunale Lees van 2 Samuel 13', PhD Dissertation, Stellenbosch University.

Van der Walt, Charlene, 2012, 'Close Encounters: Creating a Safe Space for Intercultural Bible Reading', *Scriptura* 109, pp. 110–18.

Van der Walt, Charlene, 2016, 'Danger! Ingozi! Gevaar! Why Reading Alone Can Be Bad for You', *Scriptura* 115, pp. 1–12.

Van der Walt, Charlene, 2019, 'Having Difficult Conversations: Engaging Film as a Reflective Surface to Encourage Dynamic Intersectional Encounters' in L Juliana Claassens, Charlene van der Walt and Funlola O. Olojede (eds), *Teaching for Change: Essays on Pedagogy, Gender and Theology in Africa*, Stellenbosch: SunMedia.

Van Klinken, Adriaan, 2019, *Kenyan, Christian, Queer: Religion, LGBT Activism, and Arts of Resistance in Africa*, Philadelphia, PA: Penn State University Press.

West, Gerald, Charlene van der Walt and Kapya John Kaoma, 2016, 'When Faith Does Violence: Reimagining Engagement Between Churches and LGBTI Groups on Homophobia in Africa', *HTS Teologiese Studies/Theological Studies* 72/1, pp. 1–8.

Wilson, Tim, 2021, 'NRF Awards South Africa's First SARChI Chair in Sexualities, Genders and Queer Studies Awarded to Prof Zethu Matebeni', *University of Fort Hare*, https://www.ufh.ac.za/news/News/NRFAWARDSSOUTHAFRICA, accessed 15.03.2022.

Wittig, Monique, 1992, *The Straight Mind and Other Essays*, Boston, MA: Beacon Press.

# 10

# Becoming a Queer Prophet: Desmond Tutu, Embodiment and Speaking Out for LGBTIQA+ Equality

## JACOB MEIRING

## Introduction

On the first day of 2022, the 90-year-old body of Desmond Mpilo Tutu was aquamated, his bones dried and pulverized and interred in the tiled floor of St George's Cathedral in Cape Town. This is the place where a boy born in the impoverished township of Klerkdorp (in the now Northwest province of South Africa) was enthroned on 7 September 1986 as the first black Anglican Archbishop of Cape Town in a country still under the brutal thumb of the Nationalist apartheid government.

At his official state funeral on 1 January 2022, many ordinary South Africans from various faith communities, struggle and human rights activists, church and political leaders, friends and followers on the African continent and across the globe, bid farewell to a prophet. Albeit an irritating one. But isn't that how prophets should be? Even Nelson Mandela described Desmond Tutu with these words: 'Sometimes strident, often tender, never afraid and seldom without humour, Desmond Tutu's voice will always be the voice of the voiceless' (Sparks and Tutu 2011, p. 204).

The Arch (as he was fondly known), with his trademark humour, often recounted this meeting between God and Moses, where God commands Moses to go to Pharaoh and tell him to let God's people go, with Moses replying, 'What? Me? What have I done now? Go to Pharaoh? Please, God, no! You can't be serious!', pleading 'God, you know I stammer.' Tutu then concluded that the God is the Exodus God, who liberates us from all kinds of bondage (Allen 1997, pp. 11–12).

Volker Faigle describes the Desmond Tutu he knew as someone who became 'a remarkable human partner of the great liberator God' through his deep compassion and commitment to justice (2021, p. 200). Can you imagine – Desmond Tutu, a man who in many ways 'stammered', also with his 'wounded' body, as the partner of a God, as one of the leaders who endeavoured to lead us out of the bondages of apartheid?

How did this man with his vulnerable black body become a prophet, trying to lead us not just from the bondage of racial oppression, but also from many other kinds of dehumanizing systems of oppression and relationships, while dreaming, hoping and constantly praying for more just, dignified, compassionate and peaceful societies? How did he become a passionate advocate, using his prophetic voice, for the equal inclusion of lesbian, gay, bisexual, transgender, intersex, queer, asexual and pansexual (LGBTIQA+) communities in the household of God?

How did his own embodiment, the way he made meaning with the body he had and through the body he was, contribute to this becoming, this transformation from a teacher in Munsieville High School to a courageous spiritual and human rights leader on the world stage? Was Desmond Tutu then indeed a queer prophet?

## Becoming a prophet

In August 1968, students called for the end of racist education at Ford Hare University. Desmond Tutu was the Anglican chaplain to the students while also lecturing at the nearby St Peter's Seminary. The campus erupted in protest when the rector refused to see a delegation of students wanting to persuade him to treat them as 'responsible human beings, not as a lower form of human life' (Du Boulay 1988, p. 77). Students were to be expelled, and police arrived on the campus with armoured cars, surrounding the students with guns, tear gas and police dogs. Tutu walked over from the seminary, elbowed his way through the police, saying, 'Don't try to stop me, because if you are arresting the students you can count me, as their chaplain, with them.' This confrontation was part of Tutu's awakening, slowly growing into a leadership role (Du Boulay 1988, p. 72). He was angry with God for letting this happen to students and according to the President of the Seminary, bewildered by the experience and by the brutality with which authorities man-handled students.

While he was working for the Theological Education Fund as Director for Africa, Desmond Tutu wrote that Black theology is concerned with human liberation, that it calls 'man' to 'align himself with the God who is the God of the Exodus, God the liberator, who leads his people, all his people, out of all kinds of bondage – political, economic, cultural' (1973, p. 6).

In the early 1970s, Tutu spent practically six months a year travelling throughout Africa, witnessing, among other things, the brutal repression of Idi Amin's Uganda, the overthrow of Haile Selassie in Ethiopia, the Biafran war in Nigeria. In the former Rhodesia, he was detained by security police, who found draft papers on Black theology in his luggage, shouting that his presence is about politics and not theology (Du Boulay 1988, p. 88).

For Tutu, Black theology enquires whether it is possible to be Black and a Christian, to ask on whose side God is, since it is a theology that is concerned about 'the humanisation of man, because those who ravage our humanity, dehumanise them-selves in the process' (1973, p. 6). The liberation of the 'Black man' 'is the other side of the coin of the liberation of the white man'. In these words, lay the seeds of his *Ubuntu* theology, and one of the key principles that guided the work of the Truth and Reconciliation Commission (TRC), which commenced under his leadership 22 years later.

Black theology is an assertion of the personhood of Black people, confirming an identity of Blacks, not 'an over-againstness' of anybody else, thereby declaring that Black people are fundamentally subjects and not objects. Tutu decries the degeneration of things Black and of Black persons, defined in white man's terms, and at the end, being treated 'as human but not quite as human as the white man ... treated as inferior persons' (1973, p. 2), who at the end doubts their own humanity. John Lamola, who as a young theologian worked at the SACC and the Institute for Contextual Theology (ICT), describes Tutu as 'an acknowledged pioneering exponent of South African Black Theology' (2021, p. 226).

Black theology, for Tutu, is a theology that takes the life experiences of a particular community seriously, and 'must take the scandal of its own particularity seriously' (1973, p. 4). It is not merely an academic theology that is detached from reality. He calls it 'a gut level theology, relating to the real concerns, the life and death issues of the black man' (Tutu 1973, p. 5). In this sense, Tutu's description of Black theology is also deeply incarnational, since it acknowledges that God, through Jesus, has fully entered into the human situation and that 'God speaks to us as we are and our theology is filtered through who we are' (Tutu 1973, p. 5). My interest, also from the perspective of theological anthropology (as informed by body theology), is how Tutu's theology was filtered through the person he was, through the body he had.

Since Tutu's interpretation of Black theology is also deeply incarnational, Du Boulay writes that there is no divide between the religious and the political, the material and the spiritual, and that Tutu's involvement in Black theology reinforced his instinct that Christians in South Africa 'must proclaim the injustice of apartheid and God's firm stand with the oppressed' (1988, p. 85).

Using his instinct and gut feeling was an integral part of Tutu's activism and ministry. But was he becoming a prophet? In May 1976, while the Soweto student uprising was stirring, Tutu (by then the Anglican bishop of Lesotho) wrote to the then Prime Minister, B. J. Vorster, urging him to end the oppressive apartheid system. Tutu felt that unless there was urgent action, a disaster could take place. In his letter to Vorster, Tutu wrote:

Unless something drastic is done very soon then bloodshed and violence are going to happen in South Africa almost inevitably. A people can only take so much and no more ... I am dreadfully frightened, that we may soon reach a point of no return, when events will generate a momentum of their own, when nothing will stop there reaching a bloody denouement. (2006, p. 11)

The letter was dismissed by Vorster and Tutu was regarded as nothing more than a troublemaker. However, mere weeks after penning the letter, 16 June happened. The Sharpeville massacre unfolded with police gunning down students protesting in Soweto; some were shot in the back while running away.

This letter catapulted Tutu into the public sphere. The process included a political awakening influenced by the Black Consciousness Movement of Steve Biko. Tutu fully embraced Black theology as a theology of the oppressed and as a liberation theology, while deeply rooted in his faith and spiritual discipline. These conditions created the landscape for him becoming the preacher as a prophet. In March 1978 he was elected as the General Secretary of the South African Council of Churches (SACC), replacing Beyers Naudé, the Director of the Christian Institute, as 'the political voice and face of the anti-establishment church in South Africa'. Tutu was awarded the Nobel Peace Prize in 1984 for this leading spiritual and political role (Lamola 2021, p. 225).

A decade after he wrote the paper on Black theology, Tutu reflected on the role of the preacher as a prophet. In a sermon at St Luke's Orchards, he asks the question, 'Would we want to be preachers who are prophetic?' warning that, 'We must be aware what we are letting ourselves in for. We must count the cost, for the cost is enormous' (Tutu 1983a, p. 4). Similar to the role of Black theology, he describes the prophets as being 'very concerned with the present', speaking 'specific words to a particular group in a specific time'.

He sets out the characteristics of a prophet as someone who was:

a keen observer of the contemporary scene, privy often to con-
fidential matters relating to the affairs of state such as Israel's
dealings with foreign nations. They were adept at reading the
signs of the times. They were astute men who used a lot of
common sense. (Tutu 1983a, p. 2)

Prophets believed in a moral universe, where right and wrong
mattered, where the distinction between righteousness and
injustice is paramount. They were called by God, claimed their
moral authority based on this calling with no one assuming 'the
honour of his own bat. It must surely stem from the fact that
the prophetic vocation was a painful one.'

Reading through many of his speeches, sermons and books
in the archives and library of the Desmond and Leah Tutu
Legacy Foundation, I get the impression that the above is a
description of his own life experiences, and that he himself
identified strongly with the prophet Jeremiah. Jeremiah, the
so-called weeping prophet, experienced considerable anguish
to pronounce doom 'on a people he loved (for that was another
marked characteristic of the prophet – his deep and real patriot-
ism). He complained that he had had to deliver nothing but
bitter words to his people and yet when he said he would no
longer speak up for Yahweh then God's words became like a
burning fire in his breast and he could not hold them back'
(Tutu 1983a, p. 2). Prophets had to speak unpalatable truths to
recalcitrant people, and were often subjected to much suffering
and were not usually popular persons.

Tutu (1983, p. 2) writes that, 'Jeremiah felt this keenly
because more than most he loved to be loved and enjoyed the
simple delights of villages life – and yet his own village, indeed
his own family, plotted against him.' Tutu portrays Jeremiah as
he described himself in one of his notebooks – as a man 'wanting so very much to be loved'.

He ends the sermon with the following taunting questions,
once again reflecting on his own experiences:

Are you ready to speak up boldly, criticizing evil without fear
or favour, ready to bear the consequences? Are you ready for

the suffering that is almost inevitable – the taunts that you were mixing religion with politics, that you were unpatriotic, the scurrilous attacks on your integrity, on your person and those you love? Are you ready for the suffering that is almost inevitable – that taunts that you were mixing religion with politics, that you were unpatriotic, the scurrilous attacks on your integrity, on your person and those you love? Are you ready for the sake of God's word to risk detention without trial, banning, deportation and even death? It all sounds melodramatic but look at what happened to Bishop Reeves, to Beyers Naudé et al. Are you ready to suffer being unpopular or would you rather heal the deep wound of God's people lightly? Can you bear ostracism by those you love or whose good opinions you value?

Do you have a sense of honour not to take yourself seriously remembering whatever the evidence apparently to the contrary, that this is God's world and he is in charge? If you don't fill this bill, then count out prophecy. Lull your people into false confidence. (Tutu 1983a, pp. 8–9)

There was a moment in late 1979 when far-right Anglicans called on their leaders to distance themselves from Tutu; when the president of the Methodist Church stated that Tutu was speaking without a mandate and when the interior minister of the National Party government took Tutu to task for expressing his opinion to a Danish reporter, while visiting European donors, that it was 'rather disgraceful' that Denmark was purchasing coal from South Africa (Alan 2006, p. 178). This was the start of Tutu's call for a disinvestment campaign in reaction to the forced removal of hundreds of thousands of people. At a meeting between the SACC executive committee and church leaders, chaired by Peter Storey (in the absence of Sam Buti), a consensus opinion was reached that 'in the tradition of the Old Testament prophets, Tutu had a right to express his views as a matter of personal conscience, notwithstanding differences of opinion in the churches' (Alan 2006, p. 178). The prophet was ordained.

# A queer prophet?

So let us get this out of the way. Was Tutu a queer man? There is no sensationalism intended by this question. In no way do I allude to his sexual orientation or hint that Desmond Tutu was gay, although like many gay people, his body became a site of resistance against oppression. In no way do I suggest anything about his desires; although his desiring body and his passion richly infused his spirituality, yearning to be whole. Spirituality is not a disembodied state.

James Nelson, the Christian ethicist, and the father of body theology, wrote that 'desire as an expression of the body-self is an intrinsic element in our openness to God' (1978, p. 33). Spirituality has always been 'a matter of the total self – the body and its desires included'. Much later, he concludes that desire is at the heart of spirituality, a desire which is expressed 'in the hunger for wholeness, a yearning for completion, and a craving for certainty' (2004, p. 23).

Like Black theology, body theology is informed by liberation theology – and by feminist theology. Like Black theology, body theology speaks to a specific community in a particular lifeworld. Nelson writes that 'body theology begins with the concrete' and not with doctrines or creeds or problems in tradition (1992, p. 43). It begins with the concrete and 'the fleshly experience of life – with our hungers and our passions, our bodily aliveness and deadness'.

When Desmond Tutu at the 2013 United Nations Free and Equal campaign famously said, 'I would refuse to go to a homophobic heaven. No, I would say sorry, I mean I would rather go to the other place. I would not worship a God who is homophobic and that is how deeply I feel about it' (BBC 2013), he did so in complete solidarity with LGBTIQA+ persons. He did so as a preacher that became a queer prophet.

When Tutu preached at All Saints Church in Pasadena, California in 2005, paraphrasing Jesus, exclaiming, 'Hey, do you know something? You are family. You are the human family, God's family ... This family has no outsiders. Everyone is an insider ... All! All! All! – Black, white, yellow; rich, poor; clever, not so clever; beautiful, not so beautiful. All! All! … All are to be held in this incredible embrace. Gay, lesbian, so-called "straight;" all! All!' he did so as a retired archbishop who deliberately and strategically decided to use international platforms to advocate for the human rights and equal inclusion of LGBTIQA+ communities (2005, p. 3).

When Desmond Tutu emphatically wrote that it would be unlikely that Christ would be on the side of those who ostracize people based on their race, gender or sexual orientation, making them aliens, banning them from the household of God, he did so as the struggle activist and priest that became a prophet (1997, pp. ix–x). He continued: 'If the church, after the victory over apartheid, is looking for a worthy moral crusade, then this is it: the fight against homophobia and heterosexism.'

Adriaan van Klinken and Ezra Chitando write that, as with the false theological justification of apartheid, wanting 'black people to believe that they do not fully bear God's image and are less valuable children of God, homophobic and heterosexist theologies make gay and lesbian people believe they are inferior in the eyes of God' (2021, p. 103). According to them, Tutu suggests that both theologies are fundamentally un-Christian. They explore some traces of Tutu's awakening to the rights of gay and lesbian people, from a tolerant stance on the gay issue in the 1970s (mentioning them along with drug addicts and the poor), to a steady conviction over the decades to fully accept and affirm LGBTIQA+ persons (Allen 2006, p. 372; Van Klinken and Chitando 2021, p. 100). Tutu was also sensitive to the way in which gender pronouns were used in the Anglican church's liturgy. When they were debating the use of language in liturgy, Tutu verbally expressed his opinion 'we didn't have the same problem in Nguni or Sotho language groups because the pronouns were gender neutral' (Allen 2022).

Wilma Jakobsen, who was appointed in 1995 as the Arch's last chaplain before his retirement, and the first ever woman chaplain, connects Tutu's evolution on the gay issue to the ordination of women in the Anglican church. She writes that 'his earliest public comments on this were in 1990. Towards the end of his episcopate when I was his chaplain, I noticed that he started to speak more boldly and publicly on this issue when he was overseas' (2021, p. 91). The principles of justice and equality implied that any form of discrimination against gays and lesbians was immoral, similar as that against blacks and women. After his retirement, Tutu was unequivocally clear that 'God is not a man, God is not homophobic, God is not a Christian, and all human beings, all people – all are made in the image of God' (Jakobsen 2021, p. 92).

John de Gruchy links this evolution, this becoming, to Tutu's conviction that 'the Transfiguration of Christ is fundamental for the Christian understanding of both personal and societal transformation.' Already in the early 1970s, in a conversation between the two of them, Tutu expressed his wish to write a book on the transfiguration. De Gruchy poignantly writes that for Tutu 'no person is a "nobody" because everyone is "made in the image of God" and has God-given potential to change, and no society is beyond redemption because God's purpose is to create a new humanity' (2021, p. 291). Tutu was engaged in the 'transfiguration of politics', which was an outflow of his belief in God's love and justice, being a prisoner of hope 'for the transfiguration of people and the world despite every contradiction, all opposition and rejection' – all of which Tutu experienced as a prophet (De Gruchy 2021, p. 292).

Desmond Tutu was indeed queer for his time; out of step with many Christians and leaders in the Anglican community, with fellow struggle and human rights activists, with many political – and faith – leaders and victims of apartheid, calling for retribution. No, he was not gay – he was queer; queer in the sense of destabilizing and deconstructing dominant hetero-patriarchal-political centres of power, whether in churches, synagogues, mosques, governments or households. The goal of queer theorists is to liberate everyone from contemporary constructions of sexuality and gender (Van Klinken 2015, p. 43). Queer is used to underscore a viewpoint that embraces gender and sexual plurality, wanting to transform and revolutionize existing African order, instead of assimilating into oppressive heteropatriarchal-capitalist frameworks (Van Klinken 2015, p. 39).

# The embodiment of Desmond Tutu

My research in theological anthropology, focusing on the 'embodied sensing of meaning', gathers from many influential sources. Among them are the life and words of Desmond Tutu, by the body theology of James Nelson, the theological anthropologies of Wentzel van Huyssteen and David Kelsey, the philosophies of the French phenomenologists and that of George Lakoff and Mark Johnson, and more recently, the carnal hermeneutics of Richard Kearney.

The body matters. In the model I suggest for theological anthropology as 'the embodied sensing of meaning', I propose that a theological anthropology with a sentient of the flesh is about the sensing (feeling, thinking, meaning-making) of words about God (scripture, doctrines and tradition), and how this approach resonates with a lived body in a concrete situation, and how the experiencing of that body in its life-world in turn informs the speaking of words about God (interpretation of scripture and tradition in doctrines). Such a model for theological anthropology is an ongoing progression of embodying theology and theologizing (from) the body in the process of making enquiries within theological anthropology about the embodied existence of human and nonhuman creatures before God (Meiring 2015, p. 8). This approach resonates with what Tutu (1973, p. 5) wrote about Black theology nearly 50 years ago – that 'God speaks to us as we are and our theology is filtered through who we are.'

Writing to pastors and councillors, James Nelson said that 'not only our unique personal histories live in us bodily, but also our shared religious and cultural histories' (1992, p. 113). Any religious ambiguity which is part of our personal narrative 'inevitably lives in our bodyselves' and we bring our faith stories and our body stories into our relationship. Our theologies are not disconnected from our bodies. The body Desmond Tutu had and the body he was intimately mediated his theology, spirituality and activism. Richard Kearney (2021, p. 219) writes that 'spirit exits trough nature, soul lives through the body'. Flesh (as medium) is 'the site where we are most keenly attentive to wound and scars, to preconscious memories and traumas, as even our navel reminds us' (Kearney 2021, p. 219).

Reading through Desmond Tutu's books and notebooks, often written when on a spiritual retreat, one gets the sense of his strong spiritual discipline and the process of discernment he went through in making major decisions. He was a prophet listening for the voice of God. But one also senses the struggles with himself, reflecting on growing up as a boy, his right hand paralysed by polio, lying in hospital for many months, doctors fearing for his life. During this time, and throughout his life, Father Trevor Huddleston had a profound influence on Tutu, who describes him to be 'a man full of laughter and fun, deeply committed to justice and the underdog, a champion of their rights and given to much praying' (Tutu 1983b, p. 2). Tutu, furthermore, writes about his mother, not educated beyond elementary school, a domestic servant, later working as a cook for a school for blind Black women:

> I resemble her physically – she has a large nose too. I know that she likes very much to be liked and in that I take after her very much. We have come to call her in the family 'The comforter of the afflicted' because she is very fond of siding with the person who is having the worst of an argument. Maybe some of my concern for the underdog might be taking after my mother as well. (Tutu 1983b, p. 1)

He writes about the anguished relationship with his father, later a headmaster at Munsieville High School in Krugersdorp, prone to drinking and physically abusing his mother. All this left memories, wounds, and scars on his body, which future research will explore. Reasonably, all these embodied relationships deeply influenced the way he made meaning of the world he lived in, the words he uttered, the struggles he fought, the queer prophet he became.

# Conclusion

Tutu writes as follows:

> For me this struggle is a seamless rope. Opposing apartheid was a matter of justice. Opposing discrimination against women is a matter of justice. Opposing discrimination on the basis of sexual orientation is a matter of justice. It is also a matter of love. Every human being is precious ... we cannot answer hate with hate. (2004, p. 5)

Through challenging the injustice and discrimination against Black people during apartheid, by fighting for the ordination of women in the Anglican church in southern Africa, by fervently advocating for the equal rights of gay and lesbian people, and thereby destabilizing dominant constructions of sexuality and gender, Desmond Tutu transfigured from the straight preacher to the queer prophet.

Allan Boesak earned his doctoral degree in 1977 with a thesis entitled, 'A Socio-ethical study of Black Theology and Black Power'. Under his leadership, Black Christians in the Reformed churches began to query for the first time the contradictions 'in being Black and oppressed under apartheid yet in communion with a church and tradition that has been used to justify the oppression and humiliation of their own brothers and sisters' (Lamola 2021, p. 133).

At a memorial event held for the Arch's friends and allies two days before his funeral at the Desmond and Leah Tutu Legacy Foundation, Cape Town, on 30 December 2021, his struggle companion Allan Boesak said:

> ... so many that said to me, is it true that the last hope for South Africa's future is now gone? Is it true that the last voice of conscience of this nation is now gone? Is it true that the last truth-speaker and fighter for justice is now truly gone? I must say to them no, THAT is not true ... We are angry, we are disillusioned, we feel betrayed, but what is it that that we can do? And as long as there are young people who want to do what they want to do, I will never give up hope ... So, I

think he died not just with tragedy in his heart, but he died with hope in his heart. Then I decided if there is nothing else I have to do for the rest of my life, and you that are here who mourn his passing and celebrating his life, we can't do that without making that pledge to him and his children, and to our children and to God, that we will not stop until we have raised a thousand new Tutu voices. (Desmond and Leah Tutu Legacy Foundation 2021)

May there be other queer prophets.

# References

Allen, John, 1997, *The Essential Desmond Tutu*, Cape Town: David Philips.

Allen, John, 2006, *Rabble-Rouser for Peace: The Authorised Biography of Desmond Tutu*, New York: Free Press.

Allen, John, 2022, WhatsApp message to author, 2 July 2022.

BBC, 2013, 'Archbishop Tutu Would not Worship a Homophobic God', 26 July. Available at https://www.bbc.com/news/world-africa-23464694, accessed 29 June 2022.

De Gruchy, John, 2021, 'Nothing is "Untransfigurable": Tutu and the Transfiguration of Politics' in Sarojini Nadar, Tinyiko Maluleke, Dietrich Werner, Vicentia Kgabe and Rudolf Hinz (eds), *Ecumenical Encounters with Desmond Mpilo Tutu: Visions for Justice, Dignity and Peace*, Oxford: Regnum Books International, pp. 291–4.

Desmond and Leah Tutu Legacy Foundation, 2021, 'Honouring the Arch', December 30. Available at https://www.youtube.com/watch?v=mlEop4jOI1Y, accessed 1 July 2022.

Du Boulay, Shirley, 1988, *Tutu: Archbishop Without Frontiers*, London: Hodder & Stoughton.

Faigle, Volker, 2021, '"Africa's Most Refreshing Son": Inspiring Solidarity Between the German and African Churches' in Sarojini Nadar, Tinyiko Maluleke, Dietrich Werner, Vicentia Kgabe and Rudolf Hinz (eds), *Ecumenical Encounters with Desmond Mpilo Tutu: Visions for Justice, Dignity and Peace*, Oxford: Regnum Books International, pp. 197–200.

Jakobsen, Wilma, 2021, 'Stretched Towards Inclusion: Tutu, Gender and Sexuality' in Sarojini Nadar, Tinyiko Maluleke, Dietrich Werner, Vicentia Kgabe and Rudolf Hinz (eds), *Ecumenical Encounters with Desmond Mpilo Tutu: Visions for Justice, Dignity and Peace*, Oxford: Regnum Books International, pp. 88–92.

Kearney, Richard, 2021, 'Recovering Embodied Life', *The Japan Mission Journal* 75/4, pp. 219–25.

Lamola, M. John, 2021, *Sowing in Tears: A Documentary History of the Church Struggle Against Apartheid 1960–1990*, Grant Park: African Perspective Publishing.

Meiring, Jacob, 2015, 'Theology in the Flesh – A Model for Theological Anthropology as Embodied Sensing', *HTS Teologiese Studies/Theological Studies* 7/3, Art. #2858, 8 pages. http://dx.doi.org/10.4102/hts.v7i13.2858.

Nelson, James B., 1978, *Embodiment: An Approach to Sexuality and Christian Theology*, London: Augsburg Publishing House.

Nelson, James B., 1992, *Body Theology*, Louisville, KY: Westminster John Knox Press.

Nelson, James B., 2004, *Thirst: God and the Alcoholic Experience*, Louisville, KY: Westminster John Knox Press.

Sparks, Alister and Mpho A. Tutu, 2011, *Tutu: The Authorised Portrait*, Johannesburg: Pan Macmillan South Africa.

Tutu, Desmond M., 1973, 'Black Theology', Archives of the Desmond and Leah Tutu Legacy Foundation, drawer 1, Cape Town, Paper.

Tutu, Desmond M., 1983a, 'The Preacher as Prophet, St Luke's Orchards', Archives of the Desmond and Leah Tutu Legacy Foundation, Speech.

Tutu, Desmond M., 1983b, Speech 1983–18, Untitled, Archives of the Desmond and Leah Tutu Legacy Foundation.

Tutu, Desmond M., 1997, 'Foreword' in P. Germond and Steve de Gruchy (eds), *Aliens in the Household of God: Homosexuality and Christian Faith in South Africa*, Claremont: David Philip Publishers, pp. ix–x.

Tutu, Desmond M., 2004, 'Foreword' in V. Baird, *Sex, Love and Homophobia: Lesbian, Gay, Bisexual and Transgender Lives*, London: Amnesty International UK.

Tutu, Desmond M., 2005, 'And God Smiles, a Sermon by The Most Reverend Desmond Tutu, Archbishop of Cape Town, South Africa', All Saints Church, Pasadena, California.

Tutu, Desmond M., 2006. *The Rainbow People of God: A Spiritual Journey from Apartheid to Freedom*, Cape Town: Double Storey Books.

Van Klinken, Adriaan, 2015, 'In the Image of God: Reconstructing and Developing a Grassroot African Queer Theology from Urban Zambia', *Theology & Sexuality* 21/1, pp. 36–52.

Van Klinken, Adriaan and Ezra Chitando, 2021, 'Race and Sexuality in Desmond Tutu's Theology of Ubuntu' in Sarojini Nadar, Tinyiko Maluleke, Dietrich Werner, Vicentia Kgabe and Rudolf Hinz (eds), *Ecumenical Encounters with Desmond Mpilo Tutu: Visions for Justice, Dignity and Peace*, Oxford: Regnum Books International, pp. 99–108.

## 11

# What Makes a Queer Prophet? Charisma, Authority and Counter-Knowledges in the Ministry of a Kenyan Intersex Apostle

## STEPHEN KAPINDE AND ADRIAAN VAN KLINKEN

## Introduction: about prophets and queer politics in Africa

Prophets, in popular Christian cultures in Kenya and else-where in Africa, are mostly associated with anti-queer politics. In Kenya, perhaps the most well-known example is the char-ismatic leader of the high-profile Ministry of Repentance and Holiness, Prophet David Owuor, who has become well known for addressing many perceived social evils in his preaching, including the 'immorality' of homosexuality, as part of his campaign to protect Kenya as a 'born-again nation' (Parsitau and van Klinken 2018). Likewise, the late Prophet T. B. Joshua, a highly influential Nigerian Pentecostal figure with a huge following across the continent, has claimed to conduct prayers to 'cure' people of their sexual orientation, which he believed is caused by a 'demonic spirit' from which they need to be delivered (BBC 2021). A literary representation of this anti-queer culture of Christian prophecy can be found in the beautiful novel *An Ordinary Wonder*, by the Nigerian writer Buki Papillon, which includes a narrative about the protagonist

– a young intersex boy – being traumatized after his mother takes him to an indigenous charismatic church where a prophet attempts to aggressively deliver him from the 'demon' purportedly possessing him. Thus, charismatic Christian prophets appear to play a prominent role in the politics of what has been described as 'the moral regeneration of the state' and its citizens by African Christian actors (Bompani and Valois 2018), a politics that appears to be particularly concerned with issues of gender and sexuality (van Klinken and Obadare 2018).

However, this chapter demonstrates that this emerging picture of anti-queer Christian prophecy in Africa is not the full story. Another story exists, about how the figure of the prophet can be – and in fact, already is – redeemed and claimed for queer politics, as a contribution to a broader reimagination of sexual diversity in African Christianity (van Klinken and Chitando 2021). One noteworthy example here is the self-identifying 'lesbian prophetess', Prophetess Jacinta, who is featured in the documentary film *Kenyan, Christian, Queer* (Obinyan 2020), preaching a gospel of inclusivity in the *matatus* (Kenya's minibuses) and on the streets of Nairobi. Another illustrious case, which is the focus of the present chapter, is Apostle Darlan Rukih, founder of the Bride of the Lamb Ministries International Church (BLMI-C), who openly identifies as intersex and performs gender ambiguity. Rukih has established their church as a queer space, where members of the LGBTIQA+ community freely interact and fellowship together. Although Rukih has adopted the title 'apostle' rather than 'prophet' as a self-descriptor, they operate in the same discursive register of prophetic charismatic Christianity. Building on the case of Apostle Rukih, in this chapter we explore the potential of Pentecostal-Charismatic Christianity to develop 'counter queer knowledges' that can serve as a powerful counterforce to the dominant anti-queer Christian discourse in Kenya and the continent at large.

In the following section, we begin with an outline of the two key concepts of this chapter: prophecy and counter-knowledges. Proceeding from there, we introduce Apostle Rukih and their church. The main body of the chapter consists of a section discussing the prophetic practices and discourses through which Rukih develops queer counter-knowledges and inserts them in the Kenyan religio-public sphere. The chapter then concludes by discussing the significance and some of the implications of the case of Apostle Rukih in the broader context of Christianity and sexual and gender diversity in the Kenyan and broader African setting. As a preliminary note: because Rukih variably uses both male and female pronouns and performs gender ambiguity, in this chapter we use gender-neutral pronouns (they/them) when referring to them.

## Prophecy and counter-knowledges

As much as the term 'prophet' in contemporary parlance tends to be associated with charismatic Christian figures, it is important to note that prophetic figures have a much longer history in Kenya, predating the arrival of missionary Christianity. Douglas Johnson and David Anderson refer to figures variably called diviners, oracles, spirit mediums and witch doctors among the various ethnic groups in East Africa. They subsequently conclude that 'the variety of "prophets" thus found in eastern Africa is indeed bewildering and defies easy amalgamation within a single analytical category' (1995, p. 6). Seeking to develop an analytically more precise understanding, they conceptualize the prophet as an 'inspired figure' who 'must be concerned with the wider moral community at a social or political level', and with the community recognizing their moral authority as 'inspired by a divinity or other source of spiritual or moral knowledge that influences the destiny of the community' (1995, pp. 17–19). The variety of prophetic figures has only become more diverse with the emergence of Christian-styled prophets, such as in the twentieth-century independent or spiritual churches, and in twenty-first-century (neo-)Pentecostal movements. Modern-day prophets in Kenya often make use of audio-visuals and social media in order to establish and perform religious authority (Wagner and Schulz 2022). Yet although the cultural styles of the prophet may have changed, the key elements identified by Johnson and Anderson of what makes a prophet are still relevant: spiritual inspiration, social-political commitment, and community recognition. As Ruy Llera Blanes puts it in a discussion of contemporary African prophetism, prophetic charisma 'implies a disruption of traditional political authority; it inaugurates new ways of thought and experience that are mediated simultaneously by contrary emotions of uncertainty and trust concerning the future' (2013, p. 147). As we show below, Apostle Rukih – by their persona as an openly intersex Christian prophet, but also through their prophetic utterances in religious ritual and preaching – contests established religious and political voices who are invested in maintaining hetero-orthodoxy and rigid gender binaries, and by doing so they open up new possibilities and imaginations.

In the context of this chapter, we speak about Rukih as a Kenyan queer prophet. Adding the adjective 'queer' indicates the particular spiritual, social and political vision that the prophet is invested in. This is the vision of a queer utopia, powerfully captured in the 'African LGBTI/Queer Manifesto', which states:

> As Africans, we stand for the celebration of our complexities and we are committed to ways of being which allow for self-determination at all levels of our sexual, social, political and economic lives. ... We are specifically committed to the transformation of the politics of sexuality in our contexts, as long as African LGBTI people are oppressed, the whole of Africa is oppressed. (Ekine and Abbas 2013, pp. 52–3)

Perhaps surprisingly, given the popular association of Christian prophets with anti-queer politics, we suggest that Rukih's prophetic figure and performance is one way in which this queer African revolution and reimagination is being engendered. Rukih's self-cultivated identity as an intersex prophet may be seen by many as paradoxical, yet it reflects one of the complexities that ought to be celebrated and embraced as a form of self-determination and creative imagination, as stated in the above manifesto. Adopting the concept of queer counter-knowledges (Robinson and Davies 2012), we explore the particular prophetic practices through which Rukih presents alternative religio-political imaginaries that counter anti-queer politics and open up alternative possibilities. As the queer theorist J. Halberstam (2012) suggests, such counter-knowledges often come from 'unexpected sources', and here we contend that Apostle Darlan Rukih might be such an unexpected source.

## Emergence of Apostle Darlan Rukih as a 'queer prophet'

As an intersex pastor, Darlan Rukih founded Bride of the Lamb Ministries International (BLMI-C) in 2001 as an inclusive space for both gender and sexually conforming and non-conforming persons. To understand the story of their ministry, it is essential to understand their life. Notably, BLMI-C's webpage includes a detailed account of Rukih's childhood experiences and their calling into ministry, which itself narrates their religious authority (ChurchFinder, n.d.).

According to this account, the Apostle was born in 1975 at Karungu in Homa Bay County, Western Kenya. They were born out of an affair between their mother, Marashan Raya, from the Sakwa Waora people, and their biological father, Maalan Nzambi, from the town of Zanza. Yet they grew up in the house of their mother's long-term partner, Mark Ngaw, from the Luo people, whom they believed to be their father. At birth, Rukih was recognized as a boy and, although officially named Darlan Rukih, as a child they were more commonly known as Moses. The name Moses responded to a prophecy by a woman from the Roho Israel church that they would be a servant of God like Moses, perhaps a reflection of their future prophetic ministry. Rukih was born as intersex, which troubled the mother so much that she even contemplated killing them if their grandmother had not intervened. As Darlan Rukih narrates:

I was born an intersex with both female and male sexual organs. My mother did not want the people to know my sexual identity and decided that I should be referred as a boy because she feared that people will abuse me as an intersex. As I grew up I also felt that being a boy was better although my feminine identity was also a matter of public knowledge. I developed interest in putting on my foster sister's dress against her wish although I did it innocently as a child. (Rukih, in interview with Kapinde 2021)

Growing up as an intersex person, Rukih faced hostility at home, as siblings and relatives constantly challenged their sexual and gender orientation. Like the biblical prophet Jeremiah (e.g. see Jeremiah 11.18–23), Rukih's social life was disrupted, as they faced social exclusion and discrimination including constant harassment and threats from their peers and the community at large. Rukih recounts these ordeals and other risks facing sexual minorities in Kenya and particularly, the LGBTIQA+ community. They recall some painful incidents during their elementary education as follows:

I had thought that the discrimination I faced was limited to my clan and family members at home. However, when I joined school in 1986, I faced hostility from my peers and teachers as well who questioned whether I was a girl or a boy. I was mocked during lessons and my classmate did not want to share the desk with me, with boys claiming that I was a girl and girls pushing me to sit with boys. ... I could not partici-pate in sports as teachers did not know which gender category to place me. These tribulations made me to shift from one school to another. ... I lost hope in education and felt discour-aged with schooling due to my poor performance. (Rukih, in interview with Kapinde 2021)

The Apostle's painful experience at school as well as in their family is one among many such agonizing stories of sexual and gender minorities in Kenya. Referring to this struggle, Darlan Rukih confirms that 'consolation was only through God' ('From intersex stigma' 2017). The societal stigma they faced was at least twofold. First, being born out of wedlock meant that they could not be accepted as a legitimate child by the foster father and his Luo community. Second, among Kenyan communities, an intersex child traditionally tends to be seen as a bad omen and a curse; it was supposed to be killed upon birth and a sacrifice offered to the gods to appease their spirits over the death of the child (Qarim, in interview with Kapinde 2021). Although the rights of intersex people in contemporary society have been reaffirmed by the Kenyan Supreme Court, it is documented that 'Intersex persons in Kenya continue to face human rights violations mainly centred on their legal recognition which has a negative ripple effect in the enjoyment of their other human rights and fundamental freedoms' (KNCHR n.d.).

Against this background of stigmatization, the young Darlan found comfort in their faith. The BLMI-C webpage states, in almost hagiographic language: 'Darlan Rukih was born a religious child who feared God and loved the people of God so much. This was contrary to the children in the home where she was brought up.[1] They loved secular life more than religious life' (ChurchFinder, n.d.). Yet their experiences of stigma and discrimination reinforced their religious zeal, as they realized that 'it is only God who can help a person out of his trouble' (ChurchFinder, n.d.). In 1988, Rukih received a 'calling to serve God', while attending a pilgrim service in an independent church. Due to the cultural and social stigma, being born an intersex brought numerous challenges to Rukih's Christian ministry. The biographical account on the BLMI-C website narrates multiple transitions from one church to another, sometimes because of rejection and marginalization due to being intersex, and sometimes because of doctrinal differences between Rukih and the leaders of that respective church. In the end, Rukih decided to follow their calling by starting their own church, in the town of Ndhiwa, in Homa Bay County, Nyanza Province, in Western Kenya. The church was registered in 2004 as Moses Mark Ngaw Ministries. In the year 2012, the name was changed to Bride of the Lamb Ministry International-Church because Mark Ngaw, Rukih's foster father, did not want his name associated with the ministry. At that time, Rukih also stepped down as the lead pastor and chairperson of the ministry, instead adopting the title Apostle to indicate their position as spiritual leader, with Pastor Baran Qarim being appointed as chairperson. BLMI-C has a wide following in Kenya, particularly in Nyanza province and in the Coast region, with a few branches in Tanzania. The church also established mission centres, with St Darlan Rukih Mission in Ndhiwa serving as its headquarters. Rukih's popularity is evidenced by their considerable following: religious gatherings of BLMI-C are typically attended by thousands of worshippers; on Facebook, both Rukih's individual account and the church's formal account at the time of writing have about 5,000 followers.

As discussed earlier, Rukih's conversion to Christianity was to a considerable extent informed by their experiences of marginalization and stigma due to their intersex condition. The move by the Apostle to start their own church can be seen as an attempt to create a space for sexual and gender minorities and to contextualize the struggle for sexual and gender diversity within the religious space. This mission should not be seen as a form of liberal sexual rights activism, however. Interestingly, the BLMI-C webpage in its narrative about Rukih's ministry puts a strong emphasis on the importance of born-again conversion and 'sexual purity', warns against 'lascivious deeds including lust, uncleanliness and fornication', and mentions celibacy as a religious virtue adopted by some of Rukih's followers. Rukih themself, according to this narrative, is separated from their first wife, who committed adultery, and has refused to remarry ever since, despite the pressure from fellow church leaders to find a spouse (ChurchFinder, n.d.).

Rukih has adopted the title 'Apostle' – a term that, like 'prophet', is often used by the leaders of African Independent Charismatic Churches, and which can be seen as a discursive claim towards spiritual authority rooted in a personal calling by Christ himself. Titles such as 'apostle' and 'prophet' are not clearly defined offices in African Christianity – in fact, the terminology often is fluid, and church leaders can be addressed and referred to by their followers with various names. This is the case with Rukih, whose followers see them as a prophet and who are attracted to the church precisely because of its prophetic ministry. Each church service includes time for prophecy, in which different members with the gift of prophecy are given the opportunity to share their vision, and during which the Apostle also shares their own prophecy, for instance regarding the state of the nation and about societal issues. In one service Kapinde attended, the Apostle, after meditating for about 15 minutes, talked of a vision where God reveals to them about the collapse of the Kenyan economy under a young leader. The Apostle then commanded the congregation to pray for the country before turning to warn the church over laxity when praying. Thus, Rukih meets the description of the prophet from Anderson and Johnson (1995, pp. 17–19), as their followers see them as an inspired figure whose spiritual power and authority comes from Christ, and as Rukih arguably demonstrates a concern with the moral community at a socio-political level.[2]

Based on the Apostle's spiritual powers demonstrated through healing, exorcism and miracles, Rukih's prophetic ministry has grown considerably. A number of people who identify as LGBTIQA+ or who otherwise are in the spectrum of sexual and gender diversity belong to the ministry. This is significant, because there is an ongoing debate in Kenya and elsewhere about whether intersex people should be included under the LGBTIQA+ umbrella, given that the intersex condition is not about sexual orientation. Some intersex activists frame intersex as a medical condition, and consequently deliberately dissociate themselves from other sexual and gender minority groups (Petersen 2021, p. 197). Yet despite these debates among activists and academics, apparently many Kenyan queer people are attracted to BLMI-C, most likely because of the way in which the Apostle has openly come out as intersex, questions norms of sexuality and gender, and does not hesitate to associate with other sexual and gender minorities and welcomes them in their church. For instance, one church member who identified as gay narrated how he has been at St Darlan Rukih mission centre for the last three years, considering it his home due to the hospitality extended to him by the Apostle and other pastors (fieldwork conversation with Kapinde 2021).

BLMI-C attracts criticism from some Pentecostal pastors for embracing LGBTIQA+. Such criticism places the Apostle's life in danger. Pastor Baran Qarim recalled an incident in 2017 when some Pentecostal pastors incited the local community to attack St Darlan Rukih mission centre on the pretext that it was a devil-worshipping centre (Qarim, in interview with Kapinde 2021). Qarim and other BLMI-C pastors in conversations indicated that the attack had religious, social and political motives. First, the growing popularity of BLMI-C unsettled some Pentecostal clerics who engineered propaganda to tarnish the name of the Apostle as an agent of the devil. Second, St Darlan Rukih mission centre hosts more than 115 widows and about 250 orphans, and the Apostle serves as the guardian of this vulnerable group. Culturally, however, the widows are expected to abide by the local traditions of marrying their deceased husband's brother (a kind of a levirate marriage) rather than settling in a mission centre. As a result, the Apostle is viewed as one who challenges traditions and customs of the community. Lastly, the mission centre has a huge population of electoral voters whose numbers are crucial in deciding the local county leadership. The 2017 election results suggest, to some, that the followers of the Apostle voted for one candidate linked to Rukih's ministry, much to the chagrin of the candidate's opponents, who subsequently engineered the attacks on the centre.

## Apostle Darlan Rukih's counter-knowledges to anti-queer discourses

While African Pentecostal prophets have been depicted as largely anti-queer, Apostle Darlan Rukih and BLMI-C provide an alternative image. The Apostle and their church employ multiple and overlapping strategies in challenging heteronormativity and empowering sexual and gender minorities in Kenya, which can be read as a unique set of Kenyan, Christian and queer 'arts of resistance' (van Klinken 2019). In this chapter, we limit our analysis to four main methods that the church as well as the Apostle creatively utilize in their prophetic ministry. These include the use of songs, prayer rallies or crusades, talent shows and lastly the Apostle's gendered performance marked by cross-dressing and transvestitism. What follows is a discussion of these subversive approaches, including queer sermons, which we consider as counter-knowledges and as alternative queer religio-political imaginaries.

First, the Apostle composes songs and hymns that appear to reflect queer experiences and to affirm the bodies and identities of LGBTIQA+ persons. David Elliot argues that music can be considered 'as a form and a source of knowledge' and that the artist's composition is not accidental but intentional. Indeed, music has always functioned as 'a dynamic mediator of gender and sexuality' and as a productive site of symbolic resistance to cultural hegemonies and performance of queerness (Taylor 2012, p. 1). Furthermore, the performance and consumption can help in the construction of queer identities that can reveal otherworldliness as well as arouse an alternative political imagination. Building on these notions, we analyse Rukih's songs as a gendered discourse presenting queer counter-knowledges. Given that the majority of LGBTIQA+ people in Kenya live in the closet and fear coming out, the Apostle's songs create a counter-hegemonic discourse of encouragement and affirmation. See, for instance the song *Berna Obongo Nyakalanga* ('God is good'), part of which reads:

### Luo
*Berna Obongo Nyakalanga ine ngama dwara*
*Kingi nene ihera nyakanene omiyo nichweya*
*Kingi nene ihera nyakanene omiyo nichweya*
*Ngat achiel to otingo sura saba dok iyie onyuala an*

### English translation
You are good to me, Father, you are the one I need
Lord, you loved me ever since you created me
If you were like a human being I would not have been born
One person bearing seven images I would not have been born

In this song, the Apostle implicitly alludes to their own intersex condition, claiming their queer body as part of God's design of creation. In line 2, the Apostle claims God's love as a fundamental truth and as ground of their being, and suggests that God created them in a unique way. Through songs like this, other LGBTIQA+ members of the church feel affirmed in their identity and faith. The Apostle further claims in this song that they 'bear seven images', meaning biblical personalities that signify their queer identity.[3] Rukih explained these biblical images and how they relate to their intersex condition (Rukih, in interview with Kapinde 2021). First, the Apostle argues to be created in the *image* and *likeness* of God (Gen. 1.27). Theologically, this may seem uncontested considering that God is the architecture of all creation, yet Rukih uses it to counter the popular idea that being intersex is a 'mistake' of nature ('From intersex stigma' 2017). Second, the Apostle claims to embody the image of Adam typified by the male anatomy, and third the image of Eve, by reference to her femininity as a woman. Thus, Rukih identifies as *both* male and female. Fourth, the Apostle also considers themself to represent the image of Christ. They justify this aspect with reference to the pluralistic statement by God in the creation episodes: 'Let us make man in our image and in our likeness' (Gen. 1.26) and 'And God said, the man has become like one of us' (Gen. 3.22). The plural construction of God also be understood in a Trinitarian sense (God the Father, the Son and the Holy Spirit).[4] Based on this Trinitarian understanding, the Apostle believes that they embody the image of Christ. Fifth, and based on the same understanding, they claim to also be a bearer of the Holy Spirit. Sixth, the Apostle claims that they are created in the image and likeness of the angels, which is interesting given the fact that angels are typically seen as gender-neutral. They qualify this argument by referring to the aforementioned pluralistic statement 'us' and 'our' in the creation narrative. For the Apostle, the angels were equally present during the creation, and humanity resembles them as well. Seventh and last, the Apostle claims to have been created in the image of Jesus, the messiah, which is a reference to the humanity of Jesus. Creative biblical interpretation and innovative theological reflection are quite common in African Pentecostal-Charismatic circles. Rukih's claim of bearing these seven biblical images reflects this creativity and innovation, and it presents a queer form of theologizing as they use it to affirm themself as a non-conforming person, queering the boundaries between male and female, and human and divine. Thus, they directly interrogate popular Christian belief that reinforces a pejorative attitude towards queer bodies. In that sense, the Apostle's claim towards embodiment of the seven biblical personalities represents a prophetic representation of queerness.

In other songs, the Apostle dwells on the pain, suffering and tribulations faced by the queer community, and how God is gracious to them in a rather hostile heterosexual environment. The song *Tije Ni Baba* ('Your works, Father') is reminiscent of the painful experiences of the Apostle growing up as an intersex, the opening lines reading:

**Luo**
*Kanibiro lima nene iyudo sigu kopong'o iya*
*Kanidonjo e chunya neni pudho sigu modar oweya*
*Sigu nosekona mondo atho ne jowa mochaya*

**English translation**
My heart was full of enmity when you visited me
Lord, you loved me ever since you created me
Enmity had hold of me to die because of those who hate me

In lines 1 and 2, the Apostle appreciates how God rescued them from enmity against their tormentors. While this song gives an account of life experiences of the Apostle, other members of the LGBTIQA+ community in the church can easily identify with it. Further, BLMI-C members sang this song among others touching on the Apostle's life during church services. Here, gospel music serves as a form of pastoral and spiritual healing, evoking the presence of God in difficult circumstances and assuring worshippers, including queer folks, that God is on their side.

In BLMI-C, queer hymns are frequently sung during prayer services. This includes thanksgiving hymns such as *Ngwono nyasaye* ('The mercies of God'), which, when sung through the mouth of LGBTIQA+ folks, expresses gratitude to God for protecting sexual and gender minorities. Interestingly, the songs and hymns provide a context for self-making and a resource in queer identity formation and community bonding (Taylor 2012; Jones 2021). Thus, it enables an alternative imagination for self-presentation of gender diversity in a more constricted heteronormative culture. In their composition, the Apostle flexibly plays with gendered language by often alternating the pronouns 'he' and 'she' in the songs. Exemplifying this aspect is another song titled *Pok ayudo machalo gi yesu* ('I have not met anyone like Jesus'), which smoothly shifts between both genders. Further, the aspect of 'otherness' is represented in the song and how God intervenes in everyday queer life experiences. In addition to the lyrics, the performance of songs often is gender ambiguous. See, for instance, the way Rukih dresses themselves (see the discussion below). As such, they present a confirmation of Judith Butler's (1990) argument that gender identity can be constituted through repeated performative acts. In light of these queer songs, we argue that gospel music is a key method through which the Apostle showcases non-normative expressions, affirms them pastorally and theologically, encourages and nurtures queer people of faith, and thus channels beliefs that are counter-hegemonic to the patriarchal and colonial norms of heterosexuality. Not all of the Apostle's songs are explicitly religious. In some of them, Rukih instead engages more explicitly with political themes, invoking Luo history and tradition. One of those songs, titled *Jaramogi*, praises queer legends within the Luo community such as Nyar Migondho and the legendary warrior Lwanda Magere, as well as a more recent political figure, Jaramogi Oginga, a twentieth-century Luo chief who played a prominent role in the struggle for Kenyan independence. This song, discussed in more detail below, revalorises cultural traditions and values in an implicit appeal for acceptance of queer persons, countering the popular idea that queer identities are 'un-African'.

The second approach used by the Apostle involves prayer rallies in the form of BLMI-C crusades and conventions. The crusades provide sacred spaces for the performance of prayer healings and the enactment of queer testimonies and autobiographical accounts that allow for alternative modes of being. The crusades take place in market places and major towns across the country while the annual conventions occur at St Darlan Rukih mission centre in Ndhiwa. In these crusades and prayer rallies, the Apostle usually begins the sermon with an autobiographical account of their life as an intersex person. Woven through the testimonies are queer hymns about the mercies of God they have experienced. The Apostle uses the crusades as a public site for the display of queerness. Interviews with members of BLMI-C indicated that crusades serve to create an inclusive religious environment for sexually nonconforming persons (e.g. Qarim and Darlene, in interview with Kapinde 2021). Furthermore, the crusades serve as 'spaces of reconciliation' between the queer community and the larger heterosexual society. In one instance, the Apostle reportedly rescued an intersex during a crusade at Homa Bay town who had contemplated suicide. However, listening to the testimony of the Apostle, the relatives who had been abusive to the person called for forgiveness and prayers (Qarim, in interview with Kapinde 2021).

Third and likewise, BLMI-C frequently organizes talent shows for members of the community, mostly youths, to provide queer persons with a space to claim their gender identity through artistic performance. In both contexts, participants perform their queerness in multiple ways within the space of the church. This in itself demonstrates the ways in which queer resistance can take place within (rather than only against) normative institutions. For instance, the artistic performance through dance and singing sustains a queer soundscape as an alternative voice of protest. The crusades and conventions including the talent day, enhances the visibility of queer bodies as they appropriate such spaces to frame their sexual identity and create awareness. According to Pastor Qarim, 'the Apostle initiated talent day as an important practice in our church for people who have been denied such opportunity in the past on the basis of their gender and sexual orientation' (Qarim, in interview with Kapinde 2021). The testimonies and religious expressions inspire other queer persons to come out of their closet and thus they normalize queerness as part of public culture. Yet the queer hymns and melodies serve several purposes, including exposing the struggles of the queer community in contemporary Kenya. The Apostle uses these sacred spaces to subvert hegemonic masculinity and dominant understanding of gender. The crusades have a community-building function for queer persons and are a site for counter-hegemonic discourse to heteronormativity and other damaging religious and patriarchal norms. In addition, the sacred spaces provide the Apostle with an opportunity to exercise their prophetic authority by challenging retrogressive socio-cultural practices that subordinate some genders and sexualities over others.

The fourth method through which Rukih develops queer prophetic counter-knowledges is through their own embodied performance as an intersex prophet. The Apostle through cross-dressing shifts easily between the male/female identity, often creating unstable and indeterminate subjectivities. In their style of dress, the Apostle neatly depicts a gender-ambiguous intersex personality. For instance, they frequently wear a trouser-skirt in the form of culottes, combined with a shirt and a priestly collar, and a veil that doubles as a cap. In BLMI-C, intersex members have embraced this mode of dressing as a form of intersex dress code. In a more conservative society like Kenya, the Apostle's dress is a form of subversion, and indeed people frequently question Rukih's fashion style. For the Apostle, cross-dressing is one way of performing individual autonomy and more fundamentally contesting the gendered dress code in society (Kapasula 2006). All these forms of dress provide avenues for sexual and gender subversion.

Rukih's own performance of gender ambiguity is inspired by their reading of Luo tradition, in which they identify as a mythical gender-ambiguous or queer woman. In an earlier section we mentioned the song *Jaramogi* in reference to a popular Luo politician, the father of the former Prime Minister of Kenya, Raila Odinga (2008–13). Yet in the *Jaramogi* song, Rukih explicitly appeals to the Luo community to appreciate 'othernesses' and particularly the meek and oppressed people in society. Critically, the song talks of the mythical woman in Luo tradition called 'Nyar Migondho', who was married to Nyamgondho, son of Ombare. The Apostle implicitly presents this woman as 'queer' as she lacked the feminine mystique associated with traditional Luo women. The Apostle describes the woman as having 'a male physique' and suggests no Luo man would marry her even without paying a dowry (Rukih, in an interview with Kapinde 2021). According to the myth, in his fishing expeditions in Lake Victoria, Nyamgondho met the woman and took her home as his wife. The woman brought a lot of blessing to Nyamgondho in the form of material possession. Legends have it, however, that Nyar Migondho was a goddess who brought tremendous blessing to Nyamgondho and later disappeared into Lake Victoria following abuse from her husband, Nyamgondho. Taking up another example from the *Jaramogi* song, the Apostle narrates the mythical story of Simbi Nyaima, another less fortunate woman who was despised but took revenge by cursing a local community in Southern Nyanza. Based upon these legends, oral histories and cultural anthologies enable the Apostle to foreground subjugated knowledges as essential in queering the Kenyan nation. By inviting us to traditional folklore and art, the Apostle reveals that queerness and transvestitism is not a foreign phenomenon in Africa. In fact, Frederick Lamp (2002) points out that among the Ameru community of Kenya, ritual leaders called Mugawe dress routinely as women and sometimes even marry men. Thus, the Apostle innovatively uses the stories and past events to construct a 'queer historiography' that challenges normativity in form as well as content – a way of productively challenging not only what we think we know about the past, but how we came to know it. This way, Rukih also culturally legitimates their own gender-ambiguous dressing style and persona.

By identifying as an intersex person and by performing gender ambiguity and fluidity, the Apostle interrupts gender binaries, asserts a radical allegiance to queer identity and embraces their God-given identity rather than conform to patriarchal hegemonic norms of the society. Critics of the Apostle accuse them of instrumentalizing religion for queer activism. For instance, one Pentecostal cleric argued that Rukih uses religion to normalize homosexuality in Kenya (note the equation of intersex with homosexuality here), and that BLMI-C has become one of the centres for the LGBTIQA+ community (Orucho, in conversation with Kapinde 2021). Similar views are shared by another Pentecostal cleric, Kennedy Odeny, who publicly stated that queerness is the work of the devil and that the Apostle should not be regarded as a church leader (SBS Dateline 2018). The Apostle, however, refutes these claims, arguing that denominational rivalry and ideological propaganda could be at play due to the growing popularity of their prophetic ministry in the region. Regardless of these contentions, it is clear that BLMI-C has become a sanctuary for members of the queer community, as the Apostle teaches Christ's love and compassion that transcends all sexual and gender binaries. In their teachings, the Apostle presents their church as a collaborating partner of the queer community. As a partner, the Church should open its doors to all by providing inclusive spaces for authentic dialogue and love. Calls for love and tolerance are compromised as the Apostle like other biblical prophets faces backlash. For Rukih, the backlash comes from homophobic clerics who accuse them of legitimizing homosexual relations and queer practices.

## Conclusion: what makes Darlan Rukih a queer prophet?

In view of the foregoing analysis, the subversive approaches employed by Apostle Darlan Rukih help in countering anti-queer narratives and creating a 'queer spiritual space' (Browne, Munt and Yip 2010) within the overall queer-phobic religious climate in Kenya. Furthermore, through popular culture, the Apostle challenges social norms that maintain asymmetrical gender relations and sexual normativities. Particularly, music helps to deconstruct patriarchal heteronormative gender and sexual structures that are oppressive to members of the queer community. On the other hand, the songs embody the violent and traumatic experiences of queer beings. Yet they also present a glimpse of hope through the gracious love of God to the queer community. Importantly, through Rukih's ministry, BLMI-C has become a counter-cultural space where gender and sexual non-conforming bodies are welcomed and embraced, and where they can experience the love of God and the presence of the Holy Spirit. In a unique way, Rukih and BLMI-C adopt and appropriate Pentecostal-Charismatic styles and languages, in particular prophecy, that are queer affirming. With reference to the definition of East African prophecy discussed earlier, derived from Anderson and Johnson, Rukih is indeed a queer Kenyan Christian prophet: their religious authority is claimed to be inspired by God; they are concerned with the community at a social and political level, in particular creating a community and envisioning a society that is inclusive towards those marginalized by dominant socio-cultural and religious norms of gender and sexuality; and last but not least, their followers confirm this claim of divine inspiration and authority, and share the vision of an inclusive community. A future study could examine in more detail the ways in which Rukih's prophetic charisma is received by their followers, both queer and straight. Yet from the above discussion it is clear that, by invoking both the style of Pentecostal-Charismatic Christianity and the tradition of Luo mythology, Apostle Darlan Rukih in their persona, performance and message presents a uniquely indigenized form of African, Christian and queer prophecy, inaugurating 'new ways of thought and experience' (Blanes 2013, p. 147). Notably, Rukih does so outside of the established circles of LGBTIQA+ activism in Kenya, thus not only demonstrating the plurality of Christianity but also of queer world-making practices in contemporary African contexts.

## Acknowledgement

The empirical part of this study was conducted by the first author, Stephen Kapinde, under the LUCAS-LAHRI fellowship scheme for African academics with the University of Leeds in

2021, during which he was mentored by, and worked with, the second author, Adriaan van Klinken. Together we collaborated in the analysis of and reflection on the data and in the conceptual framing of this chapter.

## Notes

1 The BLMI-C webpage here uses both female and neutral pronouns for Rukih. As explained in the introduction, as authors we have opted for neutral (they/them) pronouns when referring to Rukih.

2 Anderson and Johnson describe the moral community as a 'community whose members have reciprocal moral obligations to each other' (1995, p. 18). The purpose of Rukih's ministry can be seen as promoting precisely such a sense of moral obligation, using a religious vision to transcend the boundaries of kinship, ethnicity, class and indeed gender and sexuality.

3 This claim in the lyrics is part of a broader discourse by, and about, Rukih. For instance, in an online article about Rukih, one of their followers responds: 'Amazing man with an amazing story and what powerful songs! The man with seven images ... how true! God bless Rukih' (Oginde 2015).

4 The church on its website states its agreement with the Apostles' Creed and the Nicene Creed, which both have a Trinitarian structure.

## References

Anderson, Douglas M. and David H. Johnson (eds), 1995, *Revealing Prophets: Prophecy in Eastern African History*, London: James Currey.

BBC, 2021, 'TB Joshua: YouTube blocks Nigerian preacher over gay cure claim', *BBC*, 16 April, https://www.bbc.com/news/world-africa-56771246, accessed 17.10.2022.

Blanes, Ruy Llera, 2013, 'Extraordinary Times: Charismatic Repertoires in Contemporary African Prophetism' in Charles Lindholm (ed.), *The Anthropology of Religious Charisma*. Contemporary Anthropology of Religion, New York: Palgrave Macmillan, pp. 147–68.

Bompani, Barbara and Caroline Valois (eds), 2018, *Christian Citizens and the Moral Regeneration of the African State*, London: Routledge.

Browne, Kath, Sally R. Munt and Andrew Kam-Tuck Yip (eds), 2016, *Queer Spiritual Spaces*, London: Routledge.

Butler, Judith, 1990, *Gender Trouble: Feminism and the Subversion of Identity*, New York: Routledge.

Churchfinder, n.d., 'Apostle Darlan Rukih', https://www.churchfinder. com/churches/sel/no-city-found/bride-lamb-ministries-international/ apostle-darlan-rukih, accessed 28.09.2022.

Ekine, Sokari and Hakima Abbas (eds), 2013, *Queer African Reader*, Dakar, Nairobi and Oxford: Pambazuka Press.

'From intersex stigma to Kenya's gospel star', 2017, BBC, 19 June, https:// www.bbc.co.uk/news/av/magazine-39847299, accessed 17.10.2022.

Halberstam, J., 2012, 'Foreword' in Kerry H. Robinson and Cristyn Davies (eds), *Queer and Subjugated Knowledges: Generating Subversive Imaginaries*, Soest: Bentham Books, pp. i–ii.

Jones, Jay, 2021, 'Music, Activism and LGBTQIA+ History: The Role of Music in Queer Resistance', *The Emory Wheel*, https://emorywheel. com/music-activism-and-lgbtqia-history-the-role-of-music-in-queer-resistance-lets-be-perfectly-queer/, accessed 8.08.2022.

Kapasula, Jessie K., 2006, 'Challenging Sexual Stereotypes: Is Cross-dressing "Un-African"?', *Feminist Africa* 6, pp. 68–72.

KNCHR, n.d., 'Intersex persons in Kenya', *Kenya National Commission on Human Rights*, https://www.knchr.org/Our-Work/Special-Interest-Groups/Intersex-Persons-in-Kenya, accessed 17.10.2022.

Lamp, Frederick, 2002, 'African Art: Traditional', *GLBTQ Archive*, http://www.glbtqarchive.com/arts/af_art_traditional_A.pdf, accessed 22.09.2022.

Obinyan, Aiwan, 2020, *Kenyan, Christian, Queer* (film), London: AiAi Studios, https://www.youtube.com/watch?v=bsU6QRolfzs.

Oginde, David, 2015, Comment in response to George Barasa, 'I am Intersex, Apostle Darlan Rukih Moses comes out of the Closet', *Kuchu Times*, 1 April, https://www.kuchutimes.com/2015/04/i-am-intersex-apostle-darlan-rukih-moses-comes-out-of-the-closet/, accessed 4.01.2023.

Parsitau, Damaris and Adriaan van Klinken, 2018, 'Pentecostal Intimacies: Women and Intimate Citizenship in the Ministry of Repentance and Holiness in Kenya', *Citizenship Studies* 22/6, pp. 586–602.

Petersen, Jay K., 2021, *A Comprehensive Guide to Intersex*, London: Jessica Kingsley Publishers.

Papillon, Buki, 2021, *An Ordinary Wonder*, London: Dialogue Books.

Robinson, Kerry H. and Cristyn Davies (eds), 2012, *Queer and Subjugated Knowledges: Generating Subversive Imaginaries*, Soest: Bentham Books.

SBS Dateline, 2018, 'Meet Kenya's Intersex preacher making waves in his conservative community', *YouTube*, 21 August, https://www.you tube.com/watch?v=19r_rk7KfbU, accessed 17.10.2022.

Taylor, Jodie, 2012, *Playing it Queer: Popular Music, Identity and Queer World-Making*, Bern: Peter Lang.

Van Klinken, Adriaan, 2019, *Kenyan, Christian, Queer: Religion,*

*LGBT Activism, and Arts of Resistance in Africa*, Philadelphia, PA: Penn State University Press.

Van Klinken, Adriaan and Ezra Chitando, 2021, *Reimagining Christianity and Sexual Diversity in Africa*, London: Hurst & Co.

Van Klinken, Adriaan and Ebenezer Obadare, 2018, 'Christianity, Sexuality and Citizenship in Africa: Critical Intersections', *Citizenship Studies* 22/6, pp. 557–68.

Wagner, Nicole and Dorothea Schulz, 2022, 'Validating Prophethood: Audiovisual Media and Religious Authority in Kenyan Pentecostalism' in Ralph W. Hood and Sariya Cheruvallil-Contractor (eds), *Lesser Heard Voices in Studies of Religion: Research in the Social Scientific Study of Religion, Volume 32*, Leiden: Brill, pp. 590–615.

# Interviews

Darlene, M., 2021, Interview with Stephen Kapinde, 22 June, Ndiwa: Kenya.

Orucho, M., 2021, Informal conversation with Stephen Kapinde, 13 August, Rongo: Kenya.

Qarim, B., 2021, Interview with Stephen Kapinde, 23 June, Ndiwa: Kenya.

Rukih, D., 2021, Interview with Stephen Kapinde, 24 June, Ndhiwa: Kenya.

## 12

# Queering the Circumcision Covenant: Transgender Identity in Genesis 17

ROSA ROSS

## Introduction

As part of this volume that reimagines Jonah and his experience as well as activists living in his wake, this essay draws a comparison between biblical circumcision and gender-affirming surgery in our contemporary context. While circumcision had become a normative social practice in the world reflected in the biblical traditions, circumcision is not consistently portrayed as normative in the Hebrew Bible. While often we look forward to contemporary queer experiences, I want to look *backwards* towards Sarah and Abraham as activists, where we can see a model for understanding transgender identity in terms of a kind of embodiment based in social bodily experience but not dependent on a singular, personal bodily experience.

Just as circumcision was a marker of ethnic division in the Hebrew Bible (Exod. 6.12; Josh. 5.7), gender-affirming surgery is politically divisive in our contemporary context. This comparison is anything but cosmetic. Sometimes queer literary approaches are accused of making 'cosmetic' arguments – arguing for the sake of arguing.[1] In a similar way, many insurance providers still consider gender-affirming surgeries as 'cosmetic procedures' when in fact conforming one's gender presentation with one's gender identity is often vital to the survival of trans people. Circumcision is a repeated topic in the Hebrew Bible including a concern with religious identity as distinct from those ethnicities who are uncircumcised (Gen. 34.24; Exod. 4.24–26; 12.48; Lev. 12.3; Deut. 10.16; 30.6; Josh. 5.2–9; Jer. 4.4; 9.25–26). I focus on Genesis 17, in particular, as the centrality of covenant to that circumcision narrative provides us with ways to think about God's role in the transition from one identity to another. Turning back to this passage allows us to think anew about queer activism both for an imagined Jonah and for ourselves. In the first section, I articulate my queer hermeneutical approach to reading Genesis 17. In the next section I explain how the act of circumcision functions as a rearticulation of racial-ethnic and gender identity for Abraham and his descendants. Finally, I utilize Genesis 17's understanding of renaming in connection with the circumcision covenant as a means to explain why naming and renaming matters for both Christians and trans people alike.

## 'The call is coming from inside the ~~closet~~ house (of worship)'

There is an English phrase, based on a horror/urban legend trope, 'the call is coming from inside the house'. The narrative behind the trope goes like this: after being threatened and harassed by a mysterious, creepy caller, the protagonists have the police trace the call and find out, lo and behold, the would-be-murderer is hiding in an attic, and the story concludes with the assumption that the protagonists are now as good as dead with the threat closer to home than they thought after all. What a queer hermeneutical approach does to challenge traditional understandings of gender and sex found in so many churches is to reveal that the call – and in this case a call to action for inclusion and acceptance, nevertheless heard as a murderous threat to many wedded to patriarchy more than their own relationships – is not coming from a closet in some 'Gender and Sexuality Department office' but rather from inside the house of worship itself, right there in scripture.

As a queer reader of Genesis 17, I do not begin from outside the biblical tradition as if queer identity begins in the gay bar and stumbles its way back to the seminary the next morning. But rather I flesh out the association of queer identities and queer experiences within the biblical text. I demonstrate that the Hebrew Bible's circumcision narratives offer us something queer to discern on their own terms by not focusing on latent homosexuality in the text but, as David Tabb Stewart points out, joining queer interpreters in reading ourselves in the text (2017, p. 290).

Turning to scripture, we see that Exodus 4 offers us the image of Zipporah taking on the phallic tool apart from the penis (Graybill 2015). Here is a biblical example of gender subversion in the act of circumcision. Also in Jeremiah 4.4, the prophet invites his community to not only circumcise their bodies but their hearts as well. Circumcision of the heart implies a conception of embodied marking distinct from the physical body. While relying on imagery of bodily adaptation, Jeremiah challenges his audience to think about circumcision beyond the physical act. Circumcision is indeed not only the site of identity formation but is in fact the site of identity subversion already in the Hebrew Bible. These circumcision narratives elsewhere in the Hebrew Bible outside of Genesis inform how we should seek to understand covenant in this passage.

What it means to come to a text as a queer person is not to be on the hunt for 'correct' and 'incorrect' readings but instead to be drawn to the possibility that there are alternative ways a text could be constructed (Stone 2013, pp. 170–71). As Stone writes about queer biblical criticism, 'The point, rather, is to note the dynamics of gender and sexuality at work in both the text and its reception; and, instead of trying to control those dynamics, to let them loose through interpretation' (2013, p. 170). Likewise, Linn Tonstad thinks beyond the need for solely apologetic arguments for justifying queer existence, offering that 'One might see that living openly, while not solving every or even most of the difficulties of human existence, still has good effects in the life of a loved one' (2018, p. 17).

Andrea Long Chu, a lesbian trans woman, in her famous essay 'On Liking Women' (2018) responded to how trans women encounter rejection from transphobic feminists who often make comments that trans women simply want to 'pretend' to be women out of a sexual fetish. Chu makes use of excavating older, trans-excluding feminists like the work of Valerie Solanas for moments of questioning cisnormativity and expanding the notion of womanhood beyond biological sex. She focuses this essay as a critical reassessment of political lesbianism, looking at how the radicality of trans exclusionary radical feminism can be subverted and reworked to benefit arguments for trans inclusion. Chu's hermeneutics of subversion provides a model of what it means to deploy a corpus 'against' itself (here meaning against the traditional meanings of a text). The interpretative lens that living life as a queer person and reading the Bible grants us is an ability to see the role of circumcision in Genesis 17 not as an expectation but as an opportunity to join a different kind of family.

## Circumcising the text: circumcision as bodily discourse

In the context of the Genesis paragraph, circumcision is framed as the expectation for Abraham to have many descendants. Genesis 17.11 makes specific reference to the 'foreskin' (עָרְלָה) to be circumcised. This is a particularly embodied reference. Keeping in mind how Jeremiah calls on Israel to circumcise their heart, queering this text focuses on this embodied element of circumcision, cutting off the foreskin, which is employed metaphorically in the text to talk about being cut off from God's covenant and the people of Israel. This initial metaphorical use allows us to imagine other metaphorical possibilities around circumcision.

While circumcision plays a particular role it is not just an articulation of masculinity in a specific culture but a rearticulation of identity. In many cases circumcision is an embodied marker of racial-ethnic identity. When it is medically applied it can help determine, for example, if one is from Europe or America. When it is religiously applied, it can determine if one is Jewish or a Gentile. Further, the act of circumcision is a marking, not just of racialization but also of sexual function. Circumcised and uncircumcised penises feel different in the act of sex, so people form different preferences around cut and/or uncut penises. For some, circumcision is mutilation and for others an important socio-religious tradition. The origin myth of circumcision in Genesis 17 presents a rearticulation of gender, race and religion for the origin of the community of whom we read in the biblical traditions. Using a critical queer hermeneutic, I explore the role of circumcision in the covenant between Abraham and God as a means to forecast how circumcision could be seen as an ancient parallel for gender-affirming surgery, which can help us to think about God's masculinity beyond the limitations of the image of a cis male God.

In many ways the association of circumcision with gender-affirming surgery feels like an obvious connection: it is a medical procedure on the genitals with significant social/ideological weight. Historically, the transition in medical understanding from 'hermaphroditism' as a condition to understanding intersex experience was in reaction to circumcisions on non-normative genitalia to make the infants present more female, often at the expense of the ability to feel much sexual pleasure (Rosario 2021, p. 14). Notably, gender-affirming surgeries are not just for trans people (lest we be remiss to think that this term is just a euphemism for 'sex reassignment' or whatever outdated term), as penile transplantation has been suggested as an option for cis male victims of botched circumcisions in South Africa (Moodley and Rennie 2018). As Stewart points out, similar to the ethical considerations of how to allocate gender-affirming surgeries in response to a botched circumcision, the tension between making a choice for oneself and one's parents making a choice about your gender with regards to gender-affirming surgery is a complicated one and there is no set script for what seems to be the right decision (2017, pp. 305–6). Circumcision is a weightier subject than the small amount of foreskin removed.

Circumcision is treated with the same kind of seriousness today as in the biblical text, even with the differing social and religious contexts between the present and the ancient world.

While some have viewed God's promise to Abraham in Genesis 17 as an unconditional covenant, the formulation of an exclusion from the covenant based on the lack of circumcision is present in Genesis 17.14: 'Any uncircumcised male who is not circumcised in the flesh of his foreskin shall be cut off from his people; he has broken my covenant' (Thiessen 2009, pp. 151–2). What God is portrayed as saying in Genesis 17 stresses how important circumcision is for being a part of his people, the people of Israel, and keeping to his covenant. In order to acquire favour with God, the body must change. What undergirds this expectation is a shared sense of cutting in the connection of the bodily and divine acts.

In Genesis 17.14, there is a conceptual link between the verbs מוּל ('circumcise'), כָּרַת ('to cut off'), and פָּרַר ('to break, cast off').[2] Although they are not etymologically connected there is a shared imagery here between 'cutting off' both the contract between God and his people as well as the individual from their lineage. In order not to be cut off from the covenant, what we would now classify as a cis male follower would need to cut off his foreskin. Circumcision (literally cutting round) is a cultural marker that articulates religious identity. While identity can be articulated in many different ways, here we can read the covenant as a metaphysical binding that keeps the circumcised male wrapped around his people. See how in the Psalms the word usually used for 'to circumcise' (מוּל) is here rendered to refer to the removal, cutting down or withering of grass (Psalms 37.2; 90.6). Through this poetic employment elsewhere in the Psalms we can see how the bodily act of circumcision is conceptually tethered to the covenantal casting, breaking, cutting language used in Genesis 17.14. This thread of removal is present in all these verbs. The covenant makes it clear that the failure to meet the obligation to remove the foreskin results in a cutting off the covenant and therefore the cultural marker that unifies and binds one's cultural and gender identity.

Genesis 17.14 invites us to think about embodiment beyond a body. The covenant functions as an intermediary to position the social construction of 'follower of God' not as connected to the act of circumcision. Note the text does not enforce a biological essentialist understanding. Genesis 17.14 opens to us the possibility to think about something else. For the text, there is nothing *essential* about circumcision that *produces* ethnic and religious identity for Abraham and his descendants. Just because someone is circumcised does not necessarily make them a follower of God, a descendant of Abraham or Jewish but rather what Genesis 17.14 emphasizes is the presence of the covenant that connects the expectation of circumcision with the affiliation of the identity. Perhaps a septum piercing could be the form of bodily modification necessary to distinguish oneself as a part of the covenant. Of course, it is not, and we cannot constructively create an expectation where there is none here, but there is nothing fundamental about circumcision that produces religious identity in Genesis 17.14. Instead, it is the covenant that brings Abraham and his descendants into contract with God, with the expectation attached that the cis men of his family would undergo circumcision.

By the same token, one can imagine possibilities where the identity is not necessitated by circumcision. While circumcision is the expectation in Genesis 17, we can see how men who do not have penises, whether by accident or by becoming men through gender transition, could be exempt from this requirement. Because it is not circumcision that does the work, circumcision is the expected by-product of the inclusion of the descendants of Abraham as the people of God. Considering other passages, like Jeremiah's call to circumcise the heart, also takes circumcision beyond the bodily practice to an embodied practice where the metaphor is stronger than the physical act.[3] Likewise, we should not think of gender-affirming surgery as a necessity for transgender identity and fall into the same biological essentialist traps that enforce compulsory cisgender identity but rather think of how gender-affirming surgery functions akin to circumcision in meaning-making as a form of fulfilling a kind of covenant.

What initially appears in the text as an expectation of bodily modification to demonstrate one's connection as being God's people opens up the possibility of thinking past the text, even modifying or even circumcising the text itself to understand that this covenant language enforces the metaphorical, embodied practice as central in contrast to the physical practice of circumcision.

## Gender as covenant: renaming in Genesis 17

The close association of circumcision with renaming in Genesis 17 signals the intensity with which this new ethnic-religious identity for Abraham and Sarah has now been welcomed. Just as the new identity for Abraham and Sarah makes physical nominal demands, so does the invention of a new gender identity for transgender people.

The renaming passages of Genesis 17.5 and 15 are significant in that they are not paired right beside each other. The circumcision expectation in Genesis 17.14 actually comes between Abraham's renaming in verse 5 and Sarah's renaming in verse 15. Here, we can read this text not as God reinforcing a gender binary but instead perhaps opening up two different options for renaming. Renaming in the way of Abraham, which involves genital rearticulation, and renaming in the way of Sarah, which involves no such expectation of genital modification. We can see Abraham and Sarah as the forebearers of trans people who seek medical affirmation and trans people who do not desire (or cannot legally access or financially afford) medical procedures.

The nominal transformation of Sarah in Genesis 17.15 is followed in the next verse by God's promise to give her a son, thus establishing the importance of the lineage to the story. By making Sarai into Sarah, we see how a new name is the transformation that makes her fit, in the eyes of the writer of this verse, to become the mother of the nations. We can see a parallel in how many trans people feel unfit in their lives to even take care of themselves, but upon transitioning many find a renewed sense of love for themselves and therefore the possibility of love for others including the love of children. While Genesis 17 seems to depict cisnormative portrayals of gender, with the man's transformation being associated with male circumcision and the woman's transformation being associated with child-bearing, the fact that such transformations are even needed and are not thought of as essential to who they are opens up an interpretative possibility about what the body means for queer readers of Scripture and for reading Scripture queerly.

The ideal body for transgender people is not located anywhere. Much like the mystery of the Eucharist, the new body appears despite the old substance not changing. This is embodiment without a body. Like the women at the empty tomb, we realize in the absence of a physical body that we are the body of Christ (Matt. 27.61). This is an act of embodiment, not only despite but in fact because of the body not existing. In a similar way Abram and Sarai do not exist in their desired form, mostly from their lack of children (Gen. 15.1–2). But it is through covenant with God with its embodied expectation not through the act of circumcision itself that a kind of embodiment without a body occurs, and Abraham and Sarah are rearticulated in new identities.

If we are to consider the practical implications of embodiment without a body for contemporary readers, perhaps we can read the 'descendants' of Abraham and Sarah not only as genealogical familial descendants but as genderqueer and transgender siblings, sisters and brothers who find themselves in need of new names and new identities, just like Abram and Sarai once did leaving Ur. This is an embodied genealogy, this is an embodied descent evoking the bodily covenant the character of Abraham made with God, but there is no need for the historical reality of Abraham to be present to understand the bodily, lived experience of genderqueer and transgender people. Found family may not be connected by blood but can be forged by our experience.

Max Thornton notes that gender is legally assigned in two distinct ways (2019, p. 174). For cis people, this is a morphological observation of one's genitals by a doctor as contrasted to trans people, who seek psychological confirmation by another kind of medical official, a psychologist, to legally change the gender marker on one's driver's licence, passport, birth certificate and so on (Thornton 2019, p. 174). This pressure to prove a psychological condition feels highly subjective and is open to all kinds of criticism and doubt. If we were to think about gender as covenant, we can think about gender as an embodied discourse not on the basis of the body as it is sexed at birth but in how the ideal body functions socially with its corresponding gendered experiences, including but not limited to gender-affirming surgery and renaming.

## Conclusion

Reading Genesis 17 through a queer lens reminds us that practices that were once non-normative, like genital modification, can become so normative that it is taken for granted. The theological impetus for more conservative-minded readers should not be to dismiss gender-affirming surgery as a kind of mutilation of sacred gender roles or as a conversion exercise for the ideology of 'transgenderism' but to confront transgender people with the same grace and open-mindedness deserved by Sarai and Abram on their identity journey. Further, transgender people and our allies should keep in mind the importance of subversiveness to queerness. We should be warned never to fall into the tricky thinking that any one subversive marker or identity is what makes one 'queer', whether that is in normalizing transmedicalist narratives about gender subversion or falling into the habit of filing petty grievances with one another in the queer community.

It is important to keep looking forward to the prophetic voices today of trans activists and our allies, who are fighting back against unjust princes and principalities across the globe, who are not just debating medical access but whether or not queer existence is feasible. Invaluable work is being done to ensure a future not just where transgender people can exist but can thrive. But hope for the future can be sullied by deep anxiety. While deep political anxiety has no cure, I believe one remedy is to look backwards towards queer ancestors like Sarah and Abraham. Looking backwards is not an attempt to forge a queer orthodoxy or queer apologetics but rather to think about queer ancestry in a way that reminds us that this cornerstone of transphobes' fears about genital modification practices may be a passing fad. The call is coming from inside the house. That archetypal suburban churchgoing heterosexual couple who are frantically calling the police on the norm-defying monster that has been threatening their way of life will be shocked to learn the call is coming from the upstairs closet – from grandfather Abraham, the patriarch of the faiths, and Sarah, grandmother of the nations. If given a second chance, perhaps a third, Jonah would again come to uncircumcised Nineveh to face his fear of a people whose body orientations set them outside of normativity and potentially divine grace. The brooding Jonah at the end of his book is the figure who has to figure out what to do when he learns the call is coming from inside the house.

## Notes

1 See, for example, the erroneous criticism that so much of queer commentary is from an undisciplined place of grievance. And certainly, *some* queer theory papers are superficial, but then again so are many of the papers published in any field. See, for example, Pluckrose and Lindsay 2020.

2 BDB, מוּל s. v.; כָּרַת s. v.; פָּרַר s. v.

3 This theme of a spiritual circumcision is taken on later by Christians in the circumcision controversy in early Christianity by Paul in Romans 2.25–29 and at the Council of Jerusalem. We should be cautious not to view this queering of circumcision in supersessionist terms, as a kind of replacement meant to override or forge an undeserved equality with the deep cultural and spiritual significance of the orthodoxy of physical circumcision in Judaism.

## References

Chu, Andrea Long, 2018, 'On Liking Women', *n+1* 30, pp. 47–62.

Graybill, Rhiannon, 2015, 'Masculinity, Materiality, and the Body of Moses', *Biblical Interpretation* 23/4–5, pp. 518–40.

Moodley, Keymanthri and Stuart Rennie, 2018, 'Penile Transplantation as an Appropriate Response to Botched Traditional Circumcisions in South Africa: An Argument Against', *Journal of Medical Ethics* 44/2, pp. 86–90.

Pluckrose, Helen and James Lindsay, 2020, *Cynical Theories: How Activist Scholarship Made Everything About Race, Gender, and Identity – and Why This Harms Everybody*, Durham, NC: Pitchstone Publishing.

Rosario, Vernon, 2021, 'Gender Science Marches On', *The Gay & Lesbian Review Worldwide* 28/1, pp. 14–16.

Stewart, David Tabb, 2017, 'LGBT/Queer Hermeneutics and the Hebrew Bible', *Currents in Biblical Research* 15/3, pp. 289–314.

Stone, Ken, 2013, 'Queer Criticism' in Steven L. McKenzie and John Altner (eds), *New Meanings for Ancient Texts: Recent Approaches to Biblical Criticisms and Their Applications*, Louisville, KY: Westminster John Knox Press, pp. 155–76.

Thiessen, Matthew, 2009, 'The Text of Genesis 17:14', *Journal of Biblical Literature* 128/4, pp. 151–62.

Thornton, Max, 2019, 'Gender: A Public Feeling?' in Alexis G. Waller (ed.), *Religion, Emotion, Sensation: Affect Theories and Theologies*, New York: Fordham University Press.

Tonstad, Linn Marie, 2018, *Queer Theology: Beyond Apologetics*, Eugene, OR: Cascade Books.

# 13

# Queering the Publics: Reflections on Truth by Prophetic Practitioners

NOKUTHULA MJWARA, HANZLINE R.
DAVIDS, LOUIS VAN DER RIET AND
ASHWIN THYSSEN

## Introduction

The practice of theology is, no doubt, a rather public affair; it is not a solely private affair. In fact, in a country with such pronounced religious commitments as South Africa (where at least 90 per cent adhere to a faith tradition), religion often influences public discourses. Presently the South African Constitution prevents unfair discrimination on the grounds of sexual orientation. Legislation also allows for the recognition of civil unions (of persons of the same gender). Even so, the national religious community struggles to position itself as affirming LGBTIQA+ persons. This reality, then, calls for a discussion on the public dimensions of faith, particularly Christian theology.

Many theologians, of course, are also in agreement that religion is foundationally public – some would even argue that it is a public good. This view has in recent decades given rise to public theology, a mode of religious reflection that sets out to be in dialogue with the various publics that shape human society. Following David Tracy, the public theologian converses with three publics: first, the church, the community of believers; second, the academy, the community of technical professionals; and, third, broader society, which is composed of all the human community (2014, p. 331). This chapter presents how three religious professionals, Nokuthula Mjwara, Hanzline R. Davids and Louis van der Riet, engage in dialogue with each of these publics.

However, as the title suggests, these contributors do more than present and dialogue with these publics; quite importantly, they also actively queer these publics. Therefore, this chapter offers a queer theologically inspired consideration of how these three publics may be engaged. In this sense, queer means turning 'convention and authority on its head. It is about seeing things in a different light and reclaiming voices and sources that previously had been ignored, silenced, or discarded' (Cheng 2011, p. 6).

This chapter has a three-part focus. First, each contributor offers a narration of their queer theological journey. Second, given their role as practitioners, they respond to the question regarding the developments they witness in the respective publics. Third, the final question considers the work of hope that each of them is called to at this moment, in service of these publics. The text of this chapter comes from a live roundtable discussion. The contributors' responses appear in a manner that maintains and appreciates the integrity and moment of truth-telling, as far as possible.

## Becoming queer

**Ashwin Thyssen:** Patrick Cheng, advancing a bit of theological orthodoxy, argues that the Methodist Quadrilateral is a helpful tool for doing queer theology. The Methodist Quadrilateral, of course, keenly draws on the insight of four sources: scripture, tradition, science and experience. It is here, quite interestingly, where Cheng offers a break from orthodoxy. Cheng notes:

> Queer theology is premised upon the belief that God acts within the specific contexts of our lives and experiences, despite the fact that (LGBT) lives and experiences have been excluded from traditional theological discourse. Indeed, queer experience is an important – if not critical – source for doing theology from a queer perspective. (2011, p. 18)

In light of the preference that queer theology affords lived experience, would you share some thoughts on your journey into identifying as queer, how you became (and are becoming) a queer theologian?

**Louis van der Riet:** It is only retrospectively that the verb 'queering' has become an apt descriptor in my own attempts at theological engagement in public, and particularly in the church. I understand this as an act of both deconstruction and reconstruction of the dominant theological discourse and practices. The context in which I have been formed and have sought to do theology is a necessary framing for this contribution, and where I choose to start.

While many of my identity markers and aspects of my social location have mattered (and matter) theologically, it is perhaps most revealing that I was born in the dying hour of legislated apartheid as a cisgender, gay male, and that ethnically I am an Afrikaner, racialized as white. I have been socially privileged my entire life, with almost unrestricted access to public life. I am also an ordained minister of the Dutch Reformed Church (DRC), a majority-white denomination that is well known for its history of racialized injustice in the South African context.

Apart from dealing with the afterlife of apartheid, discourse on human sexuality has dominated the DRC's public witness more than any other subject in the post-1994 period. There has been a fixation on 'same-sex partnerships' by heterosexual, cisgender, male clergy. This is the term that functions as a discourse marker for human sexuality in the DRC. This dominance can be read against the backdrop of an Afrikaner-dilemma: morally wounded through apartheid and whiteness, yet also in a moment of cultural loss and bereavement in a post-1994 landscape. While some have used this theological and cultural inheritance to continue the use of relative power and dominant knowledge discourses to marginalize, exclude and dehumanize its LGBTIQA+ members, others have sought more humanizing avenues. Centred on the theological discourse on human dignity, there have been significant shifts towards more inclusion and affirmation of LGBTIQA+ people in the DRC. However, a division persists among clergy and church leaders, while some of the gains towards recognizing same-sex partnerships continue to be challenged in church polity.

When I was ordained in 2019, I was identified as the first openly gay clergy member to enter ministry in the DRC. While there were many other queer siblings that had gone before me, some who are still in congregational ministry, my identity was public, and therefore theologically under scrutiny in a unique way. My position within the church was thus as someone simultaneously marginalized and empowered.

I was in the final stages of completing my doctoral dissertation, which analysed how truth-telling mattered theologically in the transitional justice context of South Africa. I had a growing awareness of how being white mattered theologically, and how by virtue of my racial identity and the power it affords me socially and systemically, I was called to be responsible for racialized injustices. This forced me to confront my own power, and my own Christian witness. Moreover, this was an invitation to reflect not only on how I held this power publicly, but to question all forms of power theologically. The intersection of how the DRC has dealt with race and sexuality has thus been very formative in how I have sought to 'queer' my public theology. In a post-1994 South Africa, being white must continually be queered if any sort of moral implication is to be taken seriously.

**Nokuthula Mjwara:** Recently I have claimed the title of being a 'queer theologian'. This is usually followed by a disclaimer that the title is not one derived from academic achievements or reinforced by academic writing or formal education within theology. I am a queer theologian as I am a gender practitioner who engages, explores and critiques theology. It is through this practice of living theology in practice that I am able to claim this title of being a queer theologian.

I often introduce myself as a feminist and in the words of Sarah Koopman, 'my feminism was a doing word, a being word, long before I even knew I could assign words to it' (2018, p. 298). It was only when I was in university that I found that there was language to my lived 'disruptions' that my voice brought within my community. These lived disruptions ranged from my rebelling against dictated notions of hair and bra policies in school to the curious questioning of privilege as a black body who speaks eloquent English.

My journey in 'queering the truth' is one that starts from my younger years. My earliest memories of an incongruous biblical interpretation was when I was around the age of eight. At Sunday School, we were doing an exercise on heaven, and between the fluffing of cotton-wool balls, scribbles of images of angels, our teacher narrated a description of heaven and the afterlife. It was a life where we would be filled with the Holy Spirit, where we would be joyful and radiating, singing praises to the Lord. The uneasiness set in when she shared that we would never hunger nor tire as we are filled by the spirit. This, for an eight-year-old who loved her food and naps, led to my questioning whether this is the afterlife that I want for eternity. Faced by this cognitive dissonance, I pondered over this throughout the week. The following Sunday, I went to my Sunday School teacher and informed her that I had made the decision that I do not want to go to heaven. Surprised, she asked, 'Why?' My response was simple: I maintained that I love my food and I love my rest and although my love for God was greater than these two things, I could not fathom an eternity without them. This story always stands out for me as how one person's interpretation of how we could experience heaven led to internal turmoil and ended with a difficult decision being made. Now in my older years, I realize that my Sunday School teacher was only offering a lens into how we would experience heaven and that it is her embodied knowledge through the lens of experience, reason and tradition of denominational knowledge of Christianity.

**Hanzline Davids:** As a theological student in the Faculty of Theology at Stellenbosch University in 2007, many of the teaching staff were white, and heterosexual. The syllabi then often made me feel grateful to receive a first-class theological education. Going back to my community of Cloetesville a few kilometres from campus I was often reminded how my theological education was a mismatch to the context of Cloetesville, a community constructed by the spatial injustice policies of apartheid because people of colour could not live in central Stellenbosch. Today Cloetesville, surrounded by vineyards and mountains, is a community where drug abuse and gang violence, gender and sexual-based violence impact the stories of various bodies trying to make a life in a space where access to a better life slips through the grasp of tired fingers labouring for minimum wage. My theological education lacked liberation grit. Rather, it was a hetero-theology in vanilla clothes unable to meet the socio-economic, health and education challenges I saw every day.

Thinking back on these years I often wonder what a queer theologian of colour would have symbolized in a building, such as the Theology Faculty, that perpetuated Afrikaner nationalism, toxic masculinity and essentialist notions of gender and sexuality. Academia is still a space where racism, sexism, classism and queerphobia exist (Stockdill and Danico 2012; Naicker 2013). Bodies of colour, women and LGBTIQA+ persons over the last few decades have made modest inroads in academic discourses. At the same time, it is also a space of transformation that fosters innovative ways that justice and equality can prevail. The appointment of Mx Ashwin Thyssen, a queer person of colour, in July 2021 at the Faculty as a theological educator gives me hope. Representation in theological spaces matters.

## What do you see?

**Ashwin Thyssen:** Most helpfully, each of you has offered a lens through which to recognize and appreciate the work you are committed to. Interestingly, you have all located yourselves in particular communities – noting their influence on your formation, the role they played in shaping who you are, and the life of praxis to which you are committed. Nokuthula, you are active in society, the work of Inclusive and Affirming Ministries

(IAM), Louis you in the church space, as a clergyperson, and Hanzline you in the academy, at the Institute for Gender Studies (at the University of South Africa). What are the developments that you are seeing in the respective publics? What is the work you are presently committed to?

**Nokuthula Mjwara:** Legislation in South Africa has provided progressive legal policies that protect people in same-sex relationships, yet a paradoxical reality exists contextually when one explores the experiences of LGBTIQA+ persons within communities and Christian faith communities. Hanzline R. Davids alludes to LGBTIQA+ 'people's bodies as discursive sites' and says that we need active engagement from LGBTIQA+ persons as their very being already disrupts existing understandings of binaries, patriarchy and privileges upheld by cisgender persons (2020, p. 314). He draws on the work of Van Klinken to further demonstrate that we as queer LGBTIQA+ persons need to hear stories and personal narratives of queer theologians and academics as a process of finding their selves. This calls for the inclusion of LGBTIQA+ persons when policies that affect their lives are being discussed and voted for in conferences and synodical spaces. This, for me, substantiates the embodied work I do as a queer theologian.

As a gender practitioner working at the intersections of faith, gender and community development, I have learned and believe that transformation can be achieved when we engage authentically in conversations that allow us to question and unpack cis-heteronormativity and how we are complicit in upholding systems of oppressions. Using participatory engagement that includes the use of dialogue as a medium and embodied facilitation, we engage authentically, moving into a space of risk, sharing narratives and collectively co-creating a new narrative of humanity as opposed to the 'them vs us' narrative. I am conscious that these dialogues need enabling environments to occur, which may slow the rate of reaching large populations, but it is within these pockets of 'safe spaces' that creative and critical engagements occur, which call on participants to hold a mirror to their own learning and living within a cis-heteronormative reality. The use of personal narratives to shift internalized stereotypes and bias has been one of the methodologies IAM uses within training spaces.

**Louis van der Riet:** My sexual orientation, which cuts into my spirituality, has offered me much empathy, insight and courage to act as a marginalized person. I speak to spirituality as distinct (though not disconnected) from doctrine and ethics. It is thus other than what I believe to be good, or the contents of my belief. Here I have in mind spirituality as the source and driving force behind my lived experience as a theologian, and my involvement in bringing about greater justice for marginalized identities. It is taking seriously that God matters, and living within this reality publicly. A poem by Fr Thomas Keating has become a mantra for me in living out this spirituality this past year. In the poem 'What matters', included in the daily meditations of the Center for Action and Contemplation, Keating wrote poignantly that,

Only the Divine matters.

From this deep theological truth, he continues on to confess that, consequently, 'everything matters.'

To speak about spirituality is to speak about my relation to, and experience of, the divine. Who God is, or who I experience God to be, has been a desired theological anchor. This might seem self-evident. However, much of theology is done without such a desire, or the disclosure of such a desire. Witnessing to the truth does not always hold this confession of God as truth relationally. It has been my desire to relate to God in vulnerability that has allowed me to queer discourses of mastery, theologically so bound to whiteness. This has been a way of confessing that I am not the owner of truth, though by virtue of belonging to God, I can stand for the truth, relationally. This is an attempt at integration; integrating what I believe about God (doctrine), and how I hold those beliefs (ethically and hermeneutically). It has been the adoption of the kind of spirituality defined by Douglas Lawrie (2009, p. 142), reflecting on the life and witness of the feminist theologian Denise Ackermann:

'Spirituality is the condition of standing with your nerve ends exposed in a place from which there is no line of retreat and in a meeting of which you are not master.' My lived experience has thus led me to a theology centred on justice, and this has been born from an experience of who God is, as a God of justice for those marginalized by the church, academy and civil society.

The time spent in congregational ministry (2019–21) afforded me first-hand knowledge and experience in working towards the recognition, celebration and participation of LGBTIQA+ people in faith communities. It has allowed me to see the value of not merely pitting theological positions against one another in a binary fashion as either 'for' or 'against' full inclusion of LGBTIQA+ people in church, but to rather centre the lived experience and theological knowledge produced by queer people themselves. I am therefore more than merely an advocate for queer inclusion – I *am* queer. It has been the claiming of this identity, as part of the *imago Dei* in myself and other queer bodies, that has sustained and grounded my participation in public theology in and through the DRC. I understand the concepts of sexual orientation, gender identity, gender expression, and sex characteristics (SOGIESC) to be fluid and evolving, while the lives of queer people themselves remain primary sources of theological knowledge. Taking this position is to locate truth not merely in scripture, tradition or reason, but in the embodied experience of human lives.

While on a retreat as part of a Spiritual Direction training course in 2021, I entered a chapel with a large rainbow-coloured cross. A phrase from the work of Dietrich Bonhoeffer came to mind: 'Only a suffering God can save us.' What Bonhoeffer implied by this was that the redemptive and salvific work of Christ is made real to us through the incarnation of God who knows and is present through and in our embodied experience as those that suffer. Seeing this image of the rainbow/queer cross, was a revelation that 'only a queer God can save us (me)'. Only an image of God that has been queered from the normative images that have served patriarchy, mastery and whiteness can liberate and bring about the truth and freedom of Christ for those in queer bodies.

**Hanzline Davids:** In my 2020 article, I reflect on my coming out experience as a gay man of colour, who is an ordained minister in the Uniting Reformed Church. In this article, I use the work of Adriaan van Klinken (2018), who argues that queer persons could learn from African feminist/womanist theologians who make use of storytelling as an act of defiance and healing to counter the impact of violence caused by religious belief systems (West, Van der Walt and Kaoma 2016). Using autobiographical storytelling in my writing assisted me in an academic publication to tell my story. Representation in academic theological discourses matters.

Telling stories might seem like a simple and unimportant way to engage with systemic, structural and ideological injustices. Often injustices take our voices away and deny us as LGBTIQA+ persons to talk back. It opens worlds that were often closed by refreshing the memory of times when expression, denial and discrimination were felt against one's own skin. Stories bring proximity because they connect with other human beings. By talking we reclaim agency, finding creative and innovative ways to tell our embodied stories. Our voices shed light on our marginalization, pain and suffering, but awaken our embodied selves. Collectively our stories string together; creating a technicolour dream coat like Joseph in Genesis. Stories have a way of connecting one's heart, mind and body, and ultimately being subversive.

Where I worked previously at Inclusive and Affirming Ministries, I was offered numerous spaces to tell my story in congregations, seminaries and other civil society spaces. The work at IAM created a deep consciousness of embodiment through body theology as a lens for my work. Publishing theological texts wherein queer persons make theological meaning-making that flows out from their lived experiences disrupts the dichotomy of dualistic theologies systems of knowledge. Embodied storytelling at the intersection of gender, sexuality, faith, religion, class and race highlights how we experience the Triune God, land and humanity. Embodied storytelling as prophetic voice is pivotal to countering the impact of violence caused by religious beliefs. These types of writing are slowly culminating in a body of knowledge that can be introduced in theological education and formation. There does exist a challenge in this regard; for argument's sake let us call it an indecent wager.

## What is to be done?

**Ashwin Thyssen:** José Esteban Muñoz argues: 'Queerness is not yet here. Queerness is an ideality. Put another way we are not yet queer ... The future is queerness's domain. Queerness is a structuring and educated mode of desiring that allows us to see and feel beyond the quagmire of the present' (2009). At present we are witnessing the assault on progress for the LGBTIQA+ persons. Seemingly this moment suggests the very reversal of the human rights of the LGBTIQA+ community. What is the hopeful truth that you feel called to witness to in this moment – when queerness is simply 'not yet here'?

**Hanzline Davids:** I hold the view that we should advocate prophetically for the academy to become queer, mindful, however, of the caution that Marcella Althaus-Reid and Lisa Isherwood offer against the positionality of queer theological discourse as 'not at the centre of the theological discourses conversing with power, but at the margins' (2007, p. 304). The centring of queer theology would mean institutionalization. Althaus-Reid and Isherwood's caution is also echoed by Susannah Cornwall (2017), arguing that queer theology would become domesticated. The institutionalization and domestication of queer theology is an indecent wager.

Beloved friends of mine, Michelle Boonzaaier, Motsau Motsau and Charlene van der Walt, who are in the civil society, ecclesial and academic spaces, introduced me to the work of Marcella Althaus-Reid. Reading her ignited my theological imagination and gave me the vocabulary and a framework to analyse the sexual and gendered discourses in the church, academy and society. Althaus-Reid gave me the language of indecency to look through my queer embodiment and those of others and sense-making that there are fundamental injustices in the way the church functions on a heteronormative axis. Reading Althaus-Reid often reminds me I am queer and indecent.

The mindfulness of positionality that Althaus-Reid's work and so many others bring I would like to argue is a strange sensation of queer belonging that is always on the move. Queer belonging never stagnates in falsehoods of stableness. On the contrary, it disturbs, disrupts and transgresses, forging out new hopes, dreams and agendas for a more just world where our queer embodiment cannot be institutionalized and domesticated.

From my experience working with queer persons across Africa, pushing the boundaries at the intersection of sexuality, gender and faith, I would make the indecent wager that perhaps queer theology or rather African Queer Theology is more needed than ever before in theological academia to work towards justice for all bodies that feel the knee of heteropatriarchy on their necks!

**Nokuthula Mjwara:** Between 2013 and 2017, I worked with an LGBTIQA+ organization based in KwaZulu-Natal. I would facilitate human sexuality workshops for a diverse audience; the majority were rural-based – namely traditional healers, tribal councils (traditional leaders), clergy and communities in spaces that were often hard to reach. I was often taken aback about how easily this audience would welcome the information, with their curiosity leaning more on understanding the Western concepts of homosexuality. Yet when unpacking the concepts, the audience would openly share stories of childhood games that were of a sexual nature or narratives of gender and sexually diverse people who they lived with and how it was often seen as a 'family issue' to resolve. This type of constant feedback demonstrated to me that being queer is not a Western concept but there is a lack of indigenous terminologies that I as a Black, queer African woman still struggle to find to explain homosexuality and gender fluidity in a non-derogatory manner. Sizwe Sithole, in *Stabanisation*, explored the need to reclaim offensive terms and redefine them as points of knowledge creation about queer identities. However, this is a slow process. Not everyone of the community is comfortable using these terms to capture their identities and find comfort in the Western terms. The lack of affirming terms erases the existence of Black, African queers, isolating them to being 'othered'.

As we witness the gross human rights violations and witch-hunts occurring in Zambia, and lobbying for anti-gay bills in Uganda, my concern for the safety and security for LGBTIQA+ persons grows daily. Liberatory shifts towards greater inclusivity is rather slow, and this is impacted by the indecisive action by the South African government in holding neighbouring countries with homophobic laws accountable, which lays bare its unwillingness to act. In the meantime, we will continue working, one community at a time, and cultivating change agents that hold on to a vision of inclusive communities of faith that welcome diversity as opposed to rejecting difference.

**Louis van der Riet:** The lives of queer Christians are a gift to the church; they are able to destabilize the false securities of the ways in which gender and sexuality have been normalized and have shaped our way of being in the world, reminding us to let go of both the inferiority and superiority with which we have been conditioned in our bodies. As a gay clergy member of the DRC, my greatest allies within my church have been those individuals who have done their own work regarding their racial identity and how they have been formed by whiteness. This is the confessional and self-emptying work of introspection and contemplation. Partnering with these allies in our common identity of race has demonstrated to me the gift that queering can bring to the church – a recognition that our freedom to live and flourish in the fullness of the life is tied to all other members in the body of Christ. Recognizing power has also allowed me the awareness to engage as an ally in the church regarding issues of race, class, gender and disability; disrupting and dismantling existing power structures and empowering others by giving power away. As I hold my identity markers lightly – whether they be race, gender or sexual orientation – and allow for the healing work of God to restore who I am in community with others, I truly begin to see how 'everything matters'.

There is a long road ahead for the full recognition of LGBTIQA+ people to be realized. The protection and promotion of their/

our rights in faith communities in Africa is an ongoing process that will require continued collaboration between church, academy and civil society. I see signs of hope where the narratives of LGBTIQA+ people are allowed the freedom to matter, both for themselves and for the whole body of Christ.

## Conclusion

In each of their contributions, Nokuthula, Hanzline and Louis take seriously the public influence of faith. Their respective responses centre an ethic of dignity that lies at the heart of both the Christian faith and the constitutional democracy of South Africa. Acting prophetically in the church, academy and society – as clergyperson, academic and gender practitioner – they are witnessing to the 'not yet' that remains the future's domain. By sharing their lived experience, these practitioners offer an invitation to imagine a different reality.

In sum, their thoughtful contributions enliven the words of Marcella Althaus-Reid, who argues: 'Our task and our joy is to find or simply recognise God sitting amongst us, at any time' (2003, p. 4). Most keenly, with profound sensitivity and great appreciation, these three practitioners have and are observing God in the midst of the respective publics – oftentimes most palpably present in both the depressing cries and joyous moans of LGBTIQA+ persons.

## References

Althaus-Reid, Marcella and Lisa Isherwood, 2007, 'Thinking Theology and Queer Theory', *Feminist Theology* 15/3 (2007), pp. 302–14.
Althaus-Reid, Marcella, 2003, *The Queer God*, London: Routledge.
Cheng, Patrick, 2011, *Radical Love: An Introduction to Queer Theology*, New York: Seabury Press.
Cornwall, Susannah, 2017, 'Home and Hiddenness: Queer Theology, Domestication and Institutions', *Theology and Sexuality* 23/1–2, pp. 31–47, DOI: 10.1080/13558358.2017.1341207.

Davids, Hanzline R., 2020, 'Recognition of LGBTIQ Bodies in the Uniting Reformed Church in Southern Africa: An Indecent Proposal?', *Stellenbosch Theological Journal* 6/4, pp. 301–17.

Keating, Thomas, 2018, *The Secret Embrace*, Temple Rock Company (poem VIII).

Koopman, Sarah, 2018, 'Feminism is a Doing Word' in J. Thorpe (ed.), *Feminism is: South Africans speak their Truth*, Cape Town: Kwela Books, pp. 298–301.

Muñoz, José Esteban, 2009, *Cruising Utopia: The Then and There of Queer Futurity*, New York: New York University Press.

Naicker, Linda, 2013, 'The Journey of South African Women Academics with a particular Focus on Women Academics in Theological Education', *Studia Historiae Ecclesiasticae* 39/Supplement 1, pp. 325–36.

Stockdill, Brett C. and Mary Yu Danico (eds), 2012, *Transforming the Ivory Tower: Challenging Racism, Sexism, and Homophobia in the Academy*, Hawaii: University of Hawaii Press.

Tracy, David, 2014, 'Three Kinds of Publicness in Public Theology', *International Journal of Public Theology* 8/3, pp. 330–34.

Van Klinken, Adriaan, 2018, 'Autobiographical Storytelling and African Narrative Queer Theology', *Exchange* 47/3, pp. 211–29.

West, Gerald, Charlene van der Walt and Kapya John Kaoma, 2016, 'When Faith Does Violence: Reimagining Engagement Between Churches and LGBTI Groups on Homophobia in Africa', *Hervormde Teologiese Studies* 72/1, pp. 1–8.

# 14

# Womanist Biblical Interpretation's Prophetic Potential

## SHEURL DAVIS, MADRÉ ARENDSE AND ASHWIN THYSSEN

## Introduction

The publication of Alice Walker's *In Search of Our Mothers' Gardens: Womanist Prose* (1983) offered the world, and particularly the theological academy, a novel way of theorizing the experiences of Black women. Womanist, then, became a lens through which to see and experience the world, in a manner that takes seriously the lives of Black women – which continue to be shaped by the prevailing reality of racism. Layli Phillips helpfully notes:

> Womanism is a social change perspective rooted in Black women's and other women of color's everyday experiences and everyday methods of problem solving in everyday spaces, extended to the problem of ending all forms of oppression for all people, restoring the balance between people and the environment/nature, and reconciling human life with the spiritual dimension. (2006, p. xx)

While womanist thought has its origin in the context of the United States of America, since the introduction of womanist thought, several persons outside of North America draw upon the ideas and practices of womanist thought. For example, the Nigerian writer Chikwenye Okonjo Ogunyemi developed her conception of womanism in a manner quite different from Walker and other US Americans. Nyasha Junior notes: 'In contrast to feminism and African American womanism, Ogunyemi views her "African womanism" as less individualistic, more familial, and more focused on the distinctiveness of African struggles within a global community' (Junior 2015, p. 3). Womanist thought is, therefore, a mode of theorizing that centres the lived experiences of Black women across the world.

The far-reaching potential of womanism shapes this discussion on current biblical interpretation. The contributions of Sheurl Davis and Madré Arendse are to be read in the light of Nyasha Junior's helpful corrective. According to Junior (2015, p. 6), present efforts to offer womanist interpretations of biblical texts should be considered in the light of their informants; that is, the activism of women, and the developing womanist scholarship in fields related to religious studies (such as the biblical sciences).

This chapter has a threefold division, framed by three questions. First, Davis and Arendse offer some reflection on their journey as emerging scholars, paying particular attention to the entry into womanist biblical interpretation. Second, in the light of their respective journeys, they consider the present scholarship they are developing. Third, as emerging scholars thinking retrospectively, they offer some advice for their younger selves. The contributions of Sheurl and Madré are presented here in the written form they offered it.

## 'Ain't You a Woman?' Becoming a womanist biblical interpreter

**Ashwin Thyssen:** Sheurl and Madré, whenever I think about womanism I am always struck by the famous speech attributed to Sojourner Truth, 'Ain't I a woman?' In this speech, quite thoughtfully, Truth would offer the remark: 'If the first woman God ever made was strong enough to turn the world upside down all alone, these women together ought to be able to turn it back, and get it right side up again!' (Truth 1851). Would you share your experience of being drawn to womanist biblical interpretation, and how you may be trying to turn the world right side up?

**Sheurl Davis:** I grew up in a small town named Mafikeng, the capital of the Northwest Province. I am currently employed as a junior lecturer in Old Testament studies at the Faculty of Theology, North-West University. My context has deeply inspired my scholarship. I consider myself to be a contextual scholar. I do not see the relevance of being a theologian and not doing contextual work. What do your endless writings mean to anyone if it does not filter into our contemporary society? How do you impact and influence a context without doing the groundwork? Contextual scholarship has been disregarded and understood to be anecdotal in the normative heteropatriarchy academy.

Offering this reflection, I am quite mindful of the discomfort that accompanies this exercise. I am uncomfortable because it seems too anecdotal to write a piece about myself, without the risk of being too personal. At the same time, I am inspired by Katie Geneva Cannon, as she debunks this heteropatriarchal analysis of the anecdotalist in the academy. She made these remarks in a YouTube video uploaded by Union Theological Seminary in the City of New York that explores the ideas of the 'founding mothers of Womanist theology and Womanist ethics' (Cannon 2014). Cannon argues that people want to dismiss our truth as anecdotal. If there is no scientific database for our experience, if you cannot prove that these experiences are true for so many women, then it is not deemed worthy of the academic sphere. So the epistemological sea of forgetfulness is when people take the truth that hurts, that goes to the core of being, the truth that goes to the marrow of the bone, this truth people want to dismiss and say that if you cannot prove it scientifically, factually then it does not exist. Cannon encourages people to delve into the truth, the kind of truth that stings like a serpent's tooth, that kind of truth that makes your teeth set on edge, the kind of truth that causes some people to lose their minds up in here, up in here. So even when people call your truth a lie, tell it anyway. Tell it anyway.

**Madré Arendse:** For the first 13 years my family resided in Riebeek-West, which is found in the Riebeek Valley, where I attended Riebeek Kasteel Primary. Both places were named after the VOC (the Dutch East Indies Company) Commander in the Cape, Jan van Riebeek. Now it becomes increasingly clear the type of narratives I was told as a child. At the end of each year the school would showcase a concert where each grade would get the opportunity to perform and at the end we all huddled together and sang with pride the children's song of Carike Keuzenkamp. The lyrics are as follows:

> *en ons se, dankie, se ons Jan van Riebeek ons sal vir jou, nooit vergeet, dankie 1652, net vir hierdie dag ... Hip-hip hoerah Suid-Afrika.*
> And we say thank you to Jan van Riebeek, we will never forget you, thank you 1652, just for this day ... Hip-hip hooray South Africa.
> (Keuzenkamp 2015)

We were taught to be thankful to Jan van Riebeek and his arrival at the Cape, for that is where 'our history' began. One can imagine the horrors behind this statement and the proud propaganda that fed the Eurocentric and heteropatriarchal ego. As a Coloured child this was my reality where I too envisioned my history starting in 1652 with the arrival of the Dutch at the Cape. However, being in the space that was predominantly white, male and affluent, I always felt the need to change myself, because everyone around me looked the same. My hair was never straight enough and my skin never light enough. Being part of this community and being shaped by it, I never questioned any part of it for it was simply as it was. This is an example of what happens when the master narrative has been told and presented as the only and objective truth. The reality of the matter inevitably is that when one narrative is shown as the only truth there is, all other narratives are repressed and discarded in the process. Within my body I carry these complexities. I also carry these realities that are not my own.

# Contributing to the development of womanist biblical interpretation

**Ashwin Thyssen:** Both of you have noted the complex nature of this work; the difficulty that you carry to offer a contribution to the development of womanist biblical interpretation. Please share the ways in which you are navigating this tricky terrain, while still seeking to advance womanist biblical interpretation as a helpful manner of engaging with the Bible.

**Madré Arendse:** My research looks at these narratives presented to me as the 'truth', a master narrative that overshadows and ignores all other narratives. Refusing another to breathe as it suffocates the reality of an entire people. I look at how we have been made to believe a single narrative. Refusing to simply succumb to the silence, I research the narratives of the Coloured community, especially the women in the community. Being the children of slavery, rape and colonialism as Coloured people, our histories cannot begin with Jan van Riebeek. I look at the realities of slavery and the missing histories and narratives, how these stories have been completely silenced, and how the only way we know of some of the slave women is through their interaction with the VOC, never given the opportunity to account for their own stories but rather fall victim to the pen of the master narrator.

Robert Shell so poignantly states: 'Restoring the history of such people (slave people who have been forgotten), forgotten, ignored or suppressed by the colonial process or settler historians, should be part of the modern Cape historian's agenda. In this view, history becomes an obscure branch of democracy – restoring the historical voices that was hitherto silent' (1992, p. 168).

Taking seriously then this reality of forced silence my research turns to the Hebrew Bible to find parallels with the experiences of my community. Even more than that it opens up space as we read the biblical narratives to also bring our own stories to the fore. Reading the narrative of the Hebrew Bible opens up the opportunity to read and relate our own suffering and our own narratives but also a space where we are able to read the

Hebrew Bible through our own narratives and positionality. The Hebrew Bible has been incredibly formative in the societies we inhabit. Thus, interrogating the complexities it brings is of utmost importance for our survival to be able to tell or retell our stories, to reimagine our narrative for ourselves and to be able to centre ourselves as subjects within the narratives we tell.

The key aspect of womanist biblical interpretation is the understanding that each of us comes from a specific reading community, which has been formative in how we read the biblical texts. My positionality and context have informed the way I read the biblical texts and so too it shapes and informs my research. Interpreting the Bible within my context calls me to be cognizant of who I engage with, how I engage them and what I engage with on my research journey. All of this is dependent on my identity. Womanist theology as a whole calls for the recognizing on one's own narratives, agency and traditions. The Hebrew Bible presents an opportunity for narrativizing identity.

This, then, encompasses what I envision the future of Hebrew Bible Studies in South Africa to be. I believe that any form of theological study should raise the question: What does it mean? Enquiring and interrogating ourselves around the practical demands of our work, Madipoane Masenya so poignantly reminds us that we ought to 'Make [our] context a hermeneutical key, Let the Bible become the women's [people's] Bible.'

The work done by the Circle for Concerned African Women Theologians reminds us that the Bible is the people's Bible and that the paradoxical realities of our identities drive our work. The Circle has been immensely important for the current direction of theology and specifically Hebrew Bible studies. The work of the Circle has opened up a liberatory space for African women to find rest and to be heard. What is important to remember is that in the advocacy for justice, one voice cannot speak louder than the other. The importance of the Circle in the current climate is crucial for allowing space for those who have been oppressed to have a platform to speak and to be heard. More importantly, it is a space where one is conscientized around the issue of who speaks and who listens. More often than not, certain voices need to know when to be quiet to allow some other voices to be heard; not saying or intending to place certain voices above others. This adjustment serves precisely to establish egalitarianism with the fight and advocacy efforts for justice. Allowing space for everyone to speak and to be heard is one of the most powerful tools to reshape the narrative of oppression. For work that is so important it becomes crucial to constantly ask whose voices are we missing in the discourse, queer voices, and lay voices?

**Sheurl Davis:** Inspired also by Katie Cannon, I ground my scholarship in the contextual urgency of my time. Women's experience of God has not been prioritized enough. Even less when you are a woman of colour. Juliana Claassens points out that when considering a contextual deliberation of women's experience of God, we are on hazardous grounds because the question is whose experience of God we are dealing with (2016, p. xiii). To be human means to resist dehumanization. As such, considering myself a postcolonial feminist biblical scholar, I aspire to delve deeper into the exercise of contextual work. I recognize my positionality and how that, of course, informs my insights. Because of this, I situate myself as a politically Black woman, a culturally Coloured woman residing in a postcolonial context. As a feminist and contextual biblical scholar, I am drawn to further explore and interrogate the motivations and interpretations of the biblical texts, especially the Old Testament, which have been interpreted to serve the androcentric motivations of the patriarchal history of interpretation. I am committed to the practices of decolonizing and destabilizing forms and practices in which imperial and colonial oppression operates and is perpetuated. I am also inclined to read against the grain and read beyond what is presented, in search of the underlying ideologies embedded in the interpretation of 'underdog' women characters in the biblical texts as well as in contemporary society.

In my MTh dissertation, I interrogate the interpretation, reception and portrayal of the iconic character Krotoa in the history of South Africa, by drawing her into conversation with the biblical character Rahab. Through a postcolonial feminist framework, I set out to present an alternative reading of them. I discuss the notion of women being written into history, arguing that throughout the history of the Bible and history more generally, the lives of women have been filtered through androcentric perspectives.

This MTh dissertation then serves as a precursor for my doctoral work. Here, the focus is on Winnie Madikizela-Mandela. I read her in relation to the biblical characters Jael, Jezebel and Miriam. The objective of my doctoral project is to unpack and understand the intersections between the Bible and film in popular culture read through a postcolonial feminist framework that enhances and advances both the fields of biblical scholarship and film.

My scholarship has been inspired and shaped in my thoughts by the South African Professor in Old Testament, Madipoane Masenya, who taught for many years at UNISA and coined the term 'Bosadi approach' to describe how feminist and womanist thought have found expression in her context. She offers: 'reading the Bible in light of present-day contexts both recognizes and acknowledges the reader in her/his context' (Masenya and Ramantswana 2012, p. 599). Traditional hermeneutical scholarship makes the stern distinction between the biblical texts being used as a literary source and on the other hand how the Bible is applied in our current contexts. Masenya critically questions this notion as she believes in the two-way process of biblical reading: reading the text in terms of our experience and reading our experience in terms of the text. I concur with this train of thought; I believe that I cannot merely write and engage theologically if this does not filter down to the women in the church or the ordinary woman who does not have a theological background to engage and interrogate derogative interpretations of the biblical texts. The question I sit with remains: What does this mean to an ordinary woman like my mother? Being ingrained in contextual work has immensely shaped my contribution to the academy, and I believe it is beneficial to the discipline.

Considering the question, why pursue Old Testament studies

as opposed to a different discipline in theology? Pursuing Old Testament studies indeed poses many challenges. As a Black woman in academia one can argue that it is not a smart career choice. Old Testament studies in South Africa can be considered as principally conservative in approach, a male-dominated discipline lacking critical and contextual scholarship (Le Roux 1993, p. 26). 'In the South African context, biblical scholarship historically exemplifies both the good and the bad interested reading of the Bible' (Masenya and Ramantswana 2012, p. 600). Thus, understanding where you fit into the Old Testament discourses can be quite complex specifically when considering your positionality. My positionality and focus on contextual works deeply inform and shape my contribution to the Old Testament. The Old Testament grants the reader a fertile selection of literary genres. However, the overarching challenge the Old Testament poses is that it has a complex history that extends over 800 years (Le Roux 1993, p. 26). There is a vast historical distance between contemporary society and the historical context of the Old Testament, and given this reality, the Old Testament weathered the interrogation if it is still a relevant field of epistemology. I honestly believe Old Testament studies is the most exciting theological discipline. There is so much potential in the Hebrew biblical texts; they offer the potential for life-giving and transformative interpretations, particularly for the marginalized. This potential then is being developed by scholars who take context seriously, scholars such Dr Lerato Mokoena and Madré Arendse. So indeed, much of who I am and the work I am doing is ingrained in Old Testament studies.

Where do I consider the future of the Old Testament going in South Africa? Masenya argues that in South African Old Testament scholarship has been focused more on the ancient text rather than on contemporary issues. I concur with this sentiment and observation (Masenya and Ramantswana 2012, p. 599). Many Old Testament scholars focus their scholarship on the ancient contexts and do not see the relevance of how the Old Testament filters into contemporary society. Therefore, the question arises: Is there any potential for Old Testament studies, is there anything new and fresh that the Old Testament has to offer? I foresee much potential and growth in Old Testament scholarship. More and more scholars take seriously the contextual nature of the Old Testament and have an earnest consideration for the impact the Hebrew Bible possesses in our current context.

The Circle of Concerned Women African Theologians is doing ground-breaking work in biblical scholarship. As a young woman in academia, I am so grateful and mindful of the shoulders of transformative women that I stand on. These women have gone before us and had challenged the patriarchal nature of the Bible long before I realized that I would pursue a career in theology. I am deeply influenced by the works of the Circle. Considering the Circle offers me not only the opportunity to appreciate the transformative work done, but also alerts me to what I need to focus on at present as a contributor to the development of the Circle. I contend that the Circle needs to focus more broadly on the intersections of feminist/womanist scholarship and queer theology, and their current focus on the latter needs further investigation and commitment.

## Advice to an emerging womanist

**Ashwin Thyssen:** My sincere thanks for your keen insights into the present and future potential of womanist biblical interpretation, specifically with regard to the Hebrew Bible. We are all emerging scholars, those who are still finding our feet in this space called academia. What advice would you offer a younger version of yourself, as you commit to a life in the theological academy?

**Madré Arendse:** I would invite them not to forget who called them and who sustains them. To venture down the path less travelled in scholarship is terrifying and often I doubt my own capabilities. But I have recently realized in conversation with Sheurl Davis and Dr Lerato Mokoena that doing what is different and unknown is one of the greatest joys in scholarship. My advice would also be to unapologetically pursue what captures you.

Wilda Gafney (2017) sustains me on my journey as it is just starting. She invites us to pull up a chair at her table to dine with her and keep an open mind about the dishes she serves. In my research I wish to follow in her footsteps as I set the table, invite you to dine with me, to eat the dishes of a Coloured South African woman, the experiences of slavery, the importance of narratives, silenced voices and the resistance to survive. Finally, I embarked on this study for no person to ever have to unconsciously utter words like those in the song of Keuzenkamp ever again:

> ... *en ons se, dankie, se ons Jan van Riebeek ons sal vir jou, nooit vergeet, dankie 1652, net vir hierdie dag ... Hip-hip hoerah Suid-Afrika.*
>
> And we say thank you to Jan van Riebeek, we will never forget you, thank you 1652, just for this day ... Hip-hip hooray South Africa.

A rather unsettling couple of words but an excellent example of what happens when a single story has gone down in history, presented as the truth of the nation not recognizing the complexities and inevitable trauma that these words evoke for women of colour.

**Sheurl Davis:** I am mindful of how far I have come in trusting myself, trusting the knowledge and convictions I have acquired in the years of formation as a biblical scholar. The affirmation I have for myself and for any other young woman unsure of where they fit into the Old Testament discipline would be this: imposter syndrome is a colonizing strategy, do not give it the satisfaction! Your voice matters: your argument is valid and valuable. Do not trust your fears, they do not know your strengths. Speak up and take up space with grace and humility. Often grace and humility will not be options, because most of the tables you will sit at will offer you a seat reluctantly, testing you to the core, expecting you to be silent and observant and merely to be grateful. Turn the table, challenge the narrative, and inspired by womanist scholarship, let your voice be heard wretchedly and boldly. Take up space and let the patriarchy observe your presence in discomfort.

## Conclusion

Alice Walker offered a notable definition of a womanist:

> From womanish. A black feminist or feminist of color ... Committed to survival and wholeness of entire people, male and female ... Loves music. Loves dance. Loves the moon. Loves the Spirit. Loves love and food and roundness. Loves struggle. Loves the Folk. Loves herself. Regardless ... (Walker 1983, p. xi)

By presenting their contributions, with grace and sincerity, Sheurl Davis and Madré Arendse displayed this commitment to love. Womanist love, as Walker reminds, is directed in a number of directions – not least the self and community. Setting out to offer a contribution to the development of womanist biblical interpretation, particularly in South Africa, they are highlighting the prophetic potential of the biblical sciences. In a true sense, the contributions of Sheurl Davis and Madré Arendse are pointing the truly queer potential of womanist biblical interpretation. In fact, these two womanist theologians may be considered queer prophets in your time.

## References

Cannon, Katie Geneva, 2014, 'Journey to Liberation: The Legacy of Womanist Theology', Union Theological Seminary, *YouTube*, 26 March, https://www.youtube.com/watch?v=PjhtUGqFCWg&t=64s, accessed 7.06.2023.

Claassens, L. Juliana, 2016, 'God and Violence in the Prophets' in Carol Sharp (ed.), *The Oxford Handbook of the Prophets*, Oxford: Oxford University Press, pp. 334–50.

Gafney, Wilda, 2017, *Womanist Midrash: A Reintroduction to the Women of the Torah and the Throne*, Louisville, KY: Westminster John Knox Press.

Junior, Nyasha, 2015, *An Introduction to Womanist Biblical Interpretation*, Louisville, KY: Westminster John Knox Press.

Keuzenkamp, Carike, 2015, 'Jan Van Riebeeck', *YouTube*, 4 May 4, https://www.youtube.com/watch?v=2J_HRIs81aQ, accessed 7.06.2023.

Le Roux, Jurie H., 1993, *A Story of Two Ways: Thirty Years of Old Testament Scholarship in South Africa*, Pretoria: Verba Vitae.

Masenya, Madipoane and Hulisani Ramantswana, 2012, 'Anything New Under the Sun of South African Old Testament scholarship? African Qoheleth's review of OTE 1994–2010', *Old Testament Essays* 25/3, pp. 598–637.

Phillips, Layli, 2006, 'Womanism: On its Own' in Layli Phillips (ed.), *The Womanist Reader*, London: Routledge.

Shell, Robert, 1992, 'Rangton of Bali (1673–1720): Roots and Resurrection', *Kronos* 19, pp. 167–99.

Truth, Sojourner, 1851, 'Modern History Sourcebook: Sojourner Truth: "Ain't I a Woman?", December 1851', *Fordham University*, https://sourcebooks.fordham.edu/mod/sojtruth-woman.asp (last modified 20.01.2021; accessed 7.06.2023).

Walker, Alice, 1983, *In Search of Our Mothers' Gardens: Womanist Prose*, San Diego, CA: Harcourt.

# Index of Names and Subjects